Peace, Preference, and Property

PEACE, PREFERENCE, AND PROPERTY

Return Migration after Violent Conflict

Sandra F. Joireman

University of Michigan Press
Ann Arbor

For questions or permissions, please contact um.press.perms@umich.edu

Published in the United States of America by the University of Michigan Press
Manufactured in the United States of America
Printed on acid-free paper
First published November 2022

A CIP catalog record for this book is available from the British Library.

Library of Congress Cataloging-in-Publication data has been applied for.

ISBN 978-0-472-13326-0 (hardcover : alk. paper)
ISBN 978-0-472-03910-4 (paper : alk. paper)
ISBN 978-0-472-22073-1 (e-book)

Contents

Digital materials related to this title can be found on the Fulcrum platform via the following citable URL: https://doi.org/10.3998/mpub.12333056

Figures

Tables

Preface and Acknowledgments

While I was working in Uganda on my last book, the war in the north had just ended and people had started to return home from camps and other places of refuge. With return migration came extensive conflict over land. Newspapers, daily conversations, and radio broadcasts highlighted stories about disagreements over boundaries and land claims, including those that turned violent and led to death. At the time, I wondered why, if people were returning home, there was so much conflict. Why was it so violent? Didn't people just go back to the places their families had previously lived, reclaiming what was previously theirs? Perhaps there was a problem with the breakdown of customary institutions or the failure of mediation processes? These questions bothered me for some time.

As a social scientist, I knew there were a variety of ways to go about answering these questions. I could go and ask people where they had lived before and what land was theirs, but I might get very self-interested responses. Who would be willing to say to me, a foreign researcher, "This isn't really my land." Yet, if people were not returning to live in the same places, there should be some evidence of that fact. I investigated whether I could get data on the high-conflict areas of northern Uganda before, during, and after the war. I found high-resolution satellite images and maps that detailed the placement of homes in two areas. Using spatial statistics, my students and I were able to determine that the settlement patterns were significantly different before and after the conflict; that evidence was published in *Political Geography*. However, while we were able to determine that people were settling in different places, satellite images would not tell us why.

This was my first immersion into the question, do people want to return home after being displaced by violence? Attendant to that question are others, such as, how does conflict change people's preferences? Do people still feel an attachment to home after decades of displacement? Do their children, born in places of refuge, feel a desire to return "home"? The existing literature on postconflict return migration answered different questions: What guarantees should the displaced have under international law? How are people to be treated when they are displaced by violence? Should they get their houses back if other people are occupying them? But these questions were about rights, and I had become interested in the question of preferences.

The key argument in this book is that the decisions and preferences of people displaced by violent conflict are often misaligned with the rights they have in international law and public policy. This has implications in terms of return migration, property restitution, intergenerational wealth transfer, and the long-term development of places of origin and places of refuge. While I have a deep respect for international law and human rights, this is not a book about rights, and those wanting to read about enforcing human rights law will be frustrated by it. Instead, this a book about wrongs and the choices people make in response to the most difficult of circumstances.

Rather than looking from the top down, at the rights that people have in international and domestic law, the perspective of this text is from the ground up—examining individual and household choices after conflict. It argues that the prioritizing of return is in the interest of states, which do not want to host or resettle refugees. But return is not always the preference of displaced people and is increasingly impractical after protracted displacement. Focusing personnel and money on enabling people to return is a poor use of resources when they are unable or unwilling to do so. Better uses of funding and expertise include ensuring that the displaced remain as close to home as possible; developing better local integration solutions; and working to make home communities more appealing so that returning there is desirable.

There are two ways to identify people's preferences for return migration after conflict: you can ask them if they want to return, or you can observe the choices of those who can return. To know why people in northern Uganda, did not return to the exact places they lived before, I needed to talk to them, so I went there and began asking people about their preferences. I also worked in Liberia and Kosovo, two additional countries that had experienced massive population displacement as a result of war.

Because most of my previous research has been on law and property rights, I started investigating property restitution and its role in community reconstruction and postwar economic development. It quickly became apparent that property restitution was not the only, or even the most important, motivation behind the question of who chooses to return. In this book I unpack some of the motivations influencing people's desire to return home after violent conflict, focusing on cases that are not highly studied.

This book contains data from many interviews conducted during field research. In the interviews, if I thought there was any possibility of harm, I anonymized the information about the subject. When there was no obvious threat of harm, I gave people the opportunity to choose themselves whether they wanted me to cite them directly or to keep their names confidential. As a result, the reader will note a variety of citation styles throughout the book. Sometimes there are names, sometimes titles without a name, and sometimes a number. This strategy is used to protect people who may have already suffered a great deal as a result of violent conflict while at the same time giving voice to those who desire public acknowledgment of their experiences and opinions. I am grateful for the strength and generosity of all those who agreed to be interviewed both on and off the record about their experiences of displacement. In addition to interviews, I incorporated data on return migration and population change where it was available. Regretfully, there are multiple conflicts with large numbers of displaced people that have little available data on the preferences of the displaced. I will be highlighting areas where there is an absence of data and research throughout the book.

Effective international research is dependent on the generosity and hospitality of those in the host country—interview subjects, those who facilitate contacts, and the vital interlocutors who extend friendship to a stranger. I have a debt of gratitude to the many people who assisted me in the field research and writing of this manuscript. In 2013, I seconded myself to the Liberian Refugee Repatriation and Resettlement Commission in Monrovia, Liberia, to get on-the-ground knowledge about return migration and refugee repatriation. I am extremely grateful to the director at the time, Wheatonia Barnes, for allowing me to work there and to my colleagues, particularly Jimmy T. Toe and Kojoe Ross, who were hospitable and excellent sources of information and wisdom. Greg Kitt, who was then with the Norwegian Refugee Council, and Alexandra Hartman both shared their advice and experiences in Liberia. Jonathan Greenham and Paul Robinson were helpful kindred spirits in the field research. I am grateful to Mary Baganizi, Kilara Oruni and Ronald Atkinson in northern Uganda, all of whom provided background information, key introductions, and important comments on my findings as the work moved forward. Mirriam Lakote provided excellent research assistance with high levels of energy, helpful insights, and excellent organization and translation. While I was working in Kosovo, my academic home was the governance and public policy unit at what was then the American University of Kosovo (now RIT-Kosovo). My colleagues and students there taught me much, and I am very grateful to Michael Waschak, Shpend Ahmeti, and Brian and B. Lynn Bowen for their welcome and friendship. Arben Hoti and Anita Gubetini provided research assistance, translation, and good company. In Serbia the gracious facilitation, experience, and vigorous dialogue with the good people at the Danish Refugee Council was vital to my understanding of the situation of internally displaced people there. Milosava Smiljanic and Marina Cremonese were particularly obliging. I am also extremely grateful to Davor Rako at the United Nations High Commissioner for Refugees for assistance, collegiality, and insight into the situation of Roma internally displaced persons in Serbia. Dragan Smiljanic translated, navigated, gave helpful contextual background, and was a gracious and entertaining companion in the Serbian research. In this time when those who are fleeing violence are frequently demeaned, it was inspiring to spend time with people all over the world who are working toward the well-being of the displaced.

This book pulls together several different strands of research from the past decade. In a few of the chapters I include work that has been published elsewhere in a slightly different form and am careful to note when this is the case. Various people gave helpful comments on the prospectus, different chapters, or some of the conference papers and later articles that were the basis for the book manuscript: Sara Berry, Franziska Fay, Nancy Horn, Louisa Jansen, Ekaterina Koldunova, Neophytos Loizides, Jason Long, Randall E. Newnham, Steve Offutt, Matt Soerens, Victoria Stanley, Carl LeVan, Djordje Stefanovic, Dennis Sandole, Charles Scheiner, Rachel Vanderhill, and many, many others. Leah Anderson, Amy Reynolds, Winnie Fung, and Christa Tooley read copies of multiple chapters and provided helpful comments and redirection. Laura Yoder commented on multiple chapters and coauthored the article that provided some of the material for Chapter 5. I am grateful to Jim Clark for feeding my interest in GIS, generously giving his time and energy to equipping me to use it in research, and being an excellent role model of a teacher-scholar.

At the University of Richmond my colleagues Sheila Carapico, Monti Datta, Stephen Long, Jenny Pribble, Carol Summers, and Aleksandra Sznajder Lee were helpful conversation partners in the research and writing. Chris Brown, Kim Browne, Donald Edmonds, Taylor Holden, and Beth Zizzamia gave technical support for the maps. Samantha Guss, Luka Klimaviciute, and Annika Sampedro all provided valuable research assistance. David Pervin provided excellent advice and encouragement as the manuscript moved through the publication process. David Beckmann, my coworker in the cause of ending hunger and addressing the needs of the displaced, was a regular source of enthusiasm and encouragement.

Fieldwork for this project was enabled by a Fulbright Senior Research Fellowship and grants from the Earhart Foundation. I also owe a special debt of gratitude to Carole and Marcus Weinstein, who endowed the research chair I hold. Their ongoing generosity to the University of Richmond and international interests allowed me time for writing and the resources for field research and data analysis.

The final and deepest thanks are for my family. Paul and my children have tolerated my long absences from home with perseverance and good cheer and have on several occasions spent considerable amounts of time with me overseas while I was conducting research. Paul read every chapter of this manuscript and provided technical assistance with some of the data analysis. I benefited from the restrictions on movement during the Covid crisis, as both my mother, Carol Machael, and my son Matthias Joireman used their extra time to read through the entire manuscript and provide comments that helped me to strip the book of academic jargon and improve its overall readability.

Every major research project needs partners and supporters. I am grateful to all who have assisted me in this endeavor in large and small ways.

ONE

Forced Migration and Its Troublesome Solutions

> In 2020, 82.4 million people were forcibly displaced from their place
> of residence as a result of violence and human rights violations.[1]

Milana and her family were displaced from her village in what was then Kosovo and Metohija, an area in southern Serbia.[2] This happened in 1999, in the latter part of a war that led to the independence of the state of Kosovo.

> Everyone had to leave—the whole village, every single person. We packed some things and left, but no one knew where we were going. The process of ethnic cleansing of that area had started. We didn't use the regular road, we went through villages and fields. We started early in the morning and we arrived at 1:00 or 2:00 a.m. the next morning. Someone came and told us that our village had been burned along with two other villages. . . . We had some money but not enough to feed the kids, and that was a disgusting feeling. . . . When we left we thought we would come back, so we didn't think about bringing all the documents. We just grabbed the kids and thought about bringing things for a couple of days. It is impossible for us to go back and start our lives there again. I don't want to return.

Violence forced Milana to flee and she never wants to go back. Her children were raised outside of Kosovo and do not think of it as home. Stories like hers are common in the twenty-first century. Conflict-induced forced migration is increasing, and there is little to suggest that this problem will abate. In 2021 and 2022, large numbers of people were displaced from conflicts in Afghanistan, the Central African Republic, Myanmar, South Sudan, Syria, and Ukraine. Like Milana, many displaced people do not want to go home, despite international public policies that promote their repatriation and return. Experiences of violence and lengthy displacements change people's preferences for the future. As refugees streamed out of Ukraine in 2022, they were welcomed in countries across Europe. Most Ukrainian refugees would like the war to end so that they can go home. If Ukrainian refugees follow the pattern of those in other conflicts, they will return quickly if the war ends soon. But if the war does not end rapidly and they are displaced for five, ten, or fifteen years, people will build new lives in their places of refuge, and some will want to stay. More people are displaced than ever before, they are not returning home, and they are often unwelcome in places of refuge. This humanitarian crisis and policy puzzle is the focus of this book, which seeks to bring social science insights to bear on issues of postconflict return migration and property restitution. The following chapters highlight the importance of time, ethnicity, political change, and property restitution on decisions to return.

Three Reasons for the Increase in Forced Migration

The Ukrainian war increased the visibility of forced migration. Images of Ukrainian refugees in social and mainstream media showed desperate women and children risking their lives trying to get to safety in Poland, Romania, Moldova and across Europe. These images reprise those from 2015 and 2016 when the Syrian Civil war caused millions of people to flee to Europe for safety. In the United States the same problem is visible with a different face. Children and families from the northern triangle of Central America (El Salvador, Guatemala, and Honduras) have crossed the border into the United States in record numbers since 2014, often traveling along dangerous routes. It was not always like this. People are on the move now in ways and numbers that we have not seen since World War II, fleeing violence, and looking for opportunity. "Forced migration" describes people moving involuntarily because of violence, natural disasters, climate change, famine, and development projects. In this book, I narrow the focus to those who leave their homes due to violence and the decisions they make after the threat of violence has passed.

There are three reasons for the increase in forced displacement in recent years. First, there are some unresolved, persistent conflicts. In both Afghanistan and Somalia, displacement has occurred in waves over forty years with new displacements following fluctuations in the political and geographic dimensions of those conflicts. Violence in both countries continues to force people to flee, inhibits flourishing societies and economies, and prevents displaced people from going home. Indeed, in 2021 the withdrawal of US forces from Afghanistan led to the latest massive movement of refugees out of the country. A second cause of rising displacement is the start of new conflicts in Burundi, Central African Republic, Ethiopia, Myanmar, Nigeria, South Sudan, Syria, Ukraine, and Yemen. These more recent conflicts push people across international borders or lead them to move within their country for safety. People also face pervasive violence and displacement in countries not experiencing war. In El Salvador in 2015 there were more homicides than when civil war afflicted the country during the 1980s.[3] Third, there is a decline in the number of displaced people returning home or resettling in third countries. People remain in places of refuge for longer periods, often in situations of physical insecurity, limited political representation, and constrained economic opportunities. For those in situations of protracted displacement, the average duration of exile is 21.2 years.[4] Lengthy displacements change people's goals and aspirations, their desire to return home can wane, and their children develop different attachments to place and understandings of "home."

Some would argue that the barriers to migration are lower now than they have been in the past and that becoming a refugee is an alternative immigration strategy to enter otherwise closed countries.[5] This would be a convincing argument if states were open to refugees, with the exception of Ukrainians, they are not. Margaret Peters notes that in the face of three recent major refugee crises—Central American child refugees coming to the United States, the Rohingya refugees in Southeast Asia, and the refugees from the Syrian civil war—countries in the Global North have made it *more* difficult to claim asylum.[6] Apart from Canada, even states previously welcoming to refugees are closing their borders or restricting the number of refugees they admit. Quantitative studies have robustly proven that violence is more strongly correlated with migration decisions than economic incentive across multiple countries, contexts, age groups, and time periods.[7] Those who experience violence are more likely to flee, as are those with little hope of sustaining their livelihoods because they have lost property or have limited economic opportunities. But not everyone leaves conflict zones. Research has made it clear that political affiliation, property loss, family circumstances, economic opportunity, and the ease of flight are important in individual decision-making in response to threats.[8] These decisions take place in a context formed by the international migration regime—the collection of international laws, norms, and policies regarding migration.

Scope of the Problem

The number of refugees is the highest it has been in twenty years. Forced displacement stems from the newer or reignited conflicts noted above as well as from older and "frozen" conflicts, where return is blocked or undesirable: Bosnia, Cyprus, Democratic Republic of Congo, Eritrea, Iraq, Kosovo, Palestine/Israel, and Sri Lanka. Despite high numbers of displaced people, the number of people returning home or being resettled is smaller and, in some years, negligible. Indeed, in 2020 the UN warned of the lowest levels of resettlement ever.[9] Figure 1 tells the story.

The large section above the black line represents the number of people who are refugees in any given year. There is a peak in 1991 due to three major events: the Persian Gulf War; the Afghan civil war; and the war in Mozambique. Those were the three highest source countries for refugees that year, which also marked the beginning of the disintegration of the Somali state. Not counted in this figure are those internally displaced within their own country due to violence, climate change, or development projects. The area below the black line depicts the number of people who return home in a year. The thickness of the black dividing line indicates the number of people who resettled in third countries (usually in the Global North) in any year, which is never more than 176,700—in 1990, the highest recorded year. Few people repatriate, or return home, and fewer people are being resettled. Table 1 shows a snapshot of five years of the data.

This data is from the United Nations High Commission for Refugees (UNHCR). One might argue that there are many people returning to their home countries uncounted by the UNHCR.[10] This is possible, but even if we double, triple, or quadruple the numbers of returnees; it is still far, far below the number of those who are being displaced. Where are the millions of people who are not going home? They are in places of refuge—usually neighboring countries—some in refugee camps, but the overwhelming majority (76%) in urban areas, outside of camp settings,

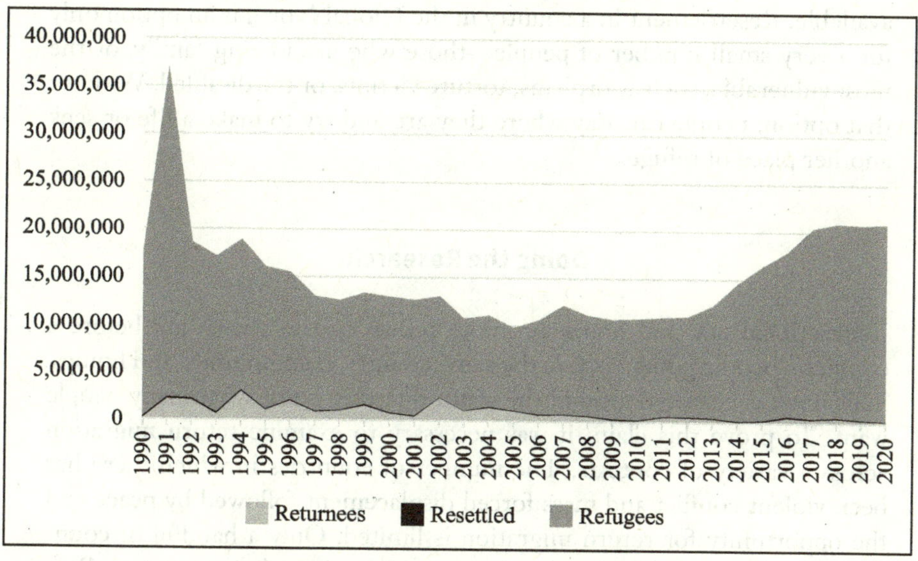

Figure 1. Refugees, Resettled, Returned. Source: UNHCR.

TABLE 1. Five Years of Refugees, Returnees, and Resettled

	2005	2006	2007	2008	2009
Refugees	8,661,994	9,877,703	11,390,930	10,489,812	10,396,538
Returnees	1,105,395	710,609	728,166	589,441	247,580
Resettled	80,797	71,703	75,300	88,800	112,472

making them more difficult to count and to reach with assistance.[11] These are Iraqi refugees resident in Jordan, Syrian refugees in Lebanon and Jordan, Somali refugees in Kenya, and so on. Many gravitate toward cities due to employment opportunities and family ties.

People stay in places of refuge years after their initial displacement because they are unable to return home or because they choose not to return. Some areas of the world, such as Afghanistan and Somalia, have been unstable for decades, and the threat of violence, though it may change over time, never completely goes away. Displaced people make decisions to return based on the conditions at home and their opportunities elsewhere. For example, in a 2008 assessment of Iraqi refugees in Syria, 89.5% had no desire to go back to Iraq because of conditions there.[12] Refugees are in a difficult situation if they do not want to repatriate; international policy is focused on their return, and there are few other permanent options available. Resettlement in a country in the Global North is an option only for a very small number of people—those who are joining family, or the most vulnerable, such as orphans, torture victims, or the disabled. Without that option, people can stay where they are and try to make a life or seek another place of refuge.

Doing the Research

International law and policy promote return to the status quo before a conflict—people going back to the same country, communities, and homes. This book is centered around the claim that this is not what many people want. To prove this claim it was necessary to examine return migration across a variety of contexts. The number of countries in which there has been violent conflict and mass forced displacement followed by peace and the opportunity for return migration is limited. Only a handful of countries meet these criteria for case selection: Afghanistan (prior to 2021), Bosnia, Colombia, Cyprus, Kosovo, Liberia, Sri Lanka, some parts of Syria, and Uganda. My choice of Liberia and Uganda was straightforward, as I have lived and worked in both countries. In Liberia, people became refugees and crossed international boundaries for safety—sometimes multiple times—or were displaced within the country. In northern Uganda, most of the displacement was within the borders of the state. I also chose to work in Kosovo as there, displacement included both refugees and internally displaced people (IDPs). That said, throughout the text there are frequent references to the experiences of Afghanistan, Bosnia, Colombia, Cyprus, and Sri Lanka. It could be argued that massive population displacement due to famine, natural disaster, or climate change would provide additional options for study, but the experience of violence is different from these other drivers of migration. Conflict-induced migration involves human perpetrators and often the specific intent to displace, making return more challenging, particularly if one must live near the perpetrators or their allies.

To write this book, I needed data on the numbers of displaced people. The UNHCR is the best available source of this data for refugees, but its data has limitations. UNHCR data includes only those who use its services in some way, such as accessing a refugee camp or seeking assistance for return home. People can leave a conflict zone or seek refuge in another country without being recorded by the UNHCR. Someone might flee Syria because of the civil war and stay with relatives in Jordan or Lebanon. Unless they seek services or support through the UNHCR or another organization, they will not get counted. Similarly, people can repatriate to their country of origin without being counted.[13] Another data problem lies in the counting of children born to refugees in their place of refuge. Are they refugees? Should they be counted as such? Dissimilar statistics regarding the numbers of refugees or years of their displacement occur because researchers answer these questions differently, not because there are a variety of sources of information.[14]

Examining data on return migration is even more challenging. Refugees "return" when they repatriate to their country of origin, even though this may not mean going back to their home communities.[15] They are also counted as having returned if they repatriate, stay for a time, and then leave again. There is limited data on people who cross a border into another country and locally integrate there. The UNHCR does not report numbers for local integration, and the lack of tracking conceals those who have found a durable solution in their place of refuge.

Though there are problems with the UNHCR data on refugees, it is far better than the data available for IDPs, those conflict-displaced people who remain within the borders of their country. One organization, the Internal Displacement Monitoring Centre, does an excellent job of reporting the best available information on IDPs, but it lacks the international mandate of the UNHCR. There is no international organization tasked with protecting the rights and welfare of IDPs, though the UNHCR understands this protection gap and assists where possible.

Recognizing these issues, the World Bank has called for an "open data" solution in which governments and international organizations share data on displaced people.[16] While this would be helpful, states and international organizations are reluctant to share information that might reveal the identity of people who are fleeing conflict or returning home—a protection of both the privacy and the security of the displaced. This need for identity protection makes data sharing a challenge. States have an additional incentive to restrict information if the state has caused displacement through actions of its armed forces. Though data collection on refugees and displaced people is currently challenging and absent in many areas, there is considerable hope for the future. New technologies are changing the options for assistance and documentation. There are websites and smartphone apps designed to help displaced people with medical advice, general assistance, and locating family members.[17] There are also new data storage techniques that protect the privacy and identity of vulnerable people. Chapter 6, suggests methods for overcoming some of the data problems that hamper both humanitarian responses and scholarly analysis.

Where it is possible, I supplement UNHCR data with demographic and spatial data. Statistics and maps of population distribution before and after conflict reveal important changes. But demographic data also has limitations. It cannot tell us why people are returning to certain areas and not to others, why some choose to repatriate while others remain where they are, and if people stay after they repatriate. Interviews and focus groups provided this important supplemental information. This mixed-method approach centers the analysis on people and the choices they make at each step in the displacement/return process. In the appendix there is a list of interviews by country, and before each case study in the chapters there is information on the fieldwork methods used to collect data and identify interview subjects.

Structure of the Book

Restoring communities after violent conflict entails the return of people and property. This book first details the international migration regime, then discusses what we know about preferences for return migration and how those are impacted by ethnicity, political change, time, and property restitution. Chapter 2 sets the context of international law and policy as it relates to refugees and IDPs. This chapter is important for those new to the topic or who have a specific interest in this area. Chapters 3, 4, and 5 present the significant new contributions to the literature, with Chapter 3 focused on the role of ethnicity and political change in forming people's choices. Chapter 4 highlights migrating children, intergenerational return migration, time, and the challenges of reclaiming property across generations. Chapter 5 focuses on postconflict property restitution and its relationship to return. The concluding chapter builds on this research with policy-focused suggestions and identification for areas of further research. Each of these chapters stands on its own and can be read independently. Throughout the text, the approach is pragmatic, examining options from the standpoint of political realities. Humanitarian or rights-based approaches to displacement and return are important, but they have not yielded progress in terms of durable solutions or interim policies. There is a need for the recent and growing social science literature on individual choice in postconflict migration.[18] Following is a brief overview of each chapter and the narrative arc of the book.

Return to place of origin is the preferred solution to forced migration. Chapter 2 describes why and identifies how return came to dominate the three "durable solutions" to ending displacement. These three solutions—voluntary repatriation to country of origin, integration into place of refuge, or resettlement in a third country—are the focus of both states and international organizations. Returning home is the preferred option, as it eliminates the need for displaced people to wait in refugee camps for a limited possibility of resettlement. It is less logistically complicated, as many people already have homes and property. Return is also symbolic of a restoration of normality; the reestablishment of the status quo before the conflict. In the case of ethnic conflict where violence has been intentionally used to move people from their homes, return to the community of origin is morally appealing.

While having displaced people return home is a priority for states and international organizations, households and individuals make their own choices regarding what to do. Determining whether to return home or stay in a place of refuge is a careful calculus of the needs and opportunities of members of the household, consideration of social networks and economic opportunity, and evaluation of the micropolitical context in the place of return. While people need to know the general security situation in the country—for example, if fighting has stopped—they also need to know if it is safe for them to return to a specific place. In cases of ethnic conflict, the safety of return can differ community by community and depend on the ethnicity of the returnee. Within the field of political science, literature on civil wars emphasizes the localized nature of violence and the importance of local conflicts, grudges, and interests within the wider civil war.[19] Local context is equally important in postconflict settings. Some localities are welcoming of returnees; in other places there are residual hostilities.

Chapter 3 highlights displacement and return in Kosovo. Not surprisingly, the victorious Albanians, in the majority, returned quickly after the 1998–1999 war. Serbs returned slowly and sporadically to certain localities—and not necessarily those we would predict. Roma, Egyptian, and Ashkali citizens did not choose to return, yet many were forced to do so when expelled from other countries. This case illuminates the ways in which ethnicity and political change construct choices regarding return migration after ethnic conflict, even in countries that are no longer at war.

Time is a critical factor in people's preferences and options for return. The passage of time can create opportunities to go home as conflicts end and political changes are consolidated. Time also changes people and families. Forced migration has become an intergenerational problem because of the length of displacements. The household composition of a family that fled a conflict may change drastically over time as older people die and young people mature, marry, and start families of their own. Ideas about "home" may change for those who have been displaced for long periods and certainly for their children. There are generations of children, raised in places of refuge, who have very different ideas about return than their parents.

Chapter 4 addresses issues of children and forced displacement. It examines the recent trend of children migrating independently, without family members or guardians, and how the international refugee regime is ill-prepared to cope with minors. In the 1980s, children were declared refugees in camps around the world and then resettled in the Global North. Today there is a much riskier strategy of children migrating independently to the Global North to seek asylum with the hope of then being declared a refugee. Chapter 4 also highlights the return challenges faced by "adult children"—those who were forcibly displaced as children and then became adults in a place of refuge. The chapter concludes with a case study of the experiences of children in northern Uganda who were raised in camps for displaced people or with rebel groups before returning home. It highlights issues of group identity, resource access, and the experience of war in decisions to return.

Studies of economic recovery after violent conflict, such as the *World Bank 2011 Development Report*, identify three key issues that need to be addressed in any postwar setting: security, justice issues that led to or stem from the conflict, and restoring jobs.[20] Restoring jobs and economic development is contingent upon return migration and property restitution. Property restitution, here referring to real property—homes, farms, businesses, and land—is the focus of Chapter 5. It is a precondition for resuming agricultural livelihoods and equally vital to those who want to return to urban homes and businesses.[21]

Reclaiming property after violent conflict can be complicated by changing political power and land governance structures. Violent actors can participate in the expropriation of land during a conflict, as happened in Colombia, pushing civilians off their traditional land.[22] Because of the importance of property in rebuilding local economies, restitution and compensation for loss is increasingly part of the postconflict landscape. Land and property issues are present in peace agreements and a focus of postconflict peacebuilding efforts.[23] Compensating people for lost property enables return or can finance settlement in a different area or country where people feel more secure. Compensation and property restitution are challenging in settings with customary land tenure, without formalized documentation of specific properties. In Chapter 5, I discuss postconflict property issues, the link between property and identity in legal theory and practice, and how customary tenure systems pose challenges in terms of restitution.

This book highlights the divergence between the choices of people displaced by violence and the expected postconflict return of displaced people to their communities of origin. Chapter 6 directly addresses these misalignments of international policy with the preferences of displaced people. If the goal of international organizations is to return displaced people to their countries and homes of origin, then available resources and incentives should focus on return. Currently, the greatest resources go into resettlement—the least likely of the possible outcomes after displacement.[24] Better-aligned policies would see a concentration of funding on both return incentives and on encouraging local integration efforts in places of first refuge, those countries and communities that provide a safe haven for displaced people. For those displaced five years or more, return home is less likely. Policies would be better focused on long-term planning for the reconstruction of lives and livelihoods in a different area of their home country or their country of refuge—not on return home or resettlement in the Global North. When the focus is only on return, host countries and international organizations do not seek local integration solutions such as permission to work, legal residency, education, and naturalization. For example, many Syrian refugees would like to locally integrate in Turkey, but the Turkish government would then need to address their employment needs and take on the education of refugee children, who do not speak Turkish. There is growing focus on developing policies that encourage local integration, and some of the policy innovations that promote it are discussed in Chapter 6.

Though there has been remarkable progress on property restitution issues in the past few decades, policies and the preferences of displaced people are not always aligned. The development of new international public policy on property restitution since the end of the Cold War is welcome. Yet the recognized rights of compensation for lost resources or return to a specific home and farm are unrealistic in many places. The nature of customary land tenure systems across much of sub-Saharan Africa, Afghanistan, and other areas where we have seen displacement precludes the simple "return what was taken" approach. More flexible options are needed, including compensation for property loss.[25]

Chapter 6 suggests policy changes that would address some of these misalignments and identifies future scholarly research areas. International policies regarding the return of displaced people do not need to be thrown out but realigned and expanded to match the choices displaced people make. They are like a house with a leaking roof and broken windows; it will do for shelter but could be improved immensely. Some of those improvements have to do with understanding the preferences of those displaced by violent conflict, recognizing that not everyone will choose to return home. Other improvements necessitate changing funding and programming to better match the choices of displaced people. Lastly, there are some areas, particularly in the protection of child migrants, in which a transformation in international law is necessary.

My goal in this book is to analyze what happens below the elevated language and ideals of human rights protection, focusing instead on local contexts and household decision-making. These are circumstances in which people make choices informed by their human rights, but often without receiving them. While the compass of this text is the political realities that shape choices, rather than human rights, I am not pessimistic about human rights. Unlike Eric Posner, who argues that human rights treaties are acts of hubris, I view human rights as essential.[26] This is not a naive perspective; it is empirical. There has been international progress on humanitarian issues.[27] Unfortunately, the human rights agreements that pertain to displacement and return are quite moderate in their promises, and there are few national and international organizations engaged in advocacy on behalf of the displaced.

In the United States there are ten refugee resettlement agencies, called "Volags"—short for "voluntary agencies." A few of these, such as World Relief, use their limited resources to engage in political advocacy. We can add to this number a handful of cultural organizations that engage in political advocacy on behalf of those displaced from their communities overseas. But this is few US advocates for the rights of the displaced. As a result, the pressure on policymakers to change domestic legislation and international agreements to benefit displaced people is limited. I hope this will change. United States media attention in 2018–2019 focused on state actions separating the children of asylum seekers from their parents. In 2021 public attention turned to the mass immigration of Afghans who assisted the US in the war and in 2022 the Ukrainian refugee crisis drew media attention. Whether these political events will result in greater advocacy for the rights and well-being of displaced people is not yet evident, and there are countervailing forces supporting closed borders and reduced immigration.

Rebuilding communities after violent conflict is contingent on two interlocking issues—returning people and property. People do not always wish to return to their country or community of origin. Those who do return face struggles reclaiming homes, businesses, and other property. These problems extend the time that it takes communities to rebuild after violent conflict. The following chapters seek to contribute to the literature on the role of individual choice in return migration, highlighting the important variables of ethnicity, political change, time, and property restitution on decisions to return.

TWO

International Law on Return

The average length of displacement has been 10–15 years since the 1990s. However, for those displaced more than 5 years, the average length of their displacement is 21.2 years.[1]

International law on refugees and displaced people articulates human rights. It provides the guidelines for how things ought to be. This chapter focuses on international law and public policy, but as those are formed by countries, it is never wholly possible to get away from the interests of states. The chapter describes existing international law with attention to its erosion in practice by the exigencies of security, capacity, and interest. For those already familiar with international law on refugees and displaced people, this chapter will be a review; for readers who are not, it is a primer on the obligations of states, their source in international law, and the way that law informs the policies of humanitarian organizations.

The discussion begins with the twentieth-century interwar period and then moves quickly to the post–World War II era and the Refugee Convention. Refugee law reached its apex in the 1951 Refugee Convention and its 1967 Protocol; nothing before or since has been as significant. The Refugee Convention is binding and requires domestication—the incorporation into the national law of signatory states. This sets it apart from previous agreements and from subsequent regional efforts or nonbinding agreements. The second part of the chapter addresses the three "durable solutions" to refugee status. These three options—return to country of origin, local integration, and resettlement—have canonical status within the UNHCR and other humanitarian organizations. They identify the options available to people who have been displaced from their homes by violence. Yet in this era of intense nationalism, these options are collapsing from three to just two—repatriation or local integration—as resettlement opportunities decline. The third section of this chapter highlights the issue of internally displaced people (IDPs). IDPs face many of the same challenges as refugees, but because they have not left their country of origin, they do not have the same protections under international law. While the UN has been able to develop guidance for states, the only significant legal protections for IDPs have occurred through regionally limited agreements such as the African Union's Kampala Convention. IDP issues are thorny because internal displacement results from civil conflict, when the state is weak, unwilling, or unable to provide civilian protections.

Refugee Law

The political upheaval and population displacement caused by World War I (1914–1918) and World War II (1939–1945) are the background for the development of the key legal protections for refugees. World War II left millions of displaced people uprooted and scattered across Europe and Asia. The borders of countries were redrawn, citizenship changed as countries ceased to exist, and millions of people lost family members, property, and employment. These circumstances incentivized states to agree on minimum standards for human rights and on the specifics of refugee protection, but the need for refugee protection was evident before World War II.

The Interwar Years

World War II was not Europe's first major refugee crisis. Violence in World War I displaced many people within Europe who then sought refuge in other states, sometimes because their country of origin ceased to exist or was unwilling to take them back. For example, the collapse of the Austro-Hungarian Empire left eight million Hungarians within the remnant state of Hungary and three million Hungarians outside of it. Many Hungarians outside of Hungary assimilated into other countries, but transfer of citizenship was not automatic and some were left stateless. At the 1919 Paris Peace Conference in Versailles, Poland agreed to give citizenship to displaced Austrians, Germans, Hungarians, and Russians residing within its territory in exchange for its recognition as a state. The Versailles Treaty also gave specific protections to the Jewish population within Poland. This was the first of the so-called Minorities Treaties instigated by the League of Nations and was the model for subsequent treaties.[2]

The Minorities Treaties were ineffective. They were poorly enforced, so minority groups did not always get citizenship, nor did they protect the human rights of Jews. The 1923 population exchange of minority religious groups between Greece and Turkey, which I will discuss in Chapter 5, happened just a few years after Greece had in its minority treaty agreed to "assure full and complete protection of life and liberty to all inhabitants of Greece without distinction of birth, nationality, language, race or religion."[3] The disintegration of empires in Europe after World War I and the ineffectiveness of the Minorities Treaties highlighted the problem of statelessness in the interwar years. Stateless people are those who cannot claim legal citizenship in any country, like the Hungarians who were not regarded as citizens in the new Polish state.

Contemporary international policy on refugees began during this time. The League of Nations was established in 1920 and appointed a high commissioner to address problems of Russian refugees created by the 1917 revolutions. The League of Nations developed the Convention Relating to the International Status of Refugees of 1933, the first effort to have states accept responsibility for refugees. The principle of *non-refoulement* was introduced into international policy in the 1933 Convention. Article 3 states:

> Each of the Contracting Parties undertakes not to remove or keep from its territory by application of police measures, such as expulsions or non-admittance at the frontier (*refoulement*), refugees who have been authorized to reside there regularly, unless the said measures are dictated by reasons of national security or public order.

Although the Convention of 1933 was only ratified by nine states, the principle of non-refoulement was the template for the 1951 Convention.

Origins of the Refugee Convention

After World War II, the United Nations took the place of the League of Nations as the critical venue for international agreements on humanitarian issues. The UN General Assembly passed the Universal Declaration of Human Rights (UDHR) in 1948, a foundational and aspirational articulation of human rights. The UDHR addressed two of the pressing issues of forced displacement evident in the interwar years and following World War II—the need for protection for those fleeing persecution and statelessness. The UDHR articulated "the right to seek and to enjoy in other countries asylum from persecution." It also declared in Article 15(1) the right to nationality or citizenship. As with other human rights, while it is important and necessary to name this as a right, the articulation in a document does not create the right in practice. There are still people in the contemporary era who are rendered stateless by national law or who exist in legal limbo because of their inability to get documentation of their citizenship. For example, in 1989 the Mauritanian government expelled tens of thousands of its black citizens, stripping them of their citizenship, or "denationalizing" them. More common are people rendered stateless by gendered citizenship laws that do not allow women to pass on their citizenship to spouses and children. For example, it was only in 2017 that Madagascar passed a law allowing both women and men to pass on their citizenship to their children.[4] Statelessness is also a contemporary problem among European Roma groups, who do not always register the birth of their children. Without a birth certificate children lack the proof of citizenship necessary to acquire national IDs, or access health services and education.

After World War II, Europe was awash in refugees and displaced persons. In western Germany alone there were millions of people displaced from the Soviet Union, Poland, France, Italy, Belgium, the Netherlands, Czechoslovakia, and Yugoslavia.

> One of the many aspects of the Second World War that make it unique among modern wars is the fact that vast numbers of civilians were taken prisoner along with the traditional military captives. Women and children, as well as men, were effectively treated as war booty. They were enslaved in a way that had not been seen in Europe since the time of the Roman Empire.[5]

Refugee flows did not subside quickly after the war ended. The number of refugees arriving from central and eastern Europe in western Europe was actually increasing through 1950.[6] While the UDHR articulated a minimal set of rights for the displaced, the United Nations also took practical steps to address the refugee problem. In 1946 the UN created the International

Refugee Organization (IRO) to protect refugees and assist with their reset-tlement. The IRO "proved to be an extremely expensive operation, and the United States and most of its Western allies became leery of making any new open-ended financial commitments to refugees."[7] The ongoing prob-lems and limited solutions led the Economic and Social Council of the UN to establish a more durable "international machinery" to ensure the pro-tection of stateless persons. In December 1949, the UN created the Office of the High Commissioner for Refugees (UNHCR) as the successor of the IRO. A few years later, the General Assembly approved the 1951 Conven-tion on Refugees. Both the Convention and the UNHCR were envisioned as temporary responses to the needs of European refugees displaced by World War II. The 1967 Protocol to the Convention on Refugees made these institutions permanent and expanded the application of the Conven-tion outside of Europe.

The 1951 Refugee Convention is the foundation of international refu-gee law. This agreement defines who is a refugee, describes their rights, outlines the legal obligations of signatories, details refugees' obligations to their host states, establishes the essential principle of non-refoulement, and identifies the durable solutions to displacement. Under the Convention, a refugee is a person who "owing to [a] well-founded fear of being perse-cuted for reasons of race, religion, nationality, membership of a particular social group or political opinion, is outside the country of his nationality and is unable or, owing to such fear, is unwilling to avail himself of the protection of that country."[8] The authors of the 1951 Convention rejected a proposal by the International Committee of the Red Cross (ICRC) that would have created a more inclusive definition of a refugee. The ICRC wanted a definition that included "every person forced by grave events to seek refuge outside his country of ordinary residence."[9] Delegates per-ceived this definition as too expansive and rejected it in favor of one that identified a much smaller group of people. The authors of the 1951 Con-vention feared the obligation of protecting an unmanageably large future refugee population. One country representative noted that the refugee definition "did not refer to refugees from natural disasters, for it was dif-ficult to imagine that fires, floods, earthquakes or volcanic eruptions, for instance, differentiated between their victims on the grounds of race, reli-gion, or political opinion."[10]

Individual countries or regions can have more expansive defini-tions of who can qualify as a refugee. The 1984 Cartagena Declara-tion on Refugees—an agreement between Latin American countries—

had a broader definition of refugee. Under the Cartagena Declaration, refugees are "persons who have fled their country because their lives, safety or freedom have been threatened by generalized violence, foreign aggression, internal conflicts, massive violation of human rights or other circumstances which have seriously disturbed public order" (Section 3, Article 3). While the Cartagena Declaration is not binding law, its refugee definition was gradually incorporated into the national law of Latin American countries.[11] The wider definition of "refugee" in the Cartagena Declaration is similar to that developed by the Organization of African Unity (OAU) 1969 Convention Governing the Specific Aspects of Refugee Problems in Africa. The OAU document also went beyond the UN definition of a refugee in Article 2.

> The term "refugee" shall also apply to every person who, owing to external aggression, occupation, foreign domination or events seriously disturbing public order in either part or the whole of his country of origin or nationality, is compelled to leave his place of habitual residence in order to seek refuge in another place outside his country of origin or nationality.

While both of these regional definitions are broader than that of the 1951 Convention and its 1967 Protocol, they are nonbinding, and, in Latin America, states often default to the narrower 1951 Convention definition.

States are not obligated to protect everyone under the Convention. They can legally expel refugees who present a security threat and can exclude anyone who is a war criminal or has committed serious nonpolitical crimes. Otherwise, they are prohibited from sending anyone back (*refouler*) to their country of origin if the person has a legitimate fear of persecution. It was through the 1951 Convention that non-refoulement gained its widespread and prominent position in international refugee policy. The Refugee Convention states: "No Contracting State shall expel or return a refugee in any manner whatsoever to the frontiers of territories where his life or freedom would be threatened on account of his race, religion, nationality, membership of a particular social group or political opinion." The understanding of non-refoulement in practice has changed with time. According to Article I(1) of the 1967 Protocol, non-refoulement is not contingent on lawful residence of a refugee in the territory of a contracting state. This means non-refoulement pertains to any country—not only the country of origin—where a refugee has reason to fear persecution.

The Refugee Convention in Practice

Every signatory to the 1951 Refugee Convention is required to "domesticate" the Convention. That means countries are required to create national law and policies for asylum that align with the Convention. This requirement made the Convention a powerful protection for refugees and asylum seekers. In the United States, the specifics of the Refugee Convention can be found in the US Code Section 1158. As of 2020, 146 countries were signatories to the 1951 Convention with the latest signatory country, South Sudan, in 2018.

The United States is not fully compliant with the international refugee law because it sets a one-year time limit on the application for asylum and limits the number of refugees it will allow in from each region every year. Someone applying after that one-year deadline could be deported—an action some would consider refoulement. Significant refugee-hosting countries, such as Jordan, have not yet signed onto the Refugee Convention or its Protocol, but follow the principle of non-refoulement. The fact that nonsignatories to the Refugee Convention adhere to non-refoulement illustrates that it has become customary international law and is now an expectation of states that exists beyond the legal requirements of the Convention.[12]

People arriving in a country apply for asylum if they are seeking to stay based on the Refugee Convention. Asylum is the legal protection of someone fleeing persecution. Asylum seekers are a category of migrants distinct from those who travel to another country for better employment opportunities—economic migrants. Asylum seekers usually arrive in a country without work visas or residency permits, so they must seek permission to stay through a legal determination to assess whether they have a well-founded fear of persecution. The exception is refugees who have gone through a prior asylum application process, were declared to be refugees, and received clearance for resettlement before arriving in the country. In their case, the asylum determination was first made in a country of refuge, usually by the UNHCR. For example, a Bhutanese refugee family coming into the United States as part of a resettlement program has already been granted political asylum and has a legal right to remain and work in the country once they arrive. Child migrants crossing the US/Mexican border from Central America, by contrast, must apply for asylum within one year of arriving in the United States and can be deported if their applications are rejected.

In the summer of 2018, US attorney general Jeff Sessions drew attention to asylum seekers by declaring that asylum would no longer be granted to those fleeing gangs and domestic violence. His argument targeted Central American asylum seekers and overturned a previous decision by the Board of Immigration Appeals. Sessions made his case for exclusion based on an interpretation of US Code 1158, arguing that

> an applicant seeking to establish persecution on account of membership in a "particular social group" must satisfy two requirements. First, the applicant must demonstrate membership in a group, which is composed of members who share a common immutable characteristic, is defined with particularity, and is socially distinct within the society in question. And second, the applicant's membership in that group must be a central reason for her persecution. When, as here, the alleged persecutor is someone unaffiliated with the government, the applicant must show that flight from her country is necessary because her home government is unwilling or unable to protect her.[13]

While Sessions clearly wanted to limit the number of asylum seekers coming to the United States, he did not, and indeed could not, opt out of the Refugee Convention, as it had become the law of the United States. Instead, the attorney general had to issue a reinterpretation of US Code.

Where is a person supposed to file an asylum claim? The Refugee Convention doesn't state a clear answer, although in Article 31(1) it says,

> The Contracting States shall not impose penalties, on account of their illegal entry or presence, on refugees who, coming directly from a territory where their life or freedom was threatened in the sense of article 1, enter or are present in their territory without authorization, provided they present themselves without delay to the authorities and show good cause for their illegal entry or presence.

Refugees often make their way through multiple countries until they get to one where they want to seek asylum. The European Union (EU) addressed this issue and streamlined the asylum process across member states through Dublin III, or what is often called the Dublin Regulation. Under the Dublin Regulation, asylum seekers must apply for asylum in the first EU member state they enter. That way only one European country will be responsible for the asylum application and people will not file multiple applications in different countries. Some refugee rights advocates viewed the Dublin Regulation as a violation of the Refugee Convention, but the European Court of Justice ruled that it could stand.

States use a variety of means to subvert their obligations under the Refugee Convention. An illustration of this is found in the case of people trying to get into the EU in 2016 via the "Balkans Route." Many of them were passing through Serbia, but did not want to apply for asylum there because they did not want refuge in Serbia. Instead, they aspired to enter the EU (Serbia was not a member), where they would have better economic opportunities. The EU countries wanted the migrants to apply for asylum in Serbia. Hungary, which was a bordering EU country, erected a large fence to prevent the movement of migrants across the border between Serbia and Hungary. If a state grants someone asylum, that person is then a refugee and must receive protection. In practice, this means that a refugee remains in that country until they can return home safely and voluntarily. James Hathaway argues that the effect of this requirement is that "governments that are financially and logistically able to prevent the arrival of asylum seekers in the first place will likely choose that option."[14] The border fence between Serbia and Hungary is an example.

In 2020 as the Covid-19 pandemic raged, large numbers of people were trying to get to Europe by crossing the Mediterranean Sea or crossing land borders on foot. Faced with the threat of disease and a large influx of migrants, some European countries detained and deported asylum seekers, refused to let boats land on their shores, or shut down their asylum processes entirely. The European Commission responded to this situation with a New Pact on Migration and Asylum to establish a common set of policies for asylum seekers to address the large numbers of irregular arrivals and the Covid-19 pandemic. The New Pact called for pre-entry screenings, faster asylum evaluations, the quick deportation of those who do not qualify, and a plan for better tracking people's movements within EU countries.[15] While the pact leaves the Dublin Regulation in place and adheres to the Refugee Convention, it also makes it clear that the EU is not as welcoming to non-European asylum seekers as it was in 2015, when German chancellor Angela Merkel opened Germany's borders to Syrian refugees, assuring Germans, "We can handle this."[16] Restrictions on non-European asylum seekers contrasts with the open door provided by the EU to Ukrainian refugees in 2022. After the Russian attack on Ukraine, a "Temporary Protection Directive" waived asylum seeker protocols for Ukrainians, allowing them to apply for protection in any EU state. This included residence permits, the right to work and social welfare benefits.[17]

Durable Solutions

When are people no longer refugees? When they find a "durable solution" The phrase "durable solutions" came into common usage in the late 1970s, institutionalized in the Working Group on the UNHCR Fund for Durable Solutions.[18] There are three durable solutions—voluntary repatriation, local integration, and resettlement—each embedded in an interpretation of the 1951 Refugee Convention. Durable solution is never clearly defined in international law, but it means a lasting restoration of human rights.[19] Certainly, that is a minimum standard. Catherine-Lune Grayson has noted that all three durable solutions "enable refugees to secure the political, economic, legal and social conditions needed to maintain life, livelihood and dignity" and fall in line with the UNHCR's mission of "seeking permanent solutions for the problem of refugees."[20] If "restoration of human rights" is the minimum threshold for a durable solution, we could set "conditions necessary to maintain life, livelihood and dignity" as the maximum. The lived reality of durable solutions is closer to the minimum—most often a safer life in a neighboring country that frequently has its own challenges of pervasive poverty and limited economic opportunities.

Voluntary Repatriation

Until 1985, resettlement in a third country, typically somewhere in the Global North, was encouraged as a possible solution for refugees. By the 2000s, few countries were willing to permanently resettle refugees. Lack of resettlement opportunities plus limitations on local integration make voluntary repatriation increasingly the *only* viable durable solution. Repatriation is appealing for multiple reasons. First, if people are returning to their country of origin, they already have citizenship and do not need to wait for a positive decision in a bureaucratic process or legal case that will allow them residency or citizenship in a different country. Second, repatriation is less logistically complex when people have homes and property to which they can return. Third, return is symbolic of a restoration of normality. Where forced migration was the goal of violence against a group of people, their return to the country of origin, and even the homes and communities of origin, has a special appeal from the standpoint of justice and postconflict reconstruction. Available data affirms the policy preference for voluntary repatriation. In the most recent data on durable solutions from 2020—an admittedly bad year due to Covid-19 and restrictive refugee policies in the United States—251,000 refugees returned to their countries of origin, while only 34,400 were resettled to third countries.[21] Resettlement opportunities are limited, decreasing, and allocated to the most vulnerable and their families. There are no available numbers for local integration.

Repatriation was first articulated as the priority solution for displacement in the aftermath of World War I, by Fridtjof Nansen, who viewed repatriation as the only option for the 1.5 million European refugees.[22] It is now the cornerstone of both UNHCR policy and state preferences for refugees and displaced people. The notion of voluntary return derives from the principle of non-refoulement. Voluntary repatriation involves a "free and informed choice" by those returning to their country and assumes return in "safety and dignity."[23] It was first addressed by the UN General Assembly in 1946. Resolution 8(1) said, "No refugees or displaced persons who have finally and definitely, in complete freedom and after receiving full knowledge of the facts, including adequate information from the Governments of their countries of origin, expressed valid objections to returning to their countries of origin . . . shall be compelled to return to their country of origin." This language suggests the decision to return is made by the individual, which can be true. Yet it is also true that states and the UNHCR decide when it is safe to return and can revoke refugee status from certain groups of people. For example, in 1978 Bangladesh forcibly repatriated two hundred thousand Rohingya refugees to Burma with the cooperation of the UNHCR.[24] This happened again in 1994. Indeed, despite the rhetoric, repatriation has not always been voluntary. It has sometimes been forced or incentivized through strategies such as the elimination of food rations.

In 1996, the UNHCR publicized the doctrine of imposed return, making it clear the organization believed that voluntary nature of repatriation faced too many constraints, leading it to acknowledge involuntary repatriation as a necessary solution under certain circumstances.[25] This is not to say that the UNHCR favors this option—only that it is a recognized reality that many returns occur "under some form of duress."[26] The UNHCR is often under political pressure to facilitate forced or premature returns when states are no longer willing to host refugees.[27] Indeed, the UNHCR has in recent years shifted some of its focus to the reintegration of refugees and displaced people, recognizing that people may be going back before they would wish to do so, sometimes to dangerous situations.[28]

Local Integration

Local integration is a durable solution in which refugees permanently remain in the country where they have sought refuge—typically the closest neighboring country. In cases of violence, people flee to the closest place of safety, often across the nearest state boundary. This happened when Ukrainians fled violence in 2022 taking refuge in neighboring states. Similarly, during the Mano River Wars in West Africa from 1989 to 2003, refugees moved back and forth across the borders of Guinea, Liberia, and Sierra Leone, finding safety wherever they could. After those conflicts ended, many refugees remained outside of their countries of origin and locally integrated there. These countries were members of the Economic Community of West African States (ECOWAS) and according to a 1979 "Free Movement" protocol, any ECOWAS member state national can live and work in any other ECOWAS state. After war ended, this regional agreement facilitated local integration. In Liberia today there are several Sierra Leonean communities in Bomi and Grand Cape Mount Counties consisting of people who were refugees from the civil war in Sierra Leone. In 2008, they had the opportunity to apply to become naturalized citizens of Liberia. Many chose to do so, thus fully integrating into their country of refuge.

This successful West African example contrasts with other circumstances in which host countries actively oppose local integration. Under the Refugee Convention, countries have no obligation to make refugees citizens or permanent residents. Countries resist the local integration of refugees for a variety of reasons, including cost, security, and political entanglements. It is expensive to take care of the needs of refugees and, while we would expect that international humanitarian organizations would shoulder this cost, that is not always the case. As the number of displaced people rises, humanitarian organizations such as the World Food Program (WFP) are challenged to meet the needs of displaced people. In 2016 the WFP announced a shortfall in funding requiring it to reduce rations across a number of countries hosting refugees.[29] In Uganda, which at that time hosted six hundred thousand refugees and asylum seekers from Burundi, South Sudan, Somalia, Rwanda, and the Democratic Republic of Congo, those who arrived before 2015 had their rations cut by 50%. Food is the most obvious need for refugees. They also need housing, medical treatment, access to education for children, jobs, and land to farm if they are to be self-supporting.

Security is an additional concern of refugee-hosting countries. After the Rwandan genocide, many of the genocidaires fled to the Democratic Republic of Congo, where they stayed in refugee camps and, in some instances, carried on with their genocidal agenda. Genocidaires were fed, provided with medical care, and protected from accountability for their crimes while in the camps.[30] Countries that consider refugees to be security threats typically will keep them in camps and not allow them to locally integrate, or seek to prevent their presence in the country. Kenya has frequently threatened to close refugee camps for Somalis and has forcibly repatriated some refugees because of its concerns that camps are safe havens for members of Al-Shabaab, a radical Islamist group operating out of Somalia.[31] In May 2016, the Kenyan government announced that it would close the Dadaab refugee camp in eastern Kenya near the Somali border after two attacks (Westgate Mall in Nairobi in 2013 and then on Garissa University in 2015) attributed to Al-Shabaab. The camp was inhabited by 280,000 people, mainly Somali refugees, some of whom had been there for twenty years.[32] As of this writing, Dadaab has not closed; it remains open as a dismal option for Somali citizens fleeing violence.

Long sojourns in refugee camps are not durable solutions. While people may find food and services there, these cities of tents are intended to be impermanent. Betts and Collier offer caustic commentary on the three durable solutions: "Around the world, refugees are effectively offered a false choice between three dismal options: encampment, urban destitution or perilous journeys."[33] Encampment is not used in every country. Practices regarding the local economic opportunities of refugees are inconsistent across countries of refuge. As noted above Ukrainian refugees in EU countries are allowed to work. Chechen refugees in Azerbaijan are not allowed to work, but Chechen refugees in Georgia can. As a result many of the Chechen refugees in Azerbaijan are women engaged in informal trade.[34] Encampment forces refugees to be dependent on international aid organizations, but local integration, usually in cities, gives refugees the opportunity to work and pursue education or training. Economic opportunities influence where refugees seek asylum. Somali refugees prefer South Africa to Kenya because South Africa allows them to work, while Kenya does not.[35]

Resettlement

People who have little hope of returning to their country of origin in safety, perhaps because of discrimination against their religious group or due to their political activities, can apply for asylum and resettlement in another country, usually somewhere in the Global North. My first job out of college was resettling refugees in St. Louis, Missouri. At that time, many Ethiopians who had been active in rebel groups trying to overthrow the military government fled to Sudan for safety, then applied for political asylum and resettlement. They could not safely return to Ethiopia, and there was no future for them in Sudan. Many of them came to the United States or went to Sweden, Canada, and other countries where they became naturalized citizens and began new lives. Many of the large Ethiopian diaspora communities in the United States and elsewhere in the Global North are a result of resettlement efforts in the late 1980s and early 1990s that were designed to provide these political refugees with a durable solution to their refugee status.

For people fleeing violence and economic privation resettlement may be the most desirable option—the promise of full citizenship rights in a country with safety and opportunity. Yet resettlement is politically divisive in the Global North, and opportunities for resettlement are declining. It is only an option for the most vulnerable refugees—less than 1%—who are chosen by the UNHCR. These are people who have been victims of torture, children at risk, LGBT and handicapped people, vulnerable women and girls and their families.[36] Single Muslim men face barriers to resettlement because they are perceived as potential threats even if they fall into a category of vulnerability, such as being LGBT or a victim of torture.[37] While the numbers of people seeking asylum have increased, there is no commensurate increase in resettlement opportunities.

In 2017, resettlement became a major political issue in the United States as President Donald Trump restricted refugees from several Muslim-majority countries. In an executive order, the administration identified Iraq, Syria, Sudan, Iran, Somalia, Libya, and Yemen as sources of terrorist threats.[38] The executive order also capped refugee admissions at 50,000 per year.[39] The UNHCR reports that in 2016, 84,995 refugees were resettled in the United States, the largest number resettled in any state. In 2017 that number dropped to 29,022, and in 2020 the government announced a cap of 15,000 for fiscal year 2021. President Trump's action followed decisions by other developed states, such as Australia, that restricted the number and place of origin of those people it would accept as asylum seekers or refugees. In Europe, as refugees and migrants streamed into Greece in 2015, some countries welcomed them, while others, such as Slovakia, insisted they could not be expected to grant refuge to those who were religiously different.

Resettlement will remain one of the hot issues of the twenty-first century. Displacement due to violence and climate change is increasing. Many people are leaving their countries in search of protection and opportunity elsewhere, yet where can they legally go? Becoming a refugee and seeking asylum used to be one way of overcoming barriers to entry in northern states, but that open door for refugees and asylum seekers is closing. The 1951 Refugee Convention was never intended to require states to give refugees permanent residence in a different country. "Refugees are instead entitled to benefit from dignified and rights-regarding protection until and unless conditions in the State of origin permit repatriation without the risk of persecution."[40] Yet even that provision of refuge is now under threat as some states seek mechanisms to prevent asylum seekers from arriving in their countries and claiming their rights under international law.

Internally Displaced People

Critical to any discussion of conflict-induced forced migration is a distinction between the two categories of displaced people: refugees, who have crossed an international border; and IDPs, who are forced to leave their homes and communities but do not cross an international boundary. The 1951 Refugee Convention addresses the treatment of refugees, but there is no similar international convention for displaced people. At first glance, this should not matter, as the fact that people remain in their state of origin means that the government still has responsibility for the protection of their rights and well-being. Yet civil wars or natural disasters preclude some states from protecting their citizens. Moreover, intentional state actions can cause forced displacement. This happens in civil wars—Colombia, Ethiopia, and Sri Lanka are examples—or when the state targets its own citizens, such as in Myanmar.

Absence of a comprehensive and binding international agreement on IDPs makes them uniquely vulnerable. First, there is no humanitarian agency tasked with their protection. While the UNHCR has stepped into the gap to fulfill some of this role, assisting IDPs is not part of its mandate. Recognizing the need, the Norwegian Refugee Council created the Internal Displacement Monitoring Centre (IDMC) in 1998 to track the numbers of IDPs around the world.[41] The IDMC shares information publicly and provides analysis of IDP crises around the world. These efforts are important, but no organization is tasked with IDP protection the way the UNHCR protects refugees. A second issue is that while *refugee* is a recognized legal status with certain rights; being an IDP is just a description. There are no benefits or obligations that states have in relation to IDPs. A third problem resulting from the lack of an international agreement on IDPs is that if government violence against civilians is the source of displacement, there is little hope for the protection of civilians who remain within the borders of the state. In those countries with the greatest numbers of displaced people—Afghanistan, Syria, Yemen, South Sudan, Colombia, and Iraq—governments are, or have been, actors in the conflict and are unable to provide the kind of civilian protections that we would expect of more stable states.

Between 1982 and 1995 the number of IDPs increased from an estimated 1.2 million people in eleven countries to 20–25 million people in over forty countries, almost twice the number of refugees. This rapid growth in IDPs drew the attention of relief organizations. As the Cold War subsided, the possibility of providing aid to people at risk within their own countries became increasingly appealing to the international community. Three NGOs—the Friends World Committee for Consultation, the Refugee Policy Group, and the World Council of Churches—campaigned for a UN representative on IDPs as well as a set of international standards to protect them. In 1992, the secretary-general appointed Francis M. Deng, a Sudanese diplomat, as the representative charged with conducting this analysis. Deng formed a team of legal experts who identified seventeen areas of insufficient protection for IDPs. The Guiding Principles on Internal Displacement (2001) emerged from the team's findings. The position of Special Rapporteur on the Human Rights of Internally Displaced Persons was created within the UN to raise awareness regarding the issue of IDPs and draw attention to the Guiding Principles.

The nature of the development of the Guiding Principles matters. Because they were created by a committee within the UN, rather than negotiated between states, they are nonbinding. States are not required to follow them because they did not formally adopt them. Despite this limitation, the Guiding Principles have been influential in regional accords on displacement, such as the African Union Convention for the Protection and Assistance of Internally Displaced Persons in Africa, known informally as the Kampala Convention. The Kampala Convention came into force in 2010 and is *the only legally binding international law on internal displacement*. So far, fifty-four African states have signed the Kampala Convention and twenty-five have ratified it. The Kampala Convention broke new ground in terms of IDP protections in two ways: it (1) established a legal definition of an IDP and, most importantly, (2) compels states to work together with international organizations and civil society groups to address the needs of IDPs when the state is unable to do so. The convention shows a pragmatic recognition that state weakness is one of the causes of displacement and that states cannot, on their own, meet the needs of displaced populations.

Distinctions between IDPs and Refugees

The way legal distinctions between IDPs and refugees are meaningful in practice is best seen by example. In 1999, Kosovo fought a war of independence from Serbia. NATO intervened in the conflict on the side of Kosovo and Kosovo became de facto independent.[42] During that war, many Albanians fled into neighboring countries such as Macedonia and Albania, where they were recognized as refugees and provided with shelter, food rations, and medical care. Serbs and Roma who fled during the conflict typically went to central Serbia. They left their homes, businesses, and occupations, in many cases with short notice and little in the way of resources. Since Serbia then claimed, and indeed still claims, Kosovo as part of its sovereign territory, it did not recognize displaced Serbs and Roma as refugees. They were not given any of the special services, such as housing and medical assistance, they would have merited if they had crossed the border into Montenegro, North Macedonia, or another neighboring state. Instead, they were considered IDPs by the Serbian state, which, in the early years after the war, wanted them to return to Kosovo and reestablish the Serbian claim there.[43] The Serbian government was not obligated to treat them any differently than other citizens, and they did not warrant international humanitarian assistance. The UNHCR recognized their situation and pressured the Serbian government to act on their behalf. Thousands remained displaced in central Serbia after Kosovo's declaration of independence. Now, two decades after that conflict, there are remaining problems for IDPs in terms of claiming pensions, getting verification of their work, or even access to jobs. Some Serbs who worked in government positions were told they could not apply for new jobs in central Serbia because they still had their jobs in Kosovo, even if they were unable to return to those jobs. One woman described the problem to me as follows:

> It is impossible, but I never formally left my job, and the first appearance here you don't have a clue what is your real status. You know that you didn't become displaced from another country. I ran away from one part of the country to another part of the country. The people from Croatia, they were refugees. But I am displaced. I am

an internally displaced person. Can you imagine that you don't have a job and when you ask for a job, you are told that you still have your job.[44]

In this case, being a displaced person created ambiguities that were harmful to those trying to rebuild their lives in new places.

IDPs and Return Migration

Comparing the return patterns of IDPs and refugees is not easy. While we generally know if refugees have repatriated, we do not have this information for IDPs. The UNHCR is diligent in tracking individuals registered as refugees, but there is no similar individual monitoring of IDPs. It may be logistically easier for IDPs to return to their place of origin, as they need not go through immigration procedures or lengthy travel to do so. When the Ugandan government wanted people to move back home from camps in northern Uganda after the area became peaceful, they closed the camps, shut down the schools, and stopped distributing humanitarian aid. This facilitated return home for camp residents.[45]

Fleeing a conflict drives rural people into cities. In Colombia, 93% of the displaced live in urban areas, where they gravitate toward informal settlements on the outskirts of major cities.[46] Rapid movement from rural to urban areas means that households lose assets and face sustained impoverishment.[47] Little research has been done on the preferences for return migration for IDPs as compared to refugees. IDPs do not have the option of resettlement in a third country, but we may safely assume that they locally integrate in larger numbers than refugees because they do not face the same barriers to work or to getting necessary documents.[48] Megan Bradley has noted the growing recognition that IDPs need durable solutions too, specifically that IDPs have the right to property restoration and return to their homes within a country.[49]

State Sovereignty, the International Arena, and Individual Preferences

States and international organizations determine the rules for return migration. Individual displaced people make decisions within the set of choices constructed by these more powerful actors. The following section identifies the preferences and constraints of international organizations, states, and displaced people. States differ in their perspectives depending on whether they are proximate to war zones, desirable places for resettlement, or those to which refugees are repatriating.

International Organizations

The UNHCR is the organization tasked with protection of refugees. It has a large budget and international presence, enabling it to address protracted refugee situations as well as developing crises. The people who work for the UNHCR are professional, compassionate, knowledgeable, but ultimately limited by the interests of the states that fund the organization. Barbara Harrell-Bond has commented on this predicament:

> As a creation of the governments, the UNHCR has never been able to act independently. The donor governments which exercise the greatest power over refugee policy have become increasingly frustrated over the growing cost of supporting the budget of this organization and have been seeking a means of reducing their obligations. In their efforts to find ways to reduce costs, the promotion of repatriation has been seized upon as the appropriate solution.[50]

International law created by states and administered by the UNHCR gives people the legal right to return to their country of origin. While they are entitled to protection if they have a legitimate fear of persecution, they have no legal right to local integration or resettlement. Yet the right to protection is significant—it is more than the rights held by IDPs. "Refugee" can be a privileged title—it is a legally defined status imbued with rights that states and international organizations are obliged to protect. If you are a refugee, you are recognized as persecuted. Those crossing borders because of climate change, poor economies, famine, or gang violence or crime do not receive the same recognition or protections, though their situations may be equally grave.

States

The interests of states alter over time and in relation to specific security threats. Changing political circumstances can lead states to reinterpret their obligations under international law. Kenya's hospitality toward Somali refugees shifted precipitously after two terrorist attacks linked to a Somali group. Despite being a signatory to the Refugee Convention, Kenya began to forcibly repatriate Somali refugees living in the Dadaab refugee camp. While the Kenyan government claimed that it was safe to return to Somalia and that refugees were returning voluntarily, this was contested by Médecins Sans Frontières, which found that 86% of refugees surveyed were unwilling to return.[51] The Kenyan government told refugees that they would only receive financial support if they "voluntarily" returned, so many did, despite the fact that this was viewed by human rights organizations to be an incident of refoulement.[52] When the UN High Commissioner for Refugees, Filippo Grandi, visited Kenya in June 2016 to discuss the matter, he "received assurances that the return of refugees to Somalia would not contravene international obligations"[53] but the UNHCR was unable to stop the Kenyan government from forcibly returning refugees, as there is no external enforcement mechanism for the Refugee Convention; it is dependent on the cooperation of states.

Kenya, like other refugee-hosting states in the Global South, has historically demonstrated a tremendous openness to refugees. Indeed, the largest refugee-hosting states are those that neighbor countries such as Afghanistan, South Sudan, Syria, and Nigeria where there are ongoing violent conflicts. At the time of this writing the war in Ukraine has just started and we see the flow of refugees into its neighbor countries.

While an openness to refugees is the norm, security concerns and the financial burden of refugees are two reasons why states in the Global South might favor repatriation. European countries, while willing to take in European refugees, are apprehensive about non-European asylum seekers due to concerns regarding the integration of refugees into their cultures and rising anti-immigrant sentiment. According to a survey conducted by the Pew Research Center in 2016, a year following the 2015 surge in asylum seekers to Europe, a significant number of European citizens believed that accommodating refugees would negatively impact the region. Evidence from the survey suggests that Europeans do not see refugees and diversity positively. In each of ten countries surveyed, no more than 40% believed that diversity improves their country, and in two countries, Greece and Italy, the majority of those surveyed said that diversity worsens their country. Regarding security, a majority of those surveyed across the ten countries (59%) feared that the increase in refugees would lead to a rise in terrorism in Europe.[54]

The willingness of states to accommodate refugees is increasingly in question. For example, Slovakia declared in 2016 that it would take in

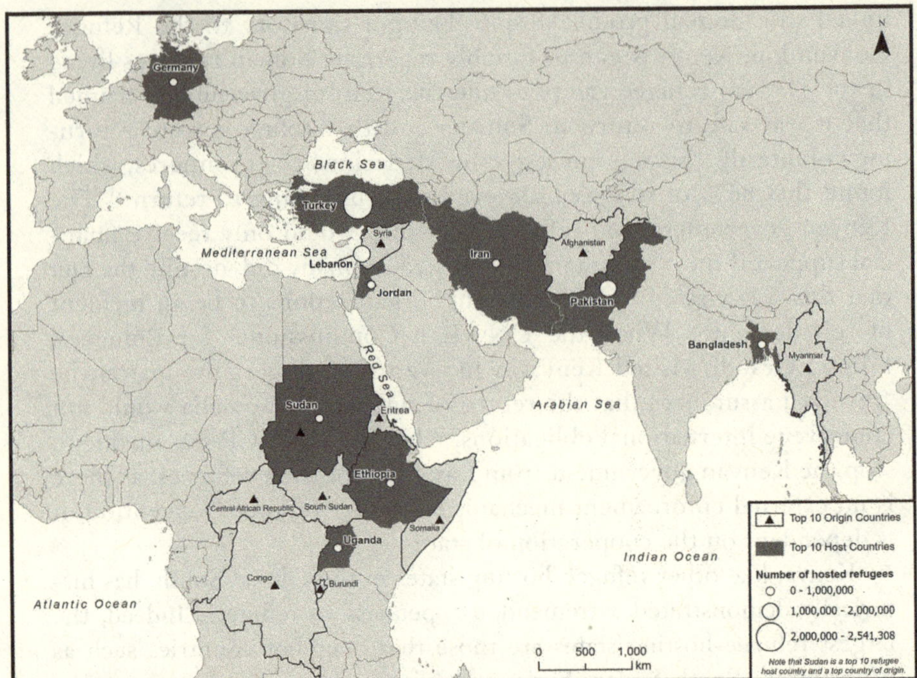

Figure 2. The Ten Countries Hosting the Largest Refugee Populations in 2020

refugees, just no Muslims.[55] In April 2016, the EU negotiated a deal with Turkey whereby it would return to Turkey asylum seekers who came to the EU from Turkey via Greece. In exchange, for each person it returned to Turkey, EU countries would take one person from Turkey who qualified as a refugee. A year after the agreement was made, the following EU countries had taken in no refugees from Turkey: Austria, Bulgaria, Croatia, Cyprus, Czech Republic, Denmark, Greece, Hungary, Ireland, Malta, Poland, Romania, Slovakia, Slovenia, and the UK.[56] Across the Atlantic, similar trends of resistance to refugee resettlement garner attention. The Trump executive order restricting refugees justified it by stating that "terrorist groups have sought to infiltrate several nations through refugee programs."[57] While the 2021 US open door to Afghanis who worked with US forces seems to disprove this trend, it is not yet clear how this will impact overall public sentiment on the accommodation of refugees.

Resistance to refugee resettlement usually takes the form of passive refusal to admit refugees, but state interests can lead to involuntary refugee repatriation. Pakistan has hosted large numbers of Afghan refugees since

1978, when a coup in Afghanistan and the Soviet invasion created conflict that has persisted in different forms since that time. The proximity of Pakistan—their long, shared border and ethnic similarities—made Pakistan a natural place of refuge. Afghan refugees, forcibly repatriated in 2016 and 2017, immediately became IDPs within Afghanistan because it was not safe for them to return to their homes. They were repatriated to Afghanistan as violence there was rising.[58] To compel repatriation, Pakistan stopped providing schooling for Afghan refugee children and announced that refugee status for Afghans would be revoked. Human Rights Watch argues that this amounted to refoulement because the conditions in Afghanistan were still insecure.[59] Involuntary repatriation occurred because Pakistan increasingly saw the refugees as a security threat.

One Afghan woman who experienced refoulement is Masooma. She fled Afghanistan in the 1980s and lived in Pakistan for the majority of her life.[60] The deterioration of Afghan-Pakistan relations accompanied by increased attacks by the Pakistani Taliban increased police harassment and new restrictions for Afghan refugees in Pakistan. In September 2016, Masooma's husband was arrested and detained for one month for not being able to produce government-issued refugee documents. When he was released, the family was given two days to leave Pakistan. Masooma and her family of ten returned to Afghanistan, where they are internally displaced because it is not safe to return to their home area. Since there is no school near their settlement, Masooma's children do not go to school as they did in Pakistan.[61]

Throughout this chapter, I have noted examples of involuntary repatriation. It is unclear whether involuntary repatriation of refugees will increase in the future, but it is something we should anticipate. B. S. Chimni has noted this unfortunate trend.

> Today, involuntary repatriation is coming to be pursued as a solution to the refugee problem because in the post Cold War era the rich Northern states see no reason to share the burden of the poor South at both the level of asylum and resources. Involuntary repatriation may thus be described as the favoured solution of the Northern states in the era of globalization which is marked by the end of the Cold War and a growing North-South divide.[62]

In cases of involuntary repatriation, state interests supersede those of individuals and the requirements of international law. States are the most powerful actors in migration because no matter what they have agreed to under international law, the choices regarding who is let into a country are made at the border by immigration officials controlled by the state. This is a hard reality. States determine whether they will accept refugees, how many they will allow in, and to whom they will give citizenship. They make decisions based on political incentives within their borders, not on the pressing needs without. Megan Bradley has observed, "The problems associated with return are troubling for anyone concerned with the rights and wellbeing of refugees, but this does not alter the political realities now underlying the international refugee regime: affluent countries lack the incentive and domestic support necessary to resuscitate large-scale resettlement programmes."[63] Indeed.

Individuals

Least powerful in terms of their ability to influence outcomes are individuals and families displaced by violence. Repatriation is the option favored by states and, therefore, the option that dominates the discourse of durable solutions and the incentive structures for households and individuals. Displaced people may want to resettle in the Global North, but there are few opportunities to do so. They might also like to remain in the country in which they have taken refuge, but this option may too be closed. Naohiko Omata argues that the return discourse "dehumanizes" refugees by neglecting their own agency in making decisions.[64] But refugee agency frequently is limited to remaining in a refugee camp or repatriating, if that is possible.

Conclusion

International law establishes minimal standards for the treatment of refugees. The Refugee Convention prohibits the forcible return of people to circumstances in which their lives might be in danger. Yet the definition of refugee is intentionally narrow—to be a refugee is to cross an international boundary due to a clearly defined danger. Looking for better economic opportunity does not make you a refugee, nor does displacement within your own country. Legal protections for IDPs are insufficient in spite of some international efforts focused on their protection, and there are no protections at all for economic or climate change migrants.

The United Nations Refugee Agency was established to ensure the protection of refugees across the world. It has identified three durable solutions to refugee status: return to country of origin, local integration, and resettlement to another country, usually in the Global North. Achieving one of these outcomes means that people are no longer classified as refugees. However, people do not have the opportunity to choose which of these outcomes they prefer. Opportunities for resettlement, always limited, are declining further due to political circumstances in Europe and the United States. Yet the number of refugees in camps or situations of temporary refuge is increasing.

International law and state preference align to channel the choices of refugees toward repatriation. Yet the longer people are away from home, the more likely they are to develop preferences other than voluntary return to their places of origin. This is due to security concerns, changing ideas of home, opportunities elsewhere, and property losses. These factors impact decisions to return for both refugees and IDPs. In the next chapter, I consider the role of individual preferences in decisions to return after conflict. This chapter has been the backdrop for that discussion, demonstrating that international law and the decisions of states constrain the set of choices available to those fleeing violence.

THREE

Challenges to Return

Preferences of Displaced People

During 2020, 251,000 refugees returned to their countries of origin, often to situations which were unsafe.[1]

States prefer refugees to return to their countries of origin. International organizations such as the UNHCR serve the interests of those states and promote repatriation. Given the lack of resettlement opportunities and restrictions on permanent residence in places of refuge, repatriation is the most viable option. States are obligated to provide an open door for their citizens to return home. Yet the idea that a return home restores the pre-conflict status quo is a chimera. In reality, communities change as a result of conflict and so do the preferences of people displaced by violence.

In 2020, there were 20.7 million refugees, and an additional 48 million internally displaced people (IDPs).[2] Repatriation numbers were higher in the 1990s, contributing to the expectation that repatriation is the anticipated end of the refugee experience.[3] Repatriation means going back to your country of origin. It does not mean a return to home community, prior circumstances, or even full-time residence. The responsibility for repatriated people becomes that of the state of origin/citizenship, though the UNHCR has begun to monitor repatriated people in some concerning situations. Repatriation appears to solve the problem of displacement; people are back where they are supposed to be. Laura Hammond identifies the trouble with this understanding.

One of the reasons that repatriation has not been problematised is that its goal has been defined primarily as the need to put people back into "their place," defined in most cases as their birthplace. It is assumed by practitioners involved in repatriation programmes, whether governmental, nongovernmental or UN personnel, that once returnees are back in their native country, their roots will be reestablished. Like seedlings replanted in the earth, they will grow and thrive with a minimum of maintenance or attention. Once the natural tie between person and place is reestablished, it is expected that other challenges (attaining economic self-sufficiency, building social networks, and becoming active and valued citizens of the community, the region and the nation) will be met *ipso facto*.[4]

Because of the many cases in which repatriation is resisted or does not follow the expected pattern of return to the home community, there is a growing literature on its merits. It is important to reiterate a definitional distinction raised in the previous chapter. Refugees who return home are repatriating; IDPs who go back to their places of origin are just returning home. I use "return" when including both groups and "repatriate" when referring to just refugees. This distinction is not helpful in cases of contested sovereignty, such as the example of Kosovo in this chapter, where the use of one term or the other is a political statement.

Repatriation is the subject of refugee studies and international law, while the return of IDPs does not generate the same scholarly and political interest because, though both groups are victims of conflict-induced, forced displacement, only refugees have legal rights. Oliver Bakewell has called upon social scientists to think beyond legal and humanitarian categories to address more fundamental issues, such as why people make the choices they do.[5] Looking beyond just refugees helps us better understand more preferences of the displaced. For example in Colombia, violence displaced people within the country. A survey of twenty-seven thousand Colombian IDPs identified that 78% did not want to return to their home communities.[6] This is consistent with previous, smaller studies from Colombia, some of which had even higher percentages of people who had no desire to return to their places of origin.[7] In other circumstances where people are displaced across international borders, there is an observable reluctance to return to the community of origin.[8] Some people choose not to return; some rural people return to cities, while others return to rural areas other than their original homes.[9]

The central claim of this chapter is that displaced people do not always want to return home. The chapter is broken into three parts. The first identifies the issues that impact the decision to return. The second part addresses when and how people return, drawing attention to the fact that often people do not go back to their home communities even if they repatriate. The last section of the chapter presents a case study of Kosovo, where a war from 1998 to 1999 displaced most of the population. The Kosovo case illustrates how return migration patterns are conditioned by ethnicity, with Albanians (the majority) returning en masse immediately after the conflict, Serbs returning in limited numbers well after the conclusion of the war, and Roma forcibly repatriated years following the end of the conflict.

This chapter constructs a complex picture of what people choose to do in the wake of violent displacement. The goal is to consider what we know and what we can discern about people's preferences, separated from the international legal structure and any assumptions about "natural" patterns of return to place of origin. Much of the literature on return migration focuses on the international legal framework. There is less scholarly investigation into the issue of preferences—who wants to repatriate after a conflict, where they want to return, and why. The research on postconflict choice is growing, and scholars focused on preferences and place-making can find themselves disturbingly at odds with the humanitarian community and "in danger of playing into the hands of governments and others who may wish to diminish or ignore the pain, suffering and therefore the rights, of those who have been forced out of their homes."[10] This need not be so. Social science inquiry into the preferences of displaced people does not contest the rights they have under international law, though it highlights the ways in which people and places are changed by violence. My hope is that this chapter brings legal rights and individual preferences together to construct a nuanced understanding of "successful return" and postconflict communities.

A Note on Methods

In this chapter I use the Kosovo case as an illustration because data from Kosovo are more available and reliable than in other settings. Cross-national quantitative data on return migration is notoriously difficult to get. The international political importance of Kosovo led to extensive funding for and monitoring of return migration. Combining the return data from the UN Refugee Agency with spatial analysis reveals a complete picture of return migration. These quantitative methods are paired with extensive interviews in Kosovo and Serbia that were designed to understand why people chose to return or not. I requested interviews from municipality officials responsible for return migration in every area of Kosovo that had Serb returns, excluding the Serb-controlled northern municipalities, and met with all who responded to me. In central Serbia, I used a standard set of open-ended questions to interview displaced Serbs, Gorani, and Roma who had not returned to their places of origin. A full list of interviews is available in the appendix. In central Serbia I found subjects to interview with the assistance of the Danish Refugee Council, the UNHCR, and a Serb self-help organization. These organizations are more likely to have contact with people who need assistance and have not successfully integrated into central Serbia, so the interviews may be more negatively biased. In this chapter I also use data from my field research in Liberia, which occurred in 2012 and 2013. In 2012, I conducted interviews and focus groups in Liberia with assistance in identifying contacts from a USAID project and the Norwegian Refugee Council. In this case the same reservations apply; people who are likely to encounter aid organizations are those in need of assistance. In the summer of 2013, I returned to Liberia and volunteered with the Liberian Refugee Repatriation and Resettlement Commission, supporting its work and unsuccessfully seeking better data on returnees to Liberia. While I did not conduct any interviews during that time because of potential conflicts of interest, I went to site visits, attended meetings with relief and development organizations, and contributed to the Commission's work.

Deciding to Return

The choice to return is influenced by environmental factors, household needs, opportunities, and individual motivation. Drivers of migration operate at varied scales, differ by location, and change over time.[11] Research on return migration has highlighted four categories of factors, which impact the return of displaced populations after security is assured: the time/ length of displacement; experience of trauma; economic opportunities; and the characteristics of the household.[12] In addition to these widely accepted categories, a number of recent studies suggest that decisions to return are also influenced by the political opinion of the displaced and which party / ethnic group / government is in authority in the home community.[13] Table 2 summarizes recent studies on the variables impacting return preferences among those displaced by violence.

TABLE 2. Selected Recent Studies of Preferences for Return Migration

Country of Origin	Date of Publication	Methodology	Variables Impacting Preference for Return	Citation
Syria	2021	Survey of refugees in Lebanon about future preferences	Exposure to violence, attachment to home, attachment to place of refuge	F. Ghosn, T. S. Chu, M. Simon, A. Braithwaite, M. Frith, and J. Jandali[1]
Syria	2021	Survey of 285 Syrian refugees living in Turkey	Positive contact with host country citizens associated with decreased desire to return	Z. Özkan, N. Ergün, and H. Çakal[2]
Lebanon	2020	Data from 209 villages in the Mount Lebanon region	Ethnicity, economic opportunity/property restitution, experience of violence	K. R. Camarena and N. Hagerdal[3]
Syria	2020	Survey of 889 Syrian refugees in Germany in 2015.	Education, experience of trauma, political situation	S. Kaya and P. Orchard[4]
Cyprus	2019	Survey of Greek and Turkish Cypriot IDPs in 2016 and 2017	Property restitution, political institutions	C. Psaltis, H. Cakal, N. Loizides, and I. Kuşçu Bonnenfant[5]
Myanmar, South Sudan	2019	Interviews with refugees	Security, destruction of property, absence of services, and livelihood opportunities	D. P. Sullivan[6]
South Sudan	2019	Perception-focused study	Security, property loss, ethnicity, livelihood options and services (education for children)	C. Huser, A. Cunningham, C. Kamau, and M. Obara[7]
Iraq, Colombia, Myanmar	2019	Quantitative analysis of refugee returns in the period 1995–2015	Security, socioeconomic factors, attachment to home	C. Sydney[8]
Sri Lankan Tamils in India	2019	Unclear methodology	Property return, socioeconomic opportunities, services (education)	A. Valcárcel Silvela[9]
Syria	2019	30 in-depth interviews	Military conscription, housing, economic issues, attachment to Lebanon, Syrian child custody laws, and political beliefs	T. Fakhoury and D. Ozkul[10]
Cyprus	2019	Survey of 1,605 displaced Greek Cypriots and 801 Turkish Cypriots	Gender, age, and views on justice in both communities. Willingness to have Turkish neighbors lower among Greek Cypriots who want to return.	C. Psaltis, N. Loizides, A. LaPierre, and D. Stefanovic[11]
Bosnia	2018	Survey of 1,007 IDPs in Bosnia conducted in 2013	Age, rural origin, ideology	S. Metivier, D. Stefanovic, and N. Loizides[12]
Bosnia	2017	Survey of 1,007 IDPs in Bosnia conducted in 2013	Age, gender, ethnicity, and traumatic experiences	D. Stefanovic and N. Loizides[13]

Country of Origin	Date of Publication	Methodology	Variables Impacting Preference for Return	Citation
Sri Lankan Tamils in India	2015	In depth interviews with 15 selected refugees	Identity, age, property restitution and support	M. George, W. Kliewer, and S. I. Rajan[14]
Kurds	2015	Survey of 370 displaced Kurd returnees and nonreturnees in Turkey	Education and degree of integration into new communities	D. Stefanovic, N. Loizides, and S. Parsons[15]
Somalia	2013	62 focus groups with a total of 410 refugees in camps in Kenya and Ethiopia plus 360 interviews with heads of refugee households	Experience of violence and length of displacement	Catherine-Lune Grayson[16]

1. Faten Ghosn et al., "The Journey Home: Violence, Anchoring, and Refugee Decisions to Return," *American Political Science Review* 115, no. 3 (2021).

2. Zafer Özkan, Naif Ergün, and Hüseyin Çakal, "Positive versus Negative Contact and Refugees' Intentions to Migrate: The Mediating Role of Perceived Discrimination, Life Satisfaction and Identification with the Host Society among Syrian Refugees in Turkey," *Journal of Community & Applied Social Psychology* 31, no. 4 (2021).

3. Kara Ross Camarena and Nils Hagerdal, "When Do Displaced Persons Return? Postwar Migration among Christians in Mount Lebanon," *American Journal of Political Science* 64, no. 2 (2020).

4. Serdar Kaya and Phil Orchard, "Prospects of Return: The Case of Syrian Refugees in Germany," *Journal of Immigrant & Refugee Studies* 18, no. 1 (2020).

5. Charis Psaltis et al., "Internally Displaced Persons and the Cyprus Peace Process," *International Political Science Review* 41, no. 1 (2019).

6. Daniel P. Sullivan, "Shared Obstacles to Return: Rohingya and South Sudanese," *Forced Migration Review*, no. 62 (2019).

7. Catherine Huser et al., "South Sudanese Returns: Perceptions and Responses," *Forced Migration Review*, no. 62 (2019).

8. Chloe Sydney, "Return Decision Making by Refugees," *Forced Migration Review*, no. 62 (2019).

9. Amaya Valcárcel Silvela, "Sri Lankan Tamil Refugees in India: Return or Integration?," *Forced Migration Review*, no. 62 (2019).

10. Tamirace Fakhoury and Derya Ozkul, "Syrian Refugees' Return from Lebanon," *Forced Migration Review*, no. 62 (2019).

11. Charis Psaltis et al., "Transitional Justice and Acceptance of Cohabitation in Cyprus," *Ethnic & Racial Studies* 42, no. 11 (2019).

12. Sean Metivier, Djordje Stefanovic, and Neophytos Loizides, "Struggling for and within the Community: What Leads Bosnian Forced Migrants to Desire Community Return?," *Ethnopolitics* 17, no. 2 (2018).

13. Djordje Stefanovic and Neophytos Loizides, "Peaceful Returns: Reversing Ethnic Cleansing after the Bosnian War," *International Migration* 55, no. 5 (2017).

14. Miriam George, Wendy Kliewer, and Sebastan Irudaya Rajan, "'Rather Than Talking in Tamil, They Should Be Talking to Tamils': Sri Lankan Tamil Refugee Readiness for Repatriation," *Refugee Survey Quarterly* 34, no. 2 (2015).

15. Djordje Stefanovic, Neophytos Loizides, and Samantha Parsons, "Home Is Where the Heart Is? Forced Migration and Voluntary Return in Turkey's Kurdish Regions," *Journal of Refugee Studies* 28, no. 2 (2015).

16. Catherine-Lune Grayson, "Durable Solutions: Perpsectives of Somali Refugees Living in Kenyan and Ethiopian Camps and Selected Communities of Return" (Nairobi: Danish Refugee Council, 2013).

Time and Trauma

Time impacts the desire to return. The average length of displacement is now seventeen years, a number skewed by protracted displacement from countries involved in seemingly intractable conflicts, such as Afghanistan and Somalia.[14] The longer the displacement, the more opportunity for households and individuals to view themselves as a part of the community in their new location and to make fresh lives for themselves. Liz Alden Wily notes, "Millions of people cannot be expected to endure or participate in the horrors of war, leaving their homes, sometimes for a decade or more, and not develop marked new awareness, skills and aspirations."[15] If places of refuge are peaceful and provide an opportunity for safety, employment, and the education of children, they may be more attractive than home communities. People adapt over time to their changed circumstances, in the best-case scenario finding employment and educational opportunities through which new social networks are established. Children are raised and educated in new communities and develop attachments there. Anthropologists highlight the way in which displaced people can and do make new homes outside of "homelands."[16]

Witnessing a death or property destruction, such as a home being set on fire, impacts willingness to return.[17] A study of Somali refugees living in camps in Ethiopia and Kenya found that those who had experienced violence were unlikely to want to return home, "regardless of the duration of their exile or their bond with Somalia."[18] Preventative displacement is a decision to leave when there is a threat of violence. Reactive displacement occurs when violence has happened.[19] People displaced reactively, rather than choosing to leave, experience greater shock and disruption to their lives.[20]

In interviews with displaced people, there was a surprising range of responses to violence. In one memorable interview, I was talking with an older Gorani woman from Kosovo, who was visibly distraught when recounting damage that had been done to her house. She was not harmed, nor were any of her family members, but the memory of the attack on her home shook her with grief almost two decades after the fact. This woman desperately wanted to return to her home community and expressed a longing to have her home rebuilt. "In Dragash we don't mix with Serbs or Albanians. We don't have problems there, everyone is Gorani. My mother, my father, my sister are buried there. I want to go back. I imagine myself back there."[21]

In other cases, violence was normalized in unexpected ways. One young woman I spoke with was seven during the war in Kosovo. When I asked about her experiences during that time, she said, "When they were bombing the area, we kids would play. So it was actually a nice memory. There was no school, so the bombing let us have more time to play. I know it is sick, but I have nice memories of that time."[22] The ambivalence in responses to violence apparent in my interviews also exists in the literature on return migration. While the experience of trauma has been noted as preventing return migration in some cases, there is not overwhelming evidence that this is always a factor.[23] Sometimes the nature of the community in the present is more important than the violence experienced there in the past.

Economic Opportunities

Critical to the desire to return are economic opportunities in the place of refuge. Not all host communities are equally hospitable to refugees. In 2015, the news media featured delightful scenes of German people welcoming Syrian refugees into their country with kind words and chocolates. Six months late public sentiment had changed, but the German welcome was quite a contrast to the closed borders and barbed wire fences restricting access to other countries at that time. Minimally, most people desire the opportunity to work and send their children to school in a place of refuge. But even these low expectations are out of reach for displaced people in many parts of the world. Ethiopia is one of the poorest countries in terms of per capita income and host to seven hundred thousand refugees from surrounding countries such as Eritrea, South Sudan, Somalia, and Burundi.[24] Ethiopia's one hundred million people live on an average of USD 619 per year and work mostly in agriculture.[25] Limited job opportunities led the government to restrict formal employment for refugees until 2017. Other countries have also restricted opportunities to work.[26] By contrast, in Uganda, another East African country hosting large numbers of refugees, there is no restriction on the right to work or movement, and refugees are given farmland. Evidence shows that Ugandan host communities have gained economically from the presence of refugees.[27] Benefits to communities are magnified when refugees receive cash assistance instead of food rations; cash assistance also positively impacts the diet and happiness of refugees.[28] Hosting refugees can advantage a country when refugees are economically active, but this is not widely understood. Security fears, xenophobia, and concerns about competition for limited jobs often restrict the employment and movement of refugees. In the United States, refugees are a small subset of all immigrants but are caught up in the politically fraught conversation over immigration, despite their positive impact on economic growth.[29] Immigrants are disproportionately more entrepreneurial and create jobs through business startups. At lower skill levels, refugees tend to take jobs that complement rather than compete with native workers. Yet political rhetoric does not always align with economic reality.

There is a debate on economic opportunity and migration more generally, with some scholars arguing that economic opportunity in the place of origin promotes migration and others suggesting it as a deterrent.[30] Conflict-induced migration is different, yet it is clear that when deciding about returning to their place of origin, displaced people weigh their economic opportunities carefully.[31] They may decide to return to the community they came from if the economic opportunities are sufficient, or they may choose to have some of the family remain in the place of refuge and some go home.[32] Economic opportunities in the place of refuge incentivize remaining there. On the contrary, if host countries prevent employment or if aid organizations reduce food rations, the impetus to return home can be strong, particularly if there are inducements in the home community such as the restitution of property.[33]

Social media plays an increasingly important role in providing the information needed to assess economic opportunities at home and in places of refuge. Smartphone technology and access to digital communication networks impact the experience of migration, displacement, and return. Syrian refugees, many of whom are well educated, own smartphones, and are experienced at accessing information online to gather information about economic opportunities and services. For example, one Syrian refugee, Ahmad Edilb, created an online community called Dubarah for other forcibly displaced Syrians. The network provides information about living conditions, legal issues, education, and job opportunities in the various countries where Syrians have found refuge.[34] Social media are only as good as the information they provide. They can also be used to promote rumors and misinformation about political situations, relief opportunities, and legal requirements.

Family Characteristics

Decisions to remain or return are made by individuals and by families as a social product of the needs and characteristics of their members.[35] Households that are vulnerable, perhaps because the household head is female or a family member has medical needs, will be influenced by more than just economic opportunity. For example, a family with a child in need of dialysis may opt to stay in a refugee camp where it is available, long after they would have otherwise returned home. Families create webs of social capital. In most settings, every family member has connections with people at work or school. They are members of clubs, dance groups, sports teams, scouts, religious communities, burial societies, and rotating credit associations. These resources of social capital assist families in decisions about refuge and return.[36] They provide information; create opportunities for loans, temporary housing, or employment connections; and demonstrate the feasibility of a move, all essential elements of a positive transition. Monica Boyd argues that "studying networks, particularly those linked to family and households, permits understanding of migration as a social product—not as the sole result of individual decisions made by individual actors, not as the sole result of economic or political parameters, but rather as an outcome of all these factors in interaction."[37] Evidence of migration as a social product can be seen in the frequent practice of families splitting up to diversify the choices available to them in terms of resettlement and return.[38] Access to news or direct communication with displaced relatives and friends provides information about the difficulties of the journey, safe routes, transportation, services available, and employment. Families separated by forced migration also use digital technologies to normalize and manage absence, connecting with one another across space and place. Robertson et al. note the common practice of digitally creating family portraits with relatives who are separated by cutting and pasting images of people who are not able to be present in one place at the same time. These reposed family images create an "imaginary co-presence."[39]

The Political Situation in Home Communities

Refugee status is revoked when the political situation in a country of origin becomes safe enough for people to return. But a determination of safety by the UNHCR does not mean that everyone feels secure. Returning may mean living near neighbors of another ethnicity who participated in ethnic cleansing or bring up memories of trauma and expulsion. In addition to these individual level impediments, there can be political issues of sovereignty, or state control, involved. It was common in the case of the Yugoslav wars of the 1990s for people displaced by ethnic cleansing to find their home area under control of a different ethnic group after the war.[40] Return may mean going back to an area where your ethnic group is now a minority or repatriating to a country that is controlled by a different political party or ethnic group. Social media allow people to get up-to-date information about the situation in home communities and places of refuge, but they may not like the changed circumstances. Indeed, in the many places where war leads to a change in sovereignty; it is more difficult for minorities to return, either because of specific policies to prevent them such as Israel/Palestine, or because people do not want to return. The Kosovo case later in this chapter illustrates how political circumstances facilitating the return of one ethnic group may prevent the return of another.

Efforts to reverse ethnic cleansing by restoring conflict areas to the same ethnic composition they had before the conflict are referred to as minority returns. Minority returns attempted in the wake of several of the 1990s Balkans conflicts were largely ineffective. For example, Annex 7 of the Dayton Peace Agreement, which ended the Bosnian War, explicitly encouraged people to return to their previous place of residence: "All refugees and displaced persons have the right freely to return to their homes of origin. They shall have the right to have restored to them property of which they were deprived in the course of hostilities since 1991 and to be compensated for any property that cannot be restored to them."[41] Still, people were very reluctant to go back to their homes on a permanent basis.[42] Similarly, in Lebanon, where there was a legacy of violence in mixed Muslim/Christian communities, Christians were less likely to return even with property restitution.[43] Adelman and Barkan have noted that it is rare to see the return of minority populations displaced by violence. Indeed, they remark that in their research "we did not find any significant refugee return to an area where that refugee group would constitute an ethnic minority, unless supported by a preponderant use of force."[44] One example of successful minority return is the return of the displaced Tutsi community to Rwanda in 1994 after the genocide. Tutsi who had been living in neighboring countries since 1959, even born and raised there, returned to Rwanda after the Rwandan Patriotic Front stopped the genocide, won the war, and established control of the state. Both before and after the genocide the Tutsi were around 15% of the Rwandan population. This was possible because while eight hundred thousand people within Rwanda, mostly Tutsi, were victims of the genocide, the large Tutsi population that had been living in neighboring countries came back when it became clear that they would be safe within a Tutsi-controlled state. This was a case of minority return, accompanied by a "preponderant use of force." In democratic countries consociational political institutions are intended to make minority returns more attractive. They provide special political representation, voice, and sometimes cultural protections for minority populations. The jury is out on whether these are effective in promoting return migration, and not all postconflict states have the robust democracies necessary to make these institutions function well.

Violent conflict changes communities. "Returnees painfully discover that in their period of absence the homeland communities and their identities have undergone transformation, and these ruptures and changes have serious implications for their ability to reclaim a sense of home upon homecoming."[45] The first issue in terms of returning home is usually the restoration of property, specifically the return or rebuilding of homes. People want their property restored, often before they return. But home means more than property, it also refers to the nature of the community. Anthropological literature emphasizes that time and the experience of violence change people's sense of home and desire to return, and the nature of their communities of origin.[46]

To sum up, previous research has identified the factors that influence decisions to return: time, trauma, family characteristics and economic opportunities. To these generally agreed-upon factors, I add the political control of an area. Those who support a political party or are part of an ethnic group that lost power in a violent conflict are not likely to want to return, even when security is restored. Where political power has shifted hands, "successful return" may mean that a small percentage of the preexisting minority population is able to reclaim their property and live in the area, even if their presence is intermittent.

Where and When Do People Return?

How do we know when a conflict is over, and people can go home? There are both formal and informal answers to this question. Informally, we know a crisis to be over when a state has recovered its ability to provide security and protect the human rights of its citizens. This fact becomes obvious formally through the development of a cessation agreement, which is a statement by the UNHCR that it is no longer necessary for refugees to be under its protection. Once return is safe, how does it occur? One might think that people would pick up and move back to their old neighborhoods and previous homes at the earliest possible point. Sometimes that happens, but it is not everywhere what we see. Return migration in Liberia illustrates some of the ways in which displacement can change people's goals regarding where they wish to live.

Liberia had two civil wars from 1989 to 1997 and then 1999 to 2003. During the conflicts, approximately 80% of the population was displaced internally and internationally.[47] After the second Liberian civil war ended in 2003 with the signing of the comprehensive peace agreement, there was an extended period of uncertainty, demobilization of soldiers, and reconstruction. People began to return home as soon as they could. "Between October 2004 and the end of December 2011, 169,630 Liberian refugees repatriated, the majority of whom (126,180) were assisted by UNHCR."[48] In 2009, the UNHCR started concerted efforts to repatriate the remaining Liberian refugees from surrounding countries. This was well after the war ended and at a point in which local services were reestablished in the Liberian countryside. In 2011, the Liberian Refugee Repatriation and Resettlement Commission struck a deal with the UNHCR regarding repatriation. It was agreed that all returning refugees, no matter what their destination, would be given a flat fee of $375 for adults and $275 for children to travel back to their homes. These were to be the last returns before the cessation agreement. The hope was to bring the remaining refugees to durable solutions by December 2011. This goal proved to be too optimistic. While some refugees were willing to repatriate, others wanted to stay in their places of refuge in Ghana, Sierra Leone, Côte d'Ivoire, and Guinea, where they had established ties. "Some people didn't return to their homes because they preferred life in the camps."[49] Others remained outside Liberia, hoping for resettlement in a third country, despite the unlikeliness of this occurring. Essumen-Johnson noted this as an impediment to their repatriation: "The prospect for resettlement in the United States is serving as a huge incentive for the Liberian refugees not to repatriate; if they repatriate to Liberia then they lose any chance of being ever considered for resettlement in the United States."[50]

A cessation agreement took effect on June 30, 2012, revoking refugee status for Liberians in neighboring states. The cessation agreement applied to refugees who fled Liberia because of the war (prima facie refugees), and not to individual asylum seekers who might have a well-founded fear of persecution that would enable them to qualify for political asylum on an individual basis. Since some people still refused to repatriate, there were accommodations made for those remaining to be considered economic migrants under the Economic Community of West African States (ECOWAS) agreement. In Ghana, they received ECOWAS passports and limited work and residence visas.[51] No one was forced to repatriate, even after the cessation agreement was signed. They lost their rights as refugees, but neighboring states, linked by economic and political ties, were not willing to transgress the norm of voluntary return.

When refugees repatriate, they do not always go back to their places of origin. Everywhere we see a tendency toward urban settlement after displacement, even when the displaced have their roots in rural areas.[52] Some people choose to return to rural areas of their country where they did not live previously, usually because of better economic opportunities such as access to more or better land for farming. In the late 1990s, when Cambodian refugees in Thailand could choose where they wanted to return in Cambodia, Battambang was a popular choice because it was "idealised by many refugees as 'the land of milk and honey,' and many opted to go there when the first survey of destinations was made in the camps."[53] Of the fifty thousand Cambodian refugees who repatriated during this time period, most returned to Anlong Veng and Battambang in the northwest of the country even though they were not originally from this area.[54]

There are additional reasons why people choose to return to an area that is not their home. After the experience of ethnic violence, many are unwilling to live in proximity to different ethnic groups, choosing instead to reside in ethnic enclaves where they can enjoy the society of their co-ethnics without fears for their own security. We see this in settings as diverse as Bosnia and Northern Ireland. In both of those places, living near co-ethnics means safety, whether that area is a neighborhood or a political district. There is reason to think that the choice to live in an ethnic enclave is more than an isolated response to fear in a few settings. People returning from displacement are sensitive to their relations with neighbors, the wider community, and the state because all these relationships were insufficiently protective in the past. They may go to great lengths to ensure that, if they repatriate, they live in a local community in which they feel safe.

Kosovo: War and Return

Another illustrative case study of displacement and return is what happened during the Kosovo war and the years following.[55] Kosovo is a tiny country in the Western Balkans with two million people. At the time of its war for independence it was part of the country of Serbia and Montenegro (Montenegro became independent in 2006). Return migration in Kosovo illuminates how ethnicity—whether a person was Albanian, Serb, or Roma—impacts when, where, and if people return to their communities of origin.

The population of Kosovo at the last census was 91% ethnic Albanian with the remainder composed of Serbs, 3.4%, and other (Roma, Ashkali, Egyptian, Gorani, and Bosniaks), 5.6%.[56] The Kosovo war in 1998–1999 was a fight for sovereignty—political control over the territory of Kosovo.

Figure 3. Kosovo and the Western Balkans, 2006

Before the conflict, sovereignty rested in the hands of Serbs, but the war changed that, as Kosovo became independent under the control of the majority Albanians. Roma were bystanders to the conflict—a small minority group caught up in the violence and displacement. Because the Kosovo war was an ethnic conflict in which political control changed from one group to another, it is an excellent example of how shifting sovereignty and ethnic identity can play a role in return migration.

A Short History of the Kosovo War

The Kosovo war took place from 1998 to 1999, in the context of the disintegrating Yugoslav state. Within Yugoslavia, the Albanian population was a politically and economically insignificant minority. Albanian factions in Kosovo began agitating for greater autonomy within Yugoslavia in 1981. By 1989 their efforts resulted in a backlash from the Serbian-controlled government, which retaliated by rescinding all of Kosovo's autonomy in the areas of security, justice, defense, and planning. In April 1990, Kosovo's assembly was dissolved, and the territory was ruled directly by the Yugoslavian state. Yugoslavia was facing nationalist pressures from other groups that led to the 1991 secession of Slovenia, Croatia, and (North) Macedonia. Then, in 1992, Bosnia became independent and descended into a brutal conflict among Bosnian Muslims, Croats, and Serbs struggling for territorial control. Ethnic cleansing was used by all sides to displace civilians. The president of Serbia, Slobodan Milošević, was an ardent Serb nationalist and supported Serb paramilitary forces within Bosnia.

As the Yugoslav Federation fragmented, Kosovo was left as part of Serbia and Montenegro. This compounded problems already in place for the Albanian population in Kosovo, which had been progressively excluded from government jobs and educational opportunities. Between 1990 and 1998 the Albanian population peacefully protested school curriculum in the Serbian language, the dismissal of Albanians from government jobs, and violations of human rights. Albanians established parallel systems for education and healthcare as part of their rejection of the state.[57]

The Kosovo Liberation Army (KLA) made its first appearance in 1996 and began attacking Serbian state symbols and security forces.[58] By the middle of 1998 the KLA controlled territory and was pursuing independence through open rebellion. In this first phase of the Kosovo war, the Serbs had the upper hand as they were much better armed and trained than the Albanians. Western countries were afraid that Kosovo would become another venue for Milošević to become "a serial ethnic cleanser."[59] Diplomatic efforts to negotiate a settlement to the war occurred in February 1999 in Rambouillet, France, but failed to end the conflict.

After Rambouillet, the second phase of the Kosovo war began with a decision by NATO to intervene. NATO began bombing Serbia on March 24, 1999, to compel Serb forces to leave Kosovo. Serbia responded with violence against the Albanian civilian population, forcing them to flee to neighboring countries. The US State Department estimated that in early 1999 there were six hundred thousand internally displaced Albanians and seven hundred thousand Albanian refugees in neighboring countries, with 90% of the Albanian population displaced from their homes.[60]

By the mid-1999, Serbia capitulated to the NATO bombing and on June 20, 1999, Serbian forces withdrew, allowing Kosovo to establish de facto autonomy. Albanian refugees in bordering states and the internally displaced were able to return to their homes, and most of them did so quickly.[61] So began the third phase of the conflict. UN Security Council Resolution 1244 called for the complete disarmament of the KLA, but this never happened. Instead, there were retaliatory attacks against Serbs remaining in Kosovo: "Groups of armed Albanians all over Kosovo took advantage of the security vacuum to perpetrate a campaign of vengeance, score-settling, and plain apolitical crime. Hundreds of homes belonging to Serbs and other minorities were burned and looted."[62] There was no police force yet established in the proto-state, and crimes of revenge against Serbs were largely tolerated.[63]

Return Migration

Approximately 220,000 Serbs were displaced by the violence in Kosovo in the third stage of the war and in later ethnic riots that occurred in 2004. Unlike the Albanian majority population, which returned quickly and en masse at the end of the war, Serbs have not returned in large numbers. The best estimates are that of the 220,000 Serbs displaced by violence in Kosovo during 1999 and after the riots in 2004, only 25,430 have returned, and not all of those who have returned have remained. [64] Additionally, there were 150,000 Roma, Ashkali, and Egyptians living in Kosovo prior to the war, some of whom were resident in Kosovo because it was a place of refuge from the Bosnian conflict.[65] The Roma, Ashkali, and Egyptian populations are often grouped together and referred to as "RAE," though few identify with this term. Serbian-speaking Roma were widely thought to be allied with the Serbs and left Kosovo for central Serbia with the Serbian armed forces in June 1999, while the Albanian-speaking Ashkali and Egyptians fled the country with the large Albanian exodus earlier in the conflict. The language issue is confusing and muddied by the fact that there was no internal distinction between the three groups (all were considered Roma) until the latter twentieth century in Kosovo, when the use of language, Serbian or Albanian, created different benefits and allies for each group. All three groups face significant socioeconomic challenges in contemporary Kosovo, with one-third the per capita income of other ethnic groups and much lower levels of education.[66]

After the war ended, the UN and the European Union assisted in reconstruction. While the institutions of the state were established, Kosovo was administered by the United Nations Interim Administration Mission in Kosovo (UNMIK). UNMIK invested personnel and monetary resources in trying to address property restitution for the displaced to encourage return migration. EU programs designed to bring Serbs back to Kosovo complemented UN efforts. The EU and the government of Kosovo have spent twenty million euros over the past decade to bring Serbs and RAE back to Kosovo and reestablish an ethnic balance like that which existed prior to the war.[67] Serbia was supportive of this policy, as "Belgrade wanted to implant sizeable communities in Kosovo, which it saw as its best way of maintaining a Serb population that would substantiate Serbia's continuing claims on territory."[68] Their position has shifted somewhat, as the government of Serbia is now assisting with the local integration of Serbs displaced by the Kosovo war who do not wish to return.[69]

The return of the Serbian population to Kosovo has been important to the EU, as Serb returns are evidence of a government commitment to a multiethnic state. While Kosovo was still under UNMIK administration, Marti Ahtisaari developed a plan for Kosovo to become independent while protecting the Serbian minority community. This plan, known as the Comprehensive Settlement Proposal, or the Ahtisaari plan, eventually became part of the Constitution of Kosovo. The constitution acknowledged the multiethnic character of the state, and the Kosovan Serb population received special consociational protections, including the creation of new municipalities with Serbian majorities. Since municipal government is the only layer of political organization other than the state government, Serbian majority municipalities allowed minority communities a substantial amount of control.[70] There are also state-level protections such as reserved seats in the assembly for the minority communities (ten for Serbs and four for RAE) and a commitment to allow the use of the Serbian language in government offices and documents. These types of consociational power-sharing arrangements have been used across other democratic, postconflict states, such as Bosnia and Cyprus, to promote minority returns.

International concern about restoring communities to the demographic balance prior to the conflict has led to five programs since 2000, funded by the EU, to encourage Serbians and other minority communities to return. These programs work with both the returnees and the host communities to establish a secure, receptive environment. They have largely failed: "15 years after the 1999 conflict, in spite of substantial international assistance and targeted programmes, large numbers of persons displaced both within and outside Kosovo remain without durable solutions. The number of returns to Kosovo is decreasing every year."[71]

What makes people want to return to home communities after conflict? The assumed narrative is that those who are displaced will want to come home. But this is not always correct. As mentioned earlier, the literature on displacement identifies four factors that impact the decision to return to a home area after basic security has been restored: time, trauma, economic opportunities and household characteristics. Kosovo has limited economic opportunities overall, and there is competition for available jobs. Regional labor statistics demonstrate lower levels of unemployment in Serbia, where, before Covid, the total unemployment rate for those over fifteen was 10.4%,[72] as opposed to Kosovo, where it hovers around 30%.[73] In this context, being a minority group member, particularly a Serb, does not bode well for employment. It is also important to note that in some areas of Kosovo, security of Serbs is still in question.

Experience of trauma impacts the desire to return home. Many Kosovan Serbs witnessed or experienced violent attacks in the third phase of the Kosovo war, when NATO bombing stopped and the KLA took control of the country. Attacks after the NATO withdrawal were retaliatory in nature, designed to displace and punish Serbs. This "reverse ethnic cleansing" occurred at a time of political transition, when the Albanians controlled the state for the first time. It is estimated that 70% of the Serbian population fled Kosovo either to avoid reprisals or to pursue better opportunities in Serbia.[74] Retaliatory violence had a dual impact in the Serbian community. It pushed some Serbs out for reasons of safety and sent a message that the Serbs would not be treated well under an Albanian-controlled state. We would expect that few Serbs would want to return to areas where they were the targets of ethnic cleansing. Indeed, we would expect the number of Serbian returns to an area to be inversely correlated with the violence experienced in the last phase of the war when Serbian forces withdrew.

Poor economic opportunities combined with a lengthy displacement make people less likely to return. While EU programs targeting resettlement of Serbs seek to overcome this reluctance through financial incentives for home reconstruction and business opportunities, barriers remain, given that the economic opportunities are better in Serbia. We know that many of the displaced Serbs were living in urban areas prior to the war, where they held key positions in government and local administration. Pristina used to be an area in Kosovo with a concentration of Serbs. We would expect that educated Serbs would be able to find employment opportunities in Pristina and other cities after the war.

This background information suggests three testable hypotheses regarding return migration: first, that Serbs will be most likely to return to urban areas; second, that the number of Serbian returns to an area will be inversely correlated with the violence experienced in the last phase of the war, when Serbian forces withdrew; and third, that Serb returns are more likely to be concentrated in the Serb-majority municipalities created under the Ahtisaari plan.

Unlike many other places where there has been violence, displacement, and return, there is data from the Kosovo war that allows us to see where violence occurred and the places people have returned. A data set on violence during the civil war in Kosovo was compiled by the Armed Conflict Location & Event Data Project.[75] The data includes 1,625 separate incidents, 1,551 of them with specific dates attached. These data points indicate a violent incident, not how many people died in each. Sometimes there is additional information regarding the number of affected people, such as a note that states, "6 people killed." In other cases, the numbers are extremely vague, for example, a general notation that a village was shelled, people killed, and villagers displaced. The issue of numbers affected has been noted elsewhere as a problem with the data, as well as insufficient information about the perpetrators and quality control in the coding.[76] All of these issues have been evident in the use of this data set and controlled for whenever possible. In the absence of other comparable data sets for Kosovo, I use this with an awareness of its limitations and flaws.

There is additional data available that shows the location of Serbian and Albanian populations within the borders of Kosovo prior to the war.[77] Data on the number and location of returnees was provided by the UNHCR in Kosovo. The data covers the years 2000 through the end of 2012, detailing returns by the year of return, ethnicity of the returnee, and the municipality to which they returned, but not the age and sex of the returnees to protect their anonymity. We cannot tell whether people are returning to the place that they left, as their municipality of origin is not included and people who returned without notifying the UNHCR and receiving its assistance would not be included in this data set.[78]

Four of the Serb-majority municipalities (Leposavić/Leposaviq, Zubin Potok, Zvečan/Zveqan, Mitrovica / Mitrovicë North)[79] are close to the border of Serbia and are something of a no-man's land of sovereignty, as they operate outside of the control of the government of Kosovo, despite being territorially within Kosovo. These areas do not report return statistics or participate in the census, but there are other Serbian municipalities in Kosovo for which there is data: Novo Brdo / Novobërdë; Gračanica/ Graçanicë; Ranilug/Ranillug; Parteš/Partesh; and Klokot/Kllokot. These are all Serb-majority municipalities created by the Ahtisaari plan that are under the control of the government of Kosovo.

We would expect that returns will inversely correlate with the number of violent incidents that occurred during the final phase of the war, when Serb armed forces abandoned the territory, leaving a vulnerable Serbian minority in Kosovo without the protection of an armed group. Those municipalities that had more violent incidents during that time would

TABLE 3. Returns and Violence

Municipality Albanian/Serbian	Number of Returnees	Violence Index All	Phase 1 Pre-NATO	Phase 2 NATO Bombing	Phase 3 Serb Forces Withdraw
Klinë/Klina	863	1.61	0.29	0.52	0.78
Novobërdë / Novo Brdo	**637**	**1.78**	**0.00**	**0.15**	**1.49**
Istog/Istok	572	1.58	0.18	0.71	0.66
Gjilan/Gnjilane	550	1.31	0.00	0.21	1.10
Vushtrri/Vučitrn	550	0.80	0.34	0.33	0.11
Prizren	492	0.52	0.10	0.15	0.26
Pejë/Peć	462	1.16	0.22	0.47	0.41
Kamenicë/Kamenica	454	0.67	0.03	0.08	0.55
Gracanicë/Gračanica	**429**	**1.03**	**0.00**	**0.09**	**0.94**
Ferizaj/Uroševac	324	0.65	0.13	0.29	0.14
Obliq/Obilić	267	1.48	0.19	0.93	0.28
Rahovec/Orahovac	263	1.05	0.16	0.46	0.39
Prishtinë/Priština	242	0.89	0.15	0.36	0.31
Viti/Vitina	230	0.64	0.09	0.11	0.45
Lipjan	224	1.68	0.12	0.76	0.78
Partesh/Parteš	**167**	**3.36**	**0.00**	**0.00**	**3.36**
Fushë Kosovë/ Kosovo Polje	159	0.83	0.14	0.29	0.26
Shtërpcë/Štrpce	**125**	**1.73**	**0.14**	**1.30**	**0.14**
Ranillug/Ranilug	**120**	**1.03**	**0.00**	**0.00**	**1.03**
Skënderaj/Srbica	83	0.96	0.31	0.57	0.06
Mitrovicë/Kosovska Mitrovica	71	0.89	0.33	0.22	0.32
Kllokot/Klokot	**68**	**2.35**	**0.00**	**0.00**	**2.35**
Average		1.03	0.18	0.32	0.49

Note: Serb-majority municipalities created under the Ahtisaari plan are in bold type.

see lower numbers of returnees. Table 3 shows a violence index for each municipality during the three phases of the war, and for the entire war. The index is the number of incidents during the period, divided by the population of the current municipality. Census data is from 2011, which is less than ideal, as it is well after the war rather than during it. A violence index has been used in other cases to note the frequency of violent incidents within geographic areas in which census information is "highly questionable."[80] All municipalities with more than ten Serb returnees are listed. Serb municipalities created under the Ahtisaari plan are in bold, and the municipalities are ordered by number of Serb returnees from 2000 to 2012 in the first column.

A correlation analysis using the same data, displayed in Table 4, shows a significant and counterintuitive result. The number of Serbian returnees

TABLE 4. Correlation between Serb Returnees and Violent Incidents in the Kosovo War

	All Periods	Phase 1 Pre-NATO	Phase 2 NATO Bombing	Phase 3 Serb Forces Withdraw
Kendall's tau b	.312**	.039	.197	.502**
Sig (two-tailed)	.008	.748	.100	.000
Spearman's rho	.437**	.051	.294	.673**
Sig (two-tailed)	.007	.766	.077	.000

*Correlation is significant at the 0.05 level (2-tailed)
**Correlation is significant at the 0.01 level (2-tailed)

after the conflict is correlated with the number of violent incidents, but positively. In other words, the greater the number of violent incidents, the more likely we are to see Serbs return. In interpreting these results we need to beware of the small sample size (the thirty-seven municipalities where we have return data). Even though the data on violent incidents is geocoded and could be easily broken down into smaller geographic areas, the UNHCR data is categorized by municipality.[81]

Kendall's tau b and Spearman's rho both measure the statistical dependence between two variables without assuming a normal distribution. Since the data is discreet and the number of cases is small, they are helpful tools for assessing correlation and minimizing the effects of outliers. As expected, there is a correlation between violent incidents and return of the Serbian population in Kosovo; however, it is counterintuitive that this correlation is positive. The more violent incidents occurred, the higher the rates of return.

We can also use the UNHCR data set to determine where returns are occurring and if Serbs are returning to large urban areas or to Serb-majority municipalities. Evidence shows that the Serbs who register with the UNHCR and return through sponsored programs are not coming back to large cities. Instead, most returnees have gone back to rural areas. The rural areas to which Serbs are returning are also places where there has been a long history of Serb presence. People returning are likely to be going back to homes and farms that have been in their families for generations. Figure 4 shows a gradient of population, the three highlighted areas being the three municipalities with the largest numbers of returnees: Klinë/Klina, Novobërdë/Novo Brdo; and Istog/Istok. These three areas are predominantly rural, as indicated by the lighter shading on the map.

Interestingly, of the three municipalities with the largest numbers of returnees, Novobërdë/Novo Brdo is the only Serb-controlled munici-

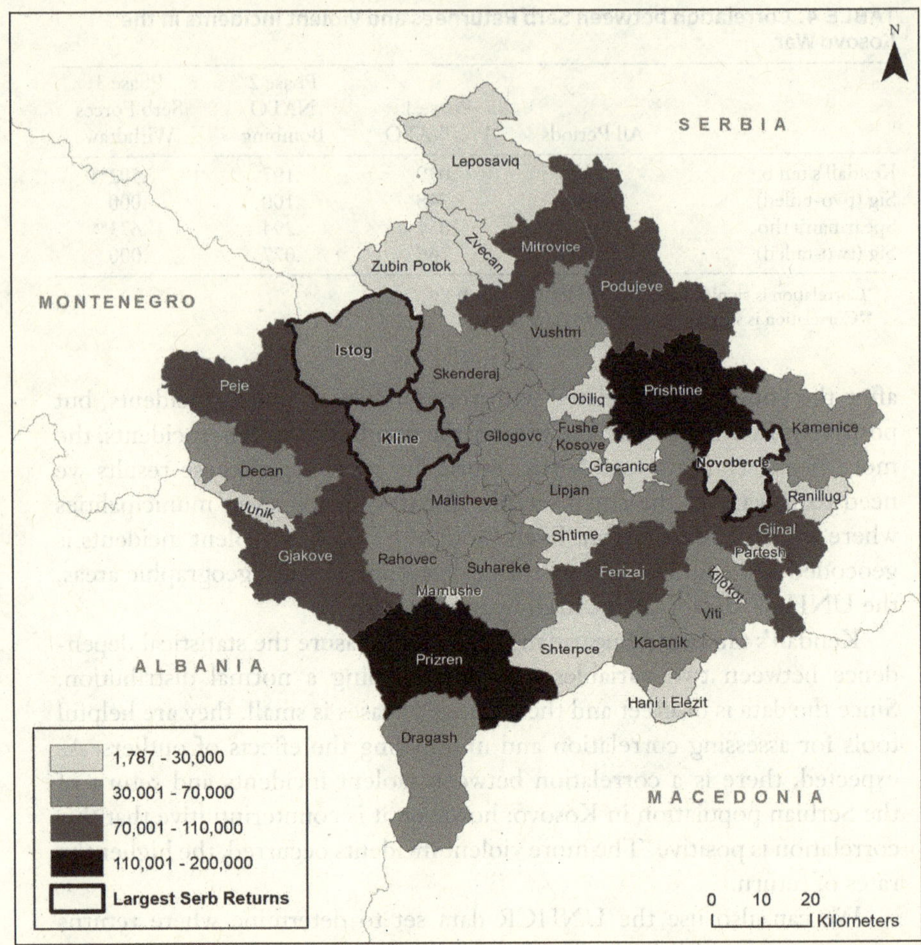

Figure 4. Serb Returnees and Population Distribution

pality. Looking back at Table 3, we can see that of the top ten receiving municipalities, only two are Serb controlled.[82]

While it might be perplexing that these municipalities received so many Serb returns, when we look at the ethnic map of Kosovo prior to the conflict, we can see that these are historic Serbian areas. The dark areas in Figure 5 indicate where Serbs were concentrated prior to the Kosovo war. I have again highlighted in black the three municipalities with the highest number of returnees. One can see from the map how they overlap with traditional Serbian areas. Other dark areas are three of the four northern municipalities (Leposavić/Leposaviq, Zubin Potok, Zvečan/Zveqan) that

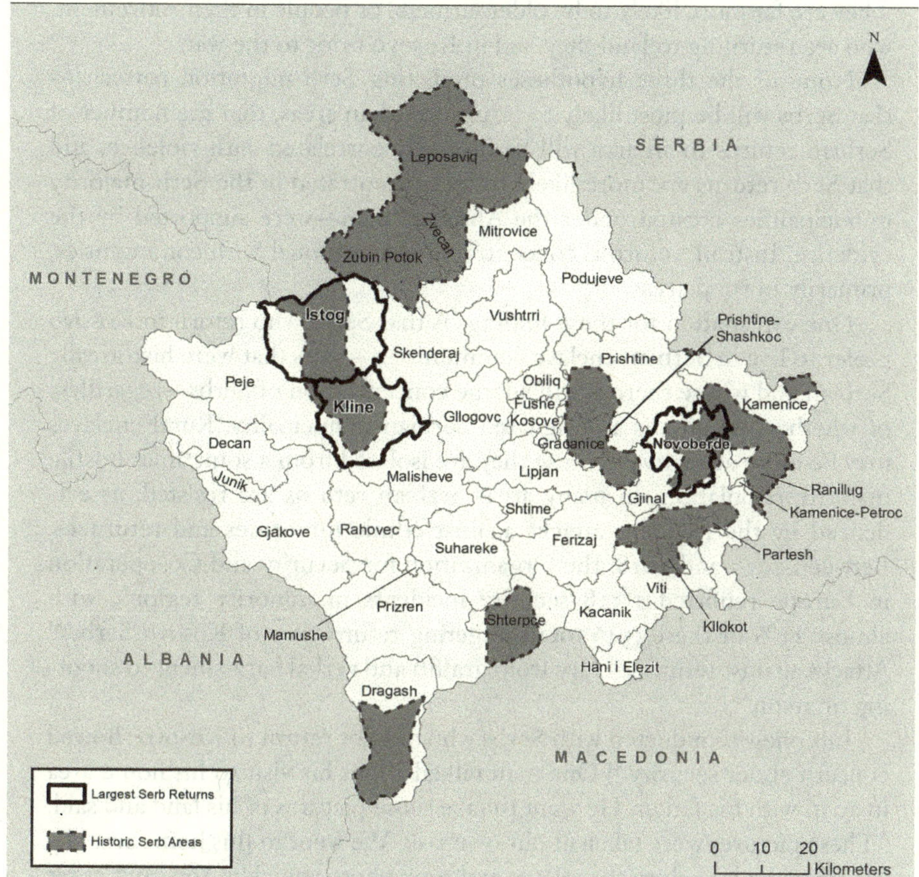

Figure 5. Serb Returnees and Ethnic Enclaves

have Serb majorities and do not report any data to the state of Kosovo because they dispute its sovereignty. Pristina, the capital, and the area around it are also dark, as it was an area where many Serbs lived prior to the war.

Serb Returnees and Ethnic Enclaves

The fact that Serb returnees prefer to return to rural areas tells us a bit about who is returning. Most of the livelihood options in rural areas of Kosovo revolve around agriculture: farming, viticulture, or the raising of livestock. Those who return to rural areas of the country are unlikely to be educated, young professionals because of the limited job opportunities.

They are far more likely to be older farmers, or people in their retirement, who are returning to land they had in Kosovo prior to the war.

None of the three hypotheses predicting Serb migration patterns—that Serbs will be most likely to return to urban areas, that the number of Serbian returns to an area will be inversely correlated with violence, and that Serb returns are more likely to be concentrated in the Serb-majority municipalities created under the Ahtisaari plan—were supported by the evidence. Instead, return is concentrated in traditional Serb communities, primarily in rural areas.

One explanation for these findings is that Serbs who return to Kosovo prefer to live in Serbian enclave communities—areas that were historically Serbian and where there is still a large concentration of Serbs—regardless of whether the area is a designated Serbian municipality. Rural enclaves may be more attractive because they are isolated from a sometimes hostile majority population. In many areas Serbian returns are resisted, as evidenced by the frequent attacks against ethnic minorities and returnees. Between 2015 and 2018, the Organization for Security and Co-operation in Europe reported 1,518 security incidents in minority regions, with almost 25% of these (346 total) targeting return sites of Kosovo Serbs.[83] Attacks against returnees vary from graffiti and verbal harassment to shooting or arson.

Interviews conducted with Serbs who did not return to Kosovo showed concern about security.[84] One man talked about his visit to his home area in 2016 with his father. He went to take some pictures of his land and said, "These pictures were taken at our own risk. We went to [his home area] by bus, then took a cab to the village and took photos quickly. You can't enter the village if you are a Serb. When the Albanians realized we were there, they organized themselves to attack us. . . . We quickly took some photos and then fled from the village."[85] His fears of safety are likely to lead him to remain in Serbia rather than return to Kosovo. Worries about security are not equally shared. Another displaced Serb who had not returned to Kosovo noted,

> Now it is absolutely peaceful, nobody causes trouble, nobody gives a damn who we are. When I go into the shops, for instance, I notice that there is an Albanian man. I started to speak in Albanian, and then he can tell that I am not an Albanian, so he started to speak in Serbian. So we don't have a problem. This is not about me but about all Serbs who go there. When we go there, we meet with old friends, coworkers, neighbors, Turks and Albanians. We all have tea.[86]

The interview excerpts illustrate that expectations regarding how neighbors might treat them was much on the minds of those contemplating return migration. Some areas of Kosovo are more welcoming to Serbs than others, and settling in an ethnic enclave means less contact with the ethnic "other." In a 2012 study of Kosovo, almost 70% of Albanians and 46.5% of Serbs reported no contact with someone outside their ethnic group in the past three months.[87] While this may not seem desirable in terms of longer-term reconciliation between ethnic groups, in the short term it enables people to feel secure in their daily environment. Enclave communities promise a community of co-ethnics, addressing the dual needs of society and security. One of the Kosovan municipality returns officers made it very clear what would make for a viable community in describing what led Serbs to return to his municipality quickly after the war.

> In 2000 it was around fifty-five families who returned and decided to stay. There are around five hundred Serbs here now, not the whole amount of people who were here before the war, but enough to make a community. They have everything they need for a community, a youth center, a secondary school, a primary school, girls for the boys to marry.[88]

A choice to return to enclave communities is similar to what happened in Bosnia. In Bosnia, when people had their property returned, many sold their homes to finance relocation to other areas where they were not in the minority.

Return of Kosovan Serbs appears to be conditioned by the nature of the community before and after the conflict. This counterintuitive finding is consistent with research on the preferences of Syrian refugees living in Lebanon[89] and similar to return preferences in Cyprus, where surveys of internally displaced Greek Cypriots reveal that among those who want to return home, experience of trauma impacts their willingness to accept neighbors who are not Greek.[90] In all this research, there is a suggestion that the nature of the local community mediates the experience of trauma in decision-making on return.

But why did people return to some ethnic enclaves and not to others? The answer could be that there is enough of a concentration of Serbs in certain areas that they are sufficiently isolated from the ethnic other while at the same time able to reproduce themselves as a society. This is certainly true in the four northern municipalities that are at present almost entirely beyond the reach of the state of Kosovo. There also could be a preference for return to areas where there are land-based livelihoods, where people have investments in tree crops such as orchards and vineyards, which are not easily restarted elsewhere. The answer to the question of why people are returning to specific enclaves does not appear to be political protections, as there is not a clear overlap between Serb-controlled municipalities and areas with the largest returns.

Roma, Ashkali, and Egyptians

After the war there were three separate trends in return migration, each defined by ethnicity. Albanians, 90% of whom were displaced during the conflict, returned immediately after the war ended. Of the 230,000 displaced Serbs, only 10% have returned. There also were approximately 150,000 RAE in Kosovo prior to the conflict, few returned, and many remain in Serbia or western Europe.[91]

> There are an estimated 35,000 to 40,000 Roma, Ashkali and Egyptians currently residing in independent Kosovo, whilst about 100,000 live abroad. Around 45,000 to 50,000 Kosovo RAE live in Serbia (23,000 as registered IDPs), 35,000 are in Germany with *Duldung* status (temporary suspension of deportation) and around 10,000 live as refugees in Montenegro, Macedonia and Bosnia Herzegovina. An uncounted number live as refugees, illegal migrants or migrant workers all over Western Europe.[92]

The RAE population and Romani peoples in general face discrimination throughout Europe. Racism and prejudice lead to their social exclusion, problems in accessing housing and education, and reduced opportunities.[93] Many of the Serb-speaking Kosovan Roma fled to central Serbia, where they are relatively well treated.[94] Others, particularly those who were Albanian speaking, went to countries such as Germany, Switzerland, and Sweden, where they originally received temporary protection. For example, RAE who went to Germany received *Duldung* status, which did not provide them with asylum but prevented their forcible return. "At the end of 2009, voluntary minority returns [of the RAE population] remain low, with 1,153 individuals returning from displacement in and outside Kosovo."[95]

European states found the slow pace of RAE return after the war to be problematic. Beginning in 2003 forcible repatriations of the RAE population from western European countries began. As of April 2010, 2,151

RAE had been deported to Kosovo and more since that time.[96] I spoke informally to several groups of Roma living in central Serbia in 2017. They mentioned a variety of reasons for their reluctance to return: the poor economy; the hostile environment for Roma; the lack of property; and the fact that they did not speak Albanian.[97] One middle-aged Roma man in Novi Sad, Serbia, told me, "No one wants to return to Kosovo. Everything is destroyed. Even if they built me a house, I would not return. If it was one year it would be different, but it has been seventeen years. The children were born here and don't speak Albanian. They are welcomed here."[98] Survey data from Roma living in central Serbia in 2015 shows that "a mere 2.4% of the displaced Roma would like to return to [Kosovo], considerably less than in 2010 when the share of those who wished to return amounted to 8.8%. The main reasons for this attitude are the security situation in [Kosovo] and fear of discrimination."[99]

An additional impediment is limited access to Serbian-speaking schools within Kosovo for their children. Forced repatriation of the RAE population is controversial because those who are returned receive very little assistance in reintegration, sometimes just a ride from the airport to their intended place of residence and money for a few days' housing.[100] Roma repatriate in families and have social welfare challenges that have not been met by the government of Kosovo. Of those children forcibly repatriated to Kosovo from Germany, 75% stopped attending school, and nearly 50% did not have essential personal documentation such as birth certificates.[101] There are other concerns regarding the provision of health services and accommodation for the forcibly returned. Sanije is an example.

> She was 12 when police turned up in the middle of the night to send her back to Kosovo, together with her older sister and widowed mother. Withdrawn and disoriented, Sanije has spent the entire year since her repatriation to Kosovo within the four walls of her ramshackle house in a village near Ferizaj. In Germany, she was a good student, but unable to write in Albanian and, without any help in Kosovo, her last day at school was the day when German police put her family on a charter flight heading to Prishtinë/Priština. After two heart attacks and suffering from lung problems, her mother is too frail to obtain Sanije's birth certificate in Germany, where she was born. She would certainly qualify for invalid pension but, due to her serious health condition, she has not found the strength to even apply. Her daughter Sanije remains undocumented to this day.[102]

Summing up the experience of the RAE populations with return migration, one things stand out. Few people returned voluntarily. The forcible repatriation of the RAE community was not factually a violation of the standard of non-refoulement, as there was no longer an active security threat in Kosovo. The hope was that services would be provided to the returning RAE population to assist them with reintegration. Unfortunately, this hope was rarely realized.

Policy Implications

What does the Kosovo experience have to teach us about return migration? First, return was conditioned by ethnicity. In this case we see radically different patterns of return, with Albanians—the majority population—returning very quickly after the end of violent conflict. Serbs returned slowly, in small numbers to ethnic enclaves within Kosovo. RAE rarely returned, and when they did, it was forcible repatriation. For both the Serb and Roma returnees there are questions about the sustainability of their return. Serbs who have returned to Kosovo frequently do not stay. One study—commissioned by the UNHCR, but not publicly distributed because of its sensitivity—made the following statement regarding returns:

> There were some 25,430 registered returns by July 2014, mostly assisted to return to Kosovo from Serbia, Montenegro and the Former Yugoslav Republic of Macedonia. There are no official data on the sustainability of return, but well-placed international stakeholders suggest the figure could be 5,000 or even fewer assisted returnees remain in Kosovo.[103]

Kosovo also illustrates the futility of trying to restore a state or community to the status quo before violent ethnic conflict. Experiences of trauma and displacement cannot be undone. No matter the strength of desire for a multiethnic state, there will be no return to the distribution of ethnic groups prior to the war because it was an ethnic conflict experienced differently by each group. Political circumstances changed dramatically in Kosovo, which is now controlled by its majority-Albanian population.

The Kosovo experience affirms the observation that minority populations rarely return after displacement. The change in sovereignty to the Albanian population in Kosovo made return difficult for Serbs because they were out of power and for Roma because of language and issues of exclusion. That said, a small number of Serbs voluntarily returned to Kosovo, reclaimed houses, apartments, and land and still live there. If the goal was to recreate a Kosovo with the ethnic composition it had prior to the war, then return/repatriation has been a failure. However, if the goal was to enable those who wish to return the ability to do so, then Kosovo is a success, a failure perhaps only for those who were forcibly repatriated.

Conclusion

While states and international organizations may have a strong preference for the return of refugees and displaced people to their places of origin, individuals and households impacted by ethnic conflict exhibit variation in their choices. International public policy needs to be responsive to the needs and desires of people whose lives have been radically changed by violence. This may mean acknowledging that some displaced people prefer local integration or recognizing that people may not want to live in the same places they did before. It also suggests privileging policies that allow the most flexibility for those who do return, such as compensation for property rather than only restitution. These issues will be covered further in the following chapters.

Conflict and displacement change people's preferences; they also change their communities of origin. Those who repatriate may avoid their home community and instead return to a city, an ethnic enclave, or a different rural area where they feel they may have better security, economic opportunities, or resource access. We also see from these examples that return migration is not always voluntary. Those unwilling to repatriate face forcible return when they are unwelcome elsewhere and have no legal claim to sanctuary.

This chapter interrogates the dominant narrative that people will return home after conflict. We see that when return becomes possible, displaced people exhibit a range of choices conditioned by ethnicity, time, and perceptions of opportunity. International policy tells us that the most desirable solution is that people should voluntarily return to their country of origin. But desirable for whom? Voluntary return is appealing to states that do not want to take on the obligation of accommodating the displaced. Displaced people should have the right to return home, but for those displaced by violence, we should not be surprised if this is not their preference.

FOUR

Children Displaced by Violence

In 2019, prior to the Covid pandemic, 400,000 asylum applications
were registered by unaccompanied and separated children. This is
considered to be a significant underestimation of the actual figure.[1]

In March 2022, media focused on the plight of Hassan, an eleven-year-old Ukrainian refugee boy who fled 600 miles to Slovakia on his own, carrying only his passport, a plastic bag, and a telephone number written on his hand.[2] Hassan became symbolic of the millions fleeing war in Ukraine. While most children migrate with their families, increasingly teenagers, and some younger children like Hassan, are migrating on their own. There are two reasons for giving children special attention in this chapter: first, the growing number of independent child migrants and the challenges of an international asylum system not designed for their needs, and second, children are growing up in places of refuge, become adults, and often must make the decision to return independent of their parents. This last point is important and understudied. Return migration is intergenerational. The decision to flee a place of violence and the decision to return may be separated by years or decades during which children who left their place of origin with their families become adults. Time plays a critical role in changing the composition of displaced families and their incentives for return.

The central claim of this chapter is that displaced children face distinct challenges and different preferences for return than displaced adults.

The chapter also highlights the problematic nature of displaced children returning as adults to areas of the world with customary land tenure. Since customary land tenure is prevalent throughout sub-Saharan Africa and Central Asia, this is a significant issue. The chapter proceeds in three sections. The first discusses the increase in children migrating alone, emphasizing that the international legal system regarding refugees is ill-equipped to address the needs of independent child migrants. The second section is devoted to children who are raised in places of refuge and then must decide as adults whether they will return home. Their decision is informed by conceptions of home that diverge from those held by their parents, who made the decision to leave. The third section is a case study of return migration to northern Uganda after the conflict between the Lord's Resistance Army and the government of Uganda. In northern Uganda, families fled violence, raising their children in camps for displaced people. After the conflict, these children (now adults) returned to their place of origin and to the problematic expectation that they would pursue the agricultural lifestyle of their parents. Evidence for the third section comes from several sources, the most important of which are interviews conducted in Gulu and Kampala in May and June 2015. Field research was augmented by secondary sources, particularly survey research conducted in northern Uganda after the conflict.

Independent Child Migrants

The suffering of children tugs at our consciences. The 2019 crisis of migrant children held in poorly equipped detention centers in the United States shocked citizens when reports of their conditions reached the news media. Do we see more stories of migrating children because there are more of them or because their pathos draws cameras and commentary? The answer is both. Children migrating on their own are greatly increasing in numbers in both North America and Europe (see Figures 6 and 7). They are also a subject of media attention and international concern because they are vulnerable and insufficiently protected.

Unaccompanied children have been present in virtually every war when children become accidentally separated from their families because of chaos caused by bombings, violence, and mass population movements. Unaccompanied children are "children who have been separated from both parents and other relatives and are not being cared for by an adult who, by law or custom, is responsible for doing so."[3] An example are the

"Lost Boys of Sudan," who fled when armed men unexpectedly attacked their villages, forcing them to run for their lives and separating them from their families. One of them, Gabriel Bol Deng, remembers how he lost contact with his family. At ten years old he was tending cattle fifteen miles from his village of Gogrial when soldiers appeared. He hid in the grass to escape them and then ran home to warn his family. "Fear gripped me as I caught a glimpse of three bloody corpses near my home. . . . they weren't my family. . . . but they were from my village; they were somebody's family. Fires raged around me. Houses burned and collapsed. The putrid smoke of burning flesh emerged out of nearby houses."[4] Deng did not find his family but continued to search for them and learned that the women and children from his village had been abducted and the men shot. As he fled on foot, he encountered other Lost Boys and began the trek to Ethiopia and safety.[5]

Sometimes the separation of children from their families is a deliberate, albeit extreme, measure to save their lives. This was evident in World War II, when Jewish families would send their children away to safe countries, often hiding their religion, nationality, and family ties. Also during World War II, residents of British cities sent their children to stay in the countryside, often with complete strangers, for safety. During the Nigerian civil war, parents were encouraged to leave their children in special safe facilities where food and education would be provided. Those children later became separated from their families because of poor record-keeping.[6]

Wherever there is war, famine, or population displacement, we see cases of unaccompanied, migrant children. The 2015 European surge in asylum seekers, largely Syrian, included many children traveling independently. Figure 6 illustrates the sharp increase at that time.

This trend is also evident in the United States, where there was an increase in the number of unaccompanied minors applying for asylum around 2013. Figure 7 illustrates the jump in unaccompanied minors crossing the southern US border (with a notable decrease in 2020, likely due to Covid-19).

This is a change; children are migrating by themselves and in groups that are composed of other children. Sixteen-year-old Yousef is an example. He was one of the thirteen hundred unaccompanied children in the refugee camp just outside of Calais, France called "the Jungle."[7] The camp, constituted of people who were trying to get to the UK from France, was on the French side of the Channel Tunnel. It existed from early 2015 until October 2016, when the French government razed it. Yousef made the difficult journey to Calais alone; his father died before the Syrian civil war broke out, his brother was killed by a sniper dur-

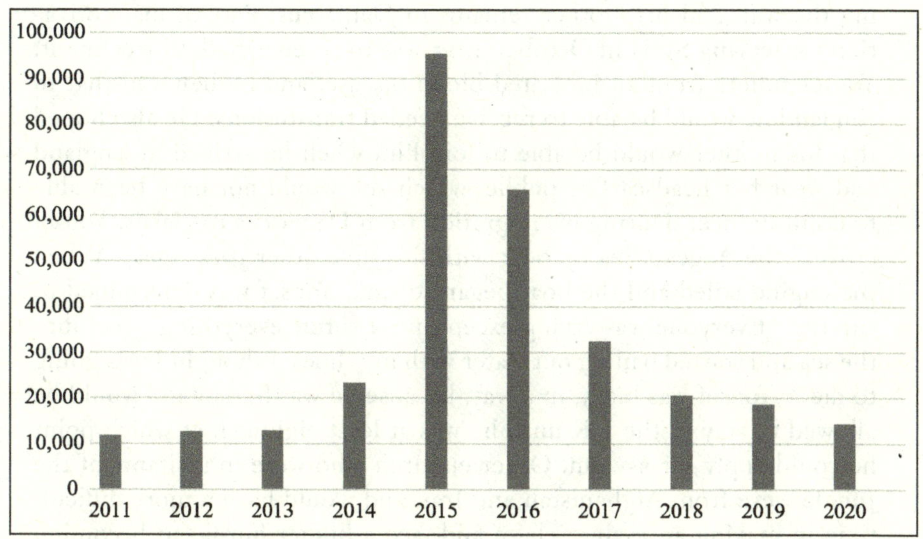

Figure 6. EU Asylum Applicants Considered to Be Unaccompanied Minors, 2011–2020. Source: Eurostat.

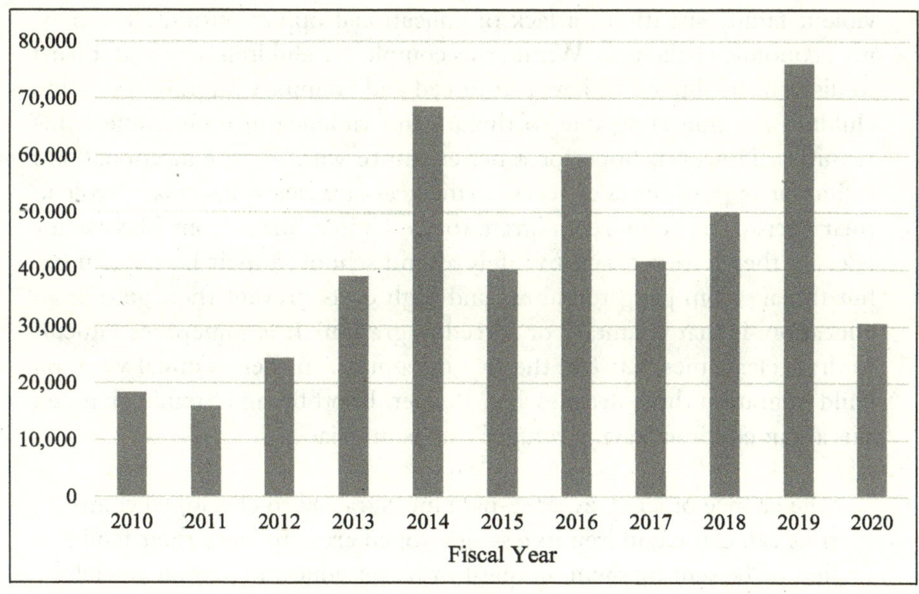

Figure 7. US Border Patrol Southwest Apprehensions of Unaccompanied Children. Source: US Customs and Border Protection, 2010–2020.

ing the war, and his mother remains in Damascus. Part of his motivation for leaving Syria in October 2015 was to receive medical treatment. Yousef suffers from an inherited blood disease, and he believed that in England he would be able to receive needed transfusions. He also hoped that his mother would be able to join him when he arrived in England and wear her headscarf in public, which she would not have been able to do in France.[8] During his migration from Damascus to Calais, Yousef crossed the Aegean Sea by boat with fifty-five other passengers. When the engine failed and the boat began to sink, Yousef was determined to survive: "Everyone was crying except me. I threw everything I had into the sea and started bailing out water with my shoes. I thought I was going to die."[9] Yousef was lucky, in a way, because he was Syrian and would be allowed to stay in the UK until he was at least eighteen, at which point he could apply for asylum. Other children who were inhabitants of the Jungle were from Afghanistan and Iran and would have a more difficult time in making an asylum claim and face a higher hurdle to becoming legal residents of a European country.[10]

The division between legitimate asylum claims under the Refugee Convention and economic migration is hard to understand and difficult for children to interpret. Children can be emerging from very complex contexts in which they may have to negotiate external threats of aggression, violent family situations, a lack of educational opportunities, and ongoing economic challenges. Within this complexity children may find it hard to discern the difference between forced and voluntary migration.[11] Some children are migrating due to threats and violence in their home communities. However, hope for a better future with more educational and economic opportunities or access to medical care clearly also plays a role in their decisions. If children migrate to the United States from El Salvador because they have a desire to safely attend school in their home country, but threats from gang recruiters and high costs prevent their getting an education, is that voluntary or forced migration? It is sometimes difficult to draw clear lines between the two categories. In their seminal work on child migration three decades ago, Ressler, Boothby, and Steinbock noted this about children leaving refugee camps in Asia:

> The chance of legal, expense-paid immigration to developed countries can cause children in less-developed areas to leave their families, or be sent by them, in quest of better education, employment, and material standards of living. In short, resettlement from less-developed to more-developed countries can itself cause child-family

separation. This is particularly true when the opportunities for later legal migration are limited.[12]

While the incentives for migration reflect what Ressler, Boothby, and Steinbock noted in the 1980s, opportunities for resettlement do not. Substantially changed since they conducted their research is the number of children migrating independently, outside of the refugee resettlement system. In other words, what they observed in the 1980s was children being declared refugees and then resettled in the Global North. What we see today are children migrating to the North to seek asylum with the hope of being declared a refugee. These children face tremendous risks. They must negotiate geographically difficult environments such as crossing the Mediterranean Sea or the Mexican desert. They must decide how to proceed and where to stop. They can fall ill or can find themselves trapped in refugee camps or informal settlements like the Jungle with no ability to get out or to go back. Children are vulnerable to traffickers and must navigate a complex bureaucratic asylum process when they arrive in a place of refuge.

If children do undertake the risk of independent migration, humanitarians would hope for their protection and generous reception when they reach their destination. Yet there is a dilemma between protecting the human rights of individual children and preventing or restricting immigration. One horn of the dilemma leads to insufficient protections for children; the other opens the country up to the burdens of responsibility for migrant children and potentially incentivizes children to risk dangerous journeys to find a better future for themselves. Jaqueline Bhabha has observed that restrictions on child migration seem to be winning out. She notes:

> One might expect that children caught up in the refugee process, particularly children traveling alone or separated from their families, would encounter an institutional environment that promoted their access to safety. But the uncomplicated concern for refugee children of the early and mid-twentieth century no longer exists.[13]

The growth in unaccompanied child migrants has made an open reception of them less likely. Countries fear an inundation of asylum seekers whether they are adults or children.

Events in the United States in the summer of 2018 highlighted the special vulnerability of children and the ways in which their well-being is compromised by wider fears about immigration, even when they are traveling with families. Attorney General Jeff Sessions determined that there would be a zero-tolerance policy for illegal migrants coming into the United States. While asylum seekers would still be able to apply for asylum, those who were illegal would be criminally prosecuted rather than facing civil deportation proceedings, as before. "If you are smuggling a child then we will prosecute you, and that child will be separated from you as required by law," Sessions said at a law enforcement conference. "If you don't like that, then don't smuggle children over our border."[14] This policy of child separation was clearly in violation of both the UN Convention on the Rights of the Child, which the US has not signed, and the policies of humanitarian organizations, which agree that

> the principle of family unity—or integrity of the family—states that all children have a right to a family, and families have a right to care for their children. Unaccompanied and separated children must be provided with services aimed at reuniting them with their parents or primary legal or customary caregivers as quickly as possible.[15]

A spokesperson from the UNHCR stated that the US policy "amounts to arbitrary and unlawful interference in family life, and is a serious violation of the rights of the child."[16] Ultimately, US public opinion and legal interventions forced a stop to the practice.

Growing national fears regarding migration exist alongside an international legal system that is not intended for children and insufficiently protects their interests. All children who become refugees are under the care and supervision of the UNHCR, which has developed a detailed process for assessing the needs of unaccompanied refugee children and helping them achieve durable solutions.[17] Yet there is no separate legal process for unaccompanied children to make asylum claims. All children must apply for asylum based on the Refugee Convention or qualify based on prima facie status.[18] The 1951 Convention provided a flexible approach to dealing with individuals and groups of refugees up until the turn of this century. It gives authority to the 146 signatory states and to the UNHCR to assess and protect refugees. However, times have changed in terms of both conflict and international climate, and this framework is less useful than it has been in the past.

The 1951 Refugee Convention was not designed to address the needs and asylum claims for unaccompanied children, yet the numbers of unaccompanied children are rising, and no legal alternatives for evaluation of their asylum claims are on the table. Legal responsibility for the protection of unaccompanied children problematically lies with the host country. But host countries are interested actors, often unwilling to take on the protection and legal guardianship of refugee children. EU countries all accept the best interests of the child as the guiding principle to follow, in keeping with the United Nations Convention on the Rights of the Child and the Charter of Fundamental Rights of the European Union. In practice, their policies differ greatly, with Portugal at one extreme, recognizing child migrants as having the same rights and benefits as any Portuguese child, and the UK, where child migrants are often held in detention centers.

This situation could be improved through specific policy interventions. Two are most obvious. First, it is critical to provide all minor asylum applicants with legal counsel. This is currently recommended, but not always followed, even in developed countries. Legal counsel would provide children with an adult representative in court who can look after their interests and make the strongest case for asylum. In the United States there have been several attempts to amend immigration law to provide legal counsel to minors; the latest was the Refugee Protection Act of 2016. However, none of the proposed changes have made it through the legislative process to become law.

A second, more controversial, policy change is that children could qualify as refugees on a prima facie basis, rather than having to apply for asylum. In other words, they would just be accepted as refugees unless there was evidence to the contrary. While this is a solution, it is politically challenging for several reasons. There is fear that this might encourage more children to leave their homes and put themselves in danger. It would also put the burden of potentially looking after large numbers of minor children on states that are ambivalent about hosting refugees in the first place.[19]

Part of the changing world in the twenty-first century is the willingness of young people to exert agency in areas we have not previously witnessed, such as migration decisions. Teenagers living in conditions of violence and deprivation are connected to the world through smartphones and the internet. They see the opportunities in other countries where access to education, job opportunities, and medical care is widely available. There are networks of intermediaries, or people traffickers, who make a profit from moving people in desperate situations—children as well as adults—to more desirable circumstances.

Children, Return, and Understandings of Home

While the number of independently migrating children has increased to the point of major international concern, it remains more common to see children forcibly displaced with their families. Families leave reactively when armed groups attack, or the government orders them out. They also leave proactively, afraid that violence, which has touched neighboring towns or kin, will be unavoidable. The primary legal responsibility for children within society rests with their parents and with states. Children are the responsibility of their parents, with the state providing the legal environment enabling family life and stepping in when the family situation warrants. That fundamental principle persists, though sensibilities regarding children's autonomy have changed over the past few decades.[20] When a family becomes refugees, humanitarian organizations assume some responsibility for children.

Lengthy displacements mean that children often mature into adulthood in places of refuge. They are raised in camps, cities, and other countries rather than their "home." This changes the nature of their socialization in ways that can be negative. For example, in northern Uganda the lengthy displacement (up to twenty years) of the Acholi people because of the conflict between the government of Uganda and the Lord's Resistance Army eroded knowledge of important cultural practices created intergenerational tensions. Julia Vorhölter notes that "according to common belief, due to fundamental changes in socialization practices the young generation never learned societal rules and norms and therefore no longer knows Acholi culture."[21] When displaced Acholi children eventually did return to a home many were not familiar with, they were young adults with their own ideas about how they wanted to live, formed by experiences of war and life in the camps. This caused conflict with the older generation.[22]

Many displaced young people are stuck in refugee camps or situations of protracted displacement with limited opportunities for education. In 2016 the secretary-general of the UN, Ban Ki Moon, convened the World Humanitarian Summit to address some of the problems in the humanitarian infrastructure. One of the specific problems on the agenda was addressing the education of displaced young people. According to the UNHCR, there are 6 million school-aged children under its mandate and 3.7 of those 6 million children do not have a school to attend.[23] Mohammed was one of the 900,000 Syrian school-aged refugee children not attending school. He fled from the war in Syria in 2015 and found temporary refuge in Turkey. Rather than attending school, Mohammed worked eleven-hour days cleaning cars, contributing some income to his family. Even before he left home, Mohammed stopped attending school in Syria because he and his family feared that the school would be bombed.[24] Mohammed lost precious years of education, as have many of the millions of school-aged refugee children.

Children who grow up in places of refuge know those places as home. Parents have identities tied to their places of origin, while children may feel stronger bonds with other identity groups and with countries of refuge. Sri Lankan Tamil refugees living in India face this problem. Young people born in India or growing up there don't always consider themselves Sri Lankan and prefer staying in India even though they are not citizens. Their parents are more interested in return to Sri Lanka, and these differences cause tensions within families. We see this in other places as well.[25] Some Sri Lankan Tamil refugee youth no longer want to be referred to as refugees, as they feel they could better integrate in India if they were not labeled as such. We see this in other places as well.[26] One 26-year-old woman I spoke with left Kosovo when she was eight years old. I interviewed her in central Serbia, where her family had taken refuge. "I feel like I am from here. It is different for me because of my age. I work. I don't want to go back. I have a desire to visit to see the place, but my friends are here, my job is here."[27] Older family members, also present at the interview, had very different feelings and wanted to return to Kosovo. Laura Hammond has also observed changed ideas of home among a resettled refugee population in Ada Bai, Ethiopia.

> Adi Bayans who were teenagers or young adults, who had come of age in the returnee settlement, were less concerned with returning to their birthplaces than they were with participating in the communities that they had helped to form in Ada Bai. Most had only vague memories of the highlands, if any, and did not feel a strong desire to return. They felt that their economic prospects were better in the returnee settlement, and that in time Ada Bai would be as compelling a home as the highlands had been for their parents.[28]

A growing literature on home-making and place-making demonstrates similar findings among other populations of displaced people.[29]

Young adults who do choose to return need to establish their own lives and livelihoods. Young people who have been displaced may want to stay in urban areas, even if their original homes were rural, because of the availability of entertainment, education, and jobs.[30] Patricia Weiss Fagan notes,

> In Colombia young people wrenched away from their homes before they came of age rarely experience the degree of nostalgia for the isolated farms where they were born. Despite continuing strong tribal identities and attachment to land ownership, the rejection of the rural social order is equally if not more pronounced among

youth in Liberia, so many of whom have spent their formative years in refugee camps and in combat.[31]

Adults raised in places of refuge face impediments to finding work if they return home. South Sudanese youth growing up in the Kakuma refugee camp in Kenya do not learn farming skills needed to return to agricultural livelihoods in South Sudan. They cannot leave the camp without permission and rely on humanitarian organizations for their food. This is not the case in all refugee camps. In Jordan's Mafraq and Zaatari camps, Syrian refugees are given work permits so they can find employment. In Kakuma it is different; if youth remain in the camp for a long time, repatriating is troublesome.

> "Nobody thinks that they can go back," said Andrew Riek Wal, 24, who lived in Kakuma for a decade before returning home in 2011, only to come back to the camp in 2013. "I am very worried about going back because I may be killed." During his brief return, Wal got a job teaching English in the capital Juba and began searching for family members. But when fighting resumed, he feared he was especially vulnerable. Because he had spent his adolescence in Kakuma, he was never given the distinctive horizontal forehead marks that distinguish Nuer men, and he feared he would be mistaken for a Dinka.[32]

The experiences of Wal illustrate one challenge faced by those who have grown up outside of their cultural home. Their socialization constrains their economic opportunities and their ability to reintegrate into their community of origin.

The possibility of asset loss is an additional problem for young people returning from places of refuge to their "home" community. Property losses from war impact economic opportunities across generations, changing the livelihood choices of adult children and their ability to finance their own durable solutions. The nature of children's property, as a future right protected by the guardianship of a parent, means that children's property rights are under the greatest threat in situations where the life of the parent is in danger or parents are separated from their children. These circumstances sever the ties that assure children of future property access.[33] No better example of this problem exists than the experience of Jewish children in World War II, so many of whom were dispossessed of their family property and never able to reclaim it.[34] Other situations that cause orphanhood, such as famines or epidemics, put the long-term economic well-being of children at risk by threatening their access to assets.[35]Being raised in a place of refuge changes the economic opportunities of adult children and shifts their understanding of home.

Children Returning in Customary Tenure Systems: A Case Study of Northern Uganda

In northern Uganda the government fought the Lord's Resistance Army (LRA) from approximately 1991 to 2006. The LRA gained notoriety for its extraordinarily malevolent practice of abducting minor children to serve as soldiers, servants, and sex slaves. By 2005, approximately 1.8 million people, including 1.2 million Acholi (90% of the population) were displaced by the conflict.[36] There were two main causes of internal displacement. First, people spontaneously fled violence as it began to affect their communities, moving to towns and trading centers close to their homes and swelling the urban population. Second, beginning in 1996 the government enacted a policy to move people into camps, forcibly displacing them for their own protection and to ensure that they did not provide support to the LRA.[37] Northern Uganda is an excellent case study of return migration because forcible displacement was lengthy and pervasive but had a distinct end and the opportunity for return of all the internally displaced people.

Life in the camps was horrific and did not provide safety from the LRA. Poor protection and miserable camp conditions inflicted damage on social relationships. The generation of children raised in the camps was disconnected from traditional norms, as roles and expectations were dramatically different there.[38]

Peace came to northern Uganda in 2006 and people began returning to their communities, first spontaneously and then encouraged by the government. The vast majority left the camps by the end of 2010. In addition to the people returning from the camps, another cohort of young adults and minors who had been kidnapped by the LRA demobilized from their forced service and returned home to civilian life. Over the twenty-year conflict, children born and raised in camps or with the LRA became adults. I refer to this group as *adult children* to capture the fact that they were children during the conflict, but they are no longer minors.[39]

Northern Uganda allows us to examine return migration across generations and in settings where there is customary law and customary land tenure. This is particularly important because customary land tenure prevails in areas where there is war; Afghanistan, the Democratic Republic of Congo, Nigeria, Somalia, South Sudan, and Syria all have customary land tenure in rural areas of the country. Access to land and the primary means of livelihood for these areas—agriculture—is contingent on customary land tenure systems.

Customary land is allocated according to customary law—a body of social rules governing personal status, communal resources, and local organization. In many parts of sub-Saharan Africa, including northern Uganda, customary law controls access to resources such as land, trees, water, and sometimes labor. It is extremely diverse and dependent on local context.[40] Customary law is unwritten, and there are few titles or written documentation for land claims under customary tenure. Without clear records, any circumstance that robs children of a parent or a guardian threatens the ability of children to claim their property rights. The lack of formal records of lineage membership and landownership exacerbate this problem in customary settings.

Customary land tenure systems are dependent on the knowledge and memory of customary leaders. When people are displaced, leaders can change or die, and the knowledge they carry with them disappears. When a community is torn by conflict and displacement, the possibility for adult children to lose assets and access to resources is magnified.[41] Self-interested behavior of older family members can prevent the land claims of the next generation because the displacement occurred when they were minors and their property rights to customary land were still future rights. Absent records, access to land is dependent on the recollection of family members, return to the community, and assent of customary leaders. In northern Uganda there were instances of older relatives taking advantage of children orphaned in the camps to subvert their land rights. These actions were condemned by those familiar with the customary system and the obligations of the clan to ensure the well-being of its children.[42] In this section of the chapter, I highlight the problems adult children faced claiming customary land.

When people left the camps and returned home, there were a host of anecdotal accounts of conflicts over land.[43] Ronald Atkinson noted, "Numerous concerns have arisen about regaining access to such land after many years of forced displacement, including the death of many knowledgeable elders during those long years of war, and the unprecedented number of widows and orphans produced by the conflict."[44] Land conflicts were frequently intergenerational in nature, occurring between adult children and their older relatives. There are three intergenerational land issues tied to return migration.

The first, and most obvious, challenge was that returning adult children did not know their land or its boundaries. "As people return to their villages, they are confronted with the realization that over a period of 20 years, clan leaders, heads of households and the elderly who would have knowledge of the previous set-up in the villages are no more."[45] Older relatives, particularly uncles who are influential in the patriarchal inheritance system, could assist with this problem if they chose to do so, but not all did. The absence of a guardian with knowledge of the rightful claims of young people and willing to defend their interests, combined with the death of some customary leaders, caused difficulty for adult children in accessing land to farm.[46] One chief I interviewed in Gulu said this was his own experience; he could not properly remember the land boundaries and no longer had a living parent to assist him.[47]

The second issue was that of young people claiming customary land only to sell it rather than use it for farming.[48] A commonly expressed intent was to use the capital from the land sale to start a business that they preferred to farming. Land sales in this area are rare. Sales are undesirable for the community because selling land moves it out of the customary system, thereby reducing the amount of land available to future generations.[49] Blame was consistently placed on young people for claiming clan land—to which they have a right if their fathers belong to the lineage—then selling it. They were not using the land for its intended purpose of providing a livelihood for themselves while stewarding the land under the control of the clan for future generations.

The third intergenerational land issue is gendered. Under customary tenure systems in northern Uganda, women have secondary rights to land *use* and men have primary claims to landownership through their clan.[50] Unmarried women and those without children can access land from their natal clan, but children make it more difficult for women to claim customary land from their family. The clan of the child's father is supposed to provide the child's mother with land so that she can raise the children of his family on his land. There have been many cases in which young mothers have returned from captivity with the LRA and their natal clan is not willing to give them land because under customary law they should receive land from the clan of the father of their child.[51] Their children are pejoratively called "Bush Children." In a 2015 study of children born of war, the Justice and Reconciliation Project (JRP) reported on a consultation it conducted with 447 people in northern Uganda, including 380 members of the Women's Advocacy Network (WAN). Women involved in WAN reported caring for 1,609 children of whom 493 (31%) were children born of war, with the overwhelming majority of those conceived from sexual violence.[52] With some cases of sexual violence, women do not know the perpetrator, thus, the identity of the father. These women face a double challenge, as they are unable to make a land claim for the child from the father's clan and face difficulty in getting land from their natal clan.[53] Women surveyed by the JRP were asked about their concerns for the future, and 51% identified land access for their children.[54] The JRP tried to identify the fathers of these "Bush Children" so that they would be able to make land claims.[55] Some natal families have accommodated the women, as they would have done in the past when land was abundant, but this is less likely to happen now because the rising value of land makes clan elders more reluctant to give it to someone without a strong claim.[56] Whyte et al. name this phenomenon "patrilineal fundamentalism," noting that "Acholi tradition is invoked to exclude people who, by all accounts, were traditionally made welcome."[57]

In northern Uganda, return led to intergenerational tensions over land. Young adults were widely perceived to be the causes of land disputes and were often the perpetrators of violence if conflicts escalated.[58] Some elders reported instances of youth threatening their older relatives to force them to give up land that the youth could then sell.[59] The youth say, "The grandfathers gave you land, but our grandfathers did not consult us."[60] Different socialization experiences and economic goals of adult children changed their life plans and perceived opportunities in ways that set them at odds with previous generations.

Forced displacement in northern Uganda was pervasive and long. People were forced off their land and into camps. Children were raised in camps or forcibly abducted and became participants in the conflict. When the conflict ended, these children were young adults with rights and claims to resources within their home communities. Their reintegration into the home community was not easy, as they did not go through the same patterns of socialization as their elders, nor did they grow up engaged in subsistence farming, as had preceding generations.

In this chapter, I have addressed three very different issues related to children and migration. The experience of northern Ugandan adult children returning from camps is unlike the experience of Kosovan Serbs raised in exile and different from the experience of migrant children making asylum claims in Europe or the United States. Yet in all of these cases children were forcibly displaced. As they matured, their ideas of home changed, their asset claims in home communities shifted, and they developed their own preferences for where they would live and what they would do.

Conclusion

Any sort of forced displaced will include children. Some of those children will be migrating on their own and others with family. The increased number of forced migrants around the world has illuminated the insufficient protection of migrating children in international law, specifically in the consideration of children as independent asylum seekers. State policies about migrating children also show gaps in the protection of basic human rights in the absence of legal representation for minors.

The longer forced displacement lasts, the more children will transition into adulthood in the place of refuge. Where those adult children have educational and work opportunities, they will be more likely to want to remain in their place of refuge. In cases where their displacement was a result of ethnic conflict, these individual choices to promote their own well-being will have the unsettling effect of cementing ethnic cleansing from an earlier generation. Serbian children displaced by the war in Kosovo and raised in Serbia have made lives there. They have gone to school, married, gotten jobs, and are now unlikely to return to Kosovo even if their parents should want to do so. This effectively prevents the Serb minority population in Kosovo, discussed in the last chapter, from returning to its previous levels.

For those refugees denied opportunities to work, the transition back to life in the place of origin may be difficult because of lost assets, different socialization, or disrupted social networks that would have provided access to resources. Children growing up in camps face challenges in returning home and reclaiming assets, such as family land to farm. The networks of relationships through which land is passed in customary tenure systems are disrupted by displacement. Adult children who have actively participated in conflict as combatants or have been its victims can face resistance to asset claims, leading to a longer-term impact on their economic well-being and that of their children—the third generation impacted by conflict and displacement.

Time changes preferences for return migration. The life choices of children raised in places of refuge highlight that truth. Those displaced as children, or born in places of refuge, have often never seen or don't remember their 'home' country or a community. A generation raised in displacement cannot be expected to choose lives like their parents had before they were impacted by violence

FIVE

Property and Return

After civil war ends, a country needs an average of 14 years to regain its previous level of income.[1]

I want to live in my own house. The one that is mine, not rented. My husband died because of sadness in missing the house and land.[2]

Rebuilding communities after violent conflict occurs slowly.[3] It takes time for displaced people to return, homes to be rebuilt, and businesses to be started anew. Chapters 3 and 4 addressed people—who returns and where they return. In this chapter the focus is on property. Clear property rights—here property means housing, land, and other physical assets—are a precondition for economic growth in any context. After conflict and displacement, property restitution encourages return migration and creates the conditions for a thriving economy.

There are four main sections to this chapter. The first section introduces the problem of property loss resulting from conflict, addressing the links between property and identity in theory and practice. The second section examines the "victor's justice" approach that characterized the first half of the twentieth century, in which the winning party in a conflict determined rights to property. That changed after the end of the Cold War, and the third section identifies the norms of property restitution and compensation that developed in international public policy, with illustrations of how these policies have worked in the Western Balkans and Iraq. The final section addresses property restitution in settings with customary land tenure, where property claims are informal. In this section, a case study of Liberia highlights the ways in which customary law and customary land tenure can accommodate different return preferences.[4] Throughout the chapter, I consider the linkages between property and identity and the ways that violence and displacement change them. The central claim of this chapter is that postconflict property restitution options should enable the choices of the displaced either to return to their homes or to choose new locations and livelihoods. This is a simple idea made complex by the limitations of international norms and the drastically different circumstances in which return migration occurs.

Property and Identity

A 2015 Hollywood movie, *Woman in Gold*, tells the story of Maria Altmann, who found out when she was eighty-two years old that her family's paintings, stolen by the Nazis, were in the possession of the Austrian government. One of the paintings, Gustav Klimt's famous *Portrait of Adele Bloch-Bauer*, or *Portrait of a Woman in Gold*, was of Altmann's aunt. Altmann fought a protracted legal battle with the Austrian government and was eventually awarded ownership of that painting and four others stolen from her family. Maria Altmann's efforts to recover family property made for a good film because of the iconic nature of the paintings and her persistence. Losses of property in conflict are common and take a variety of forms. Homes are destroyed, damaged, or confiscated, businesses looted, documentation lost. Sales of property can be compelled, and people can be forced to sell homes and businesses far below market value. A less sensational, but more representative, example of property loss during World War II is that of Miriam Tasini and her sister Alisa Sorkin, who have been unable to reclaim family property in Poland because of a loss of documentation and legal impediments. The sisters were toddlers in 1940 when they fled Poland. The family left behind their business, a factory complex in Krakow that supplied local bakeries; since the end of communism in 1989, Tasini and Sorkin have been trying to reclaim it.[5] Prior to 2021, Poland lacked legislation on the restitution of private property losses from World War II, forcing those who wanted to reclaim their property to go through lengthy court processes requiring extensive documentation and expense. The Polish government resisted restitution or compensation efforts, estimating it would cost $30 to $40 billion and create a debt crisis that would have a negative impact on Poland's citizens.[6] When Poland did eventually legislate on property restitution in 2021, the law set a thirty-year limitation on claims, effectively preventing any further restitution for World War II property losses.[7]

The Polish property restitution case highlights the rival nature of claims to individual property restitution and general social justice. The cost of restituting individual property claims, mostly to people living outside the country, would fall on the state, which has competing claims to providing public goods to current citizens. A tension exists between individual corrective justice (reparations) and social justice (provision of basic needs). Both of these World War II examples also raise the important factor of time and whether property claims deteriorate over time, a topic that has been a subject of debate in normative political theory.[8]

We see present-day property losses in numerous contexts experiencing conflict. The Syrian civil war led to the destruction of homes, loss of businesses, forced sales, and loss of documents. Half of southern Syrian refugees reported homes that were destroyed or damaged beyond repair, and a majority of IDPs reported missing property documentation.[9] The Syrian government added to the property losses of refugees, issuing a series of urban development or reconstruction laws that alienated the property of displaced people.[10] In Nigeria, violence by Boko Haram displaces people in agricultural areas, leading them to abandon their farms and leave land unoccupied, allowing neighbors to take it over.[11] When that conflict ends, these property losses will pose a challenge to postconflict community reconstruction. In Somalia, conflict since the 1990s has led to property losses and competing property claims.[12] These patterns repeat in Ukraine, Myanmar, Ethiopia, Afghanistan, Sudan, and anywhere people leave their communities because of violence.

Legal Theory

Loss or damage to a home in a conflict can cause a particular kind of harm because of the ways that homes are bound up with memory and identity. Margaret Jane Radin is a legal scholar who studies the connections between property and individual identity. She recognized the obligation of states to distinguish certain types of "personal property" (e.g., house, car) with stronger property rights because they have a more significant role in defining the individual's personhood.[13] Radin argued that people's relationship to their home is sacred and crucial for personal development, demanding special legal attention and protection because it is linked to identity through memories and experience. This is true whether home is an apartment in a city or a rural home that has been in the family for generations. Legal protection of home is legal protection of personhood. Radin's work resonates in both politics and literature. Ties to the land among rural people—farmers and indigenous peoples—often feature prominently in popular representations. In John Steinbeck's *Grapes of Wrath* a tenant-farmer notes the links between a person and property:

> Funny thing how it is. If a man owns a little property, that property is him, it's part of him, and it's like him. If he owns property only so he can walk on it and handle it and be sad when it isn't doing well, and feel fine when the rain falls on it, that property is him, and some way he's bigger because he owns it. Even if he isn't successful he's big with his property. That is so.[14]

But this is not just true for rural people. Homes, cars, and other property mean something to us in terms of our self-identification. Because property relates to identity, the destruction or theft of property can have a more significant impact than the theft of money or some other form of fungible capital like stocks. The second epigraph at the beginning of the chapter illustrates this link. It is easier to imagine someone "dying of sadness" from the loss of a home than if they lost money or stock.

The connection between property and identity is highlighted in legal scholarship related to dispossession. Bernadette Atuahene has argued that certain types of takings—the legal term for when a government acquires someone's property without paying compensation—are the result of a larger strategy of dehumanization. In these cases, taking people's property is dehumanizing to them in some manner. She refers to these as "dignity takings."[15] Examples of dignity takings are treaty violations that robbed Native Americans and other indigenous people of their land claims—the land theft was part of a larger strategy of dehumanization. Property loss resulting from ethnic cleansing is another example, as is destruction of the homes of people who live in slums or informal settlements. Atuahene argues that people who suffer dignity takings need more than a restoration of their property or compensation, but some sort of affirmation of identity—a dignity restitution—in the form of an apology, rebuilding, or additional measure that leads to the restoration of dignity as well as property. This suggests that compensation, or the monetary equivalent of property value, would be insufficient to right the wrong of property destruction of homes or because of ethnic cleansing. Money alone is an insufficient equivalent of the harms to safety, identity, and security.

In 1972, when Idi Amin expelled the Ugandan Asian population, the property of the departing families was taken by the government and redistributed to Ugandans of African descent. The Amin government paid compensation to the Asians who lost their property. After Amin was deposed, some Asians returned to Uganda and legally reclaimed their property, even though they had already received payment for it. The return of property in addition to the payment amounted to a dignity restitution. It was both an acknowledgment of harm done and a reparation.

The crucible of conflict can change a person's relation to specific property from constitutive of identity to just a commodity. When this happens, compensation—money awarded as restitution for a harm—becomes an acceptable solution to property loss, not the best solution, but a good solution. The best solution would be, as Atuahene argues, return of property or compensation accompanied by a public recognition of harm that restores people's dignity. In the postconflict settings that are the subject of this book, this is unlikely to occur. Reconciling gestures might be a good thing for those who have lost property or been displaced, but they are improbable in settings with more serious losses, such as deaths and long-term physical harms. Megan Bradley has argued that property restitution, compensation, apologies, and truth commissions all create the conditions for a "just return" of refugees by restoring the legitimacy of the state of origin.[16] Just return and dignity restorations are healing actions but demand more than postconflict states are often able or willing to give, particularly if those states were a party to the conflict. Restitution or compensation is easier to achieve than an apology, and it can be an important mechanism in enabling people to finance their choices regarding where they will live and what they will do after a conflict.

Victor's Justice

Internationally recognized rights to property restitution are recent. A robust international human rights agenda began after World War II and grew after the end of the Cold War. Before World War II, the ethnic homogenization of states was a goal and this meant restrictions on citizenship, particularly in Europe. During and after wars, minority populations were particularly vulnerable to loss of citizenship and property.

Hannah Arendt has famously lamented this situation in her book *The Origins of Totalitarianism*, which has startling relevance to today's forced migration crisis. Arendt observed that "the moment human beings lacked their own government and had to fall back upon their minimum rights, no authority was left to protect them and no institution was willing to guarantee them."[17]

A compelling example of victor's justice regarding property occurred after the Greek loss in the Greco-Turkish War of 1919–1922. Turkey and Greece agreed to the compulsory exchange of their minority citizens, expelling 1.3 million Greek Orthodox from Turkey and five hundred thousand Muslims from Greece. The population exchange happened after a brutal war in which many were killed or displaced. Both Greek Muslims and Turkish Christians were stripped of their citizenship and property in the name of ethnic and religious homogeneity. The expelled lost their rights to land and homes. At that time, the Greek population was only 4.5 million and Greece had to absorb more than one-quarter of its existing population in people expelled from Turkey. The 1923 Lausanne Peace Treaty and its Convention Concerning the Exchange of Greek and Turkish Populations makes it clear that this expulsion was permanent.

> As from the 1st May, 1923, there shall take place a compulsory exchange of Turkish nationals of the Greek Orthodox religion established in Turkish territory, and of Greek nationals of the Moslem religion established in Greek territory.
>
> These persons shall not return to live in Turkey or Greece respectively without the authorisation of the Turkish Government or of the Greek Government respectively.[18]

In this agreement, ethnic identity—defined by religion—was more important than citizenship. Both countries willingly purged religious minority groups from their territory. There was no right of return and no property protections.

Under the terms of the agreement, those forced to move were to receive full value for immovable property they left behind. The exchange vacated houses in each country that new migrants could occupy. The League of Nations was to facilitate the population exchange and oversee compensation payments. It established a commission of Greeks, Turks, and others that would value the property left by the refugees and provide for the compensation to the respective government. While this appears pragmatic, it was unworkable in practice. Many people had to finance their own journey and survived on whatever assets they had with them. There were problems on both sides. The massive influx of impoverished refugees into recently defeated Greece brought disease, hunger, and homelessness. Bruce Clark reports that in Turkey, "In theory, every family was supposed to receive housing and land that bore some relation to what had been forfeited in Greece. Initially, however, all the authorities could promise was property worth 17.5 per cent of the amount left behind. There was a vague assurance that further handouts would follow as soon as Greece and Turkey had settled all their mutual claims."[19] Negotiations on the financial settlement went on for years following the expulsions, and promises of fair compensation for lost property were unrealized.

The 1923 "population exchange" between Greece and Turkey was successful in creating more religiously homogeneous states. Both countries saw it as advantageous in eliminating a religious minority group perceived as a threat. Such was the attitude of the times that the agreement was facilitated by the League of Nations, and this massive creation of refugees received the sanction of the first High Commissioner for Refugees, Fridtjof Nansen.[20] People unfortunate enough to be part of the exchange lost their property; many also died due to disease and poverty when they reached their destination.

What are the rights to property after conflict? A victor's justice approach would tell us there are none for the losers, the refugees, or the forcibly displaced. Yet, the post–World War II development of the human rights agenda, beginning with the Universal Declaration of Human Rights (UDHR) in 1948, eventually touched on property. Article 17 of the UDHR articulates the right to own property and the protection against arbitrary deprivation of property. This would presumably prevent anything like the Lausanne Peace Treaty in the current era. Still, it was another fifty years after the UDHR that any specific policy addressing property in postconflict situations was developed.

International Public Policy on Property Restitution

In 1997, a process for developing international standards regarding property restitution began within the UN system. At that time, property issues were an ongoing postwar problem in both Bosnia and Tajikistan, where there had been substantial population displacement and property return was contentious. The UN Sub-Commission on the Promotion and Protection of Human Rights took up the study of property rights and displacement. It recruited Brazilian political scientist and diplomat Paulo Sérgio Pinheiro to write a report. Pinheiro oversaw the development of the first summative statement regarding property rights in postconflict settings—the Pinheiro Principles.

The Pinheiro Principles were endorsed by the Sub-Commission on the Promotion and Protection of Human Rights in 2005. That same year, the UN General Assembly approved the Basic Principles and Guidelines on the Right to a Remedy and Reparation for Victims of Gross Violations of International Human Rights Law and Serious Violations of International Humanitarian Law, which addressed property return as a legal remedy. This meant that the harm or damage of property dispossession was recognized, as was the need for a solution to that harm. In cases where state action has led to property loss, another UN agreement, the 2001 Responsibility of States for Internationally Wrongful Acts applies. Under this agreement,

> Victims have a prima facie entitlement to some compensation for their losses, and perpetrators have a prima facie obligation to provide such compensation, but the determination of exactly how much is owed to victims by a culpable agent depends on various other moral considerations beyond those of victims' damages and perpetrators' culpability.[21]

The agreement identifies the obligation of perpetrators while also acknowledging the tension between individual claims to compensation and overall societal needs.

All these guidelines and agreements recognize the right of people, who unlawfully or arbitrarily lost their property, to have that property restored to them or to be compensated for its loss. The Pinheiro Principles in particular have guided property restitution efforts in postconflict settings. They focus on housing, apply to both refugees and internally displaced people, and have an appealing simplicity—return that which was lost or taken. Perhaps because they are widely used and referenced, the Pinheiro Principles have also been attacked as an overly optimistic set of policies that transplant human rights law into the goal of social development and peacebuilding.[22] Optimism is admirable, but legal transplantation has not worked well in the past, as simply stating rights does not often lead to social absorption and enforcement. Nor has local development and peacebuilding always proceeded as intended or achieved the goal of restoring the communities to what they were.

The most recent international agreement to address postconflict property rights is the 2012 Voluntary Guidelines on the Responsible Governance of Tenure of Land, Fisheries and Forests in the Context of National Food Security (VGGT). The VGGT resulted from a wide consultative process led by the UN Committee on World Food Security. They consider land governance and resource access in all contexts, not just postconflict. They are more adaptable than the Pinheiro Principles and avoid some of the criticisms regarding legal transplantation. Because they are less directive in terms of the mechanisms that must be used, the VGGT are useful in settings with customary law and customary land tenure. For example, the Pinheiro Principles state very specifically that claims for restitution should be submissible in person, by post, or by proxy. The VGGT do not specify the ways in which people have to be informed, but they directly address customary tenure systems and allow for compensation through the return of different plots of land. Article 14.2 notes,

> Where possible, the original parcels or holdings should be returned to those who suffered the loss, or their heirs, by resolution of the competent national authorities. Where the original parcel or holding cannot be returned, States should provide prompt and just compensation in the form of money and/or alternative parcels or holdings, ensuring equitable treatment of all affected people.[23]

The VGGT focus on agricultural land and productive resource access rather than the focus on housing we see in the Pinheiro Principles. In rebuilding economies after conflict, both housing and productive resources are important, particularly in environments where subsistence farming or smallholder agriculture is the prevailing livelihood. Housing may be the most immediate concern, but other real property such as agricultural land or business premises are essential to fully restoring lost livelihoods. Moreover, while housing can be destroyed, land can always be restored.

In numerous studies from contexts as varied as Bosnia and Afghanistan, returnees have noted property as critical in their decision to return home or to remain in their place of refuge.[24] The availability of shelter, at a minimum, and preferably previous homes, businesses, or land to farm helps people to envision return to their communities of origin.

Property Restitution in Practice

Articulation of the Pinheiro Principles occurred when postwar property issues in Bosnia and Tajikistan were high on the international agenda. While the Dayton Peace Agreement, which ended the Bosnian War, informed the development of the Pinheiro Principles, it also illustrated their shortcomings. During the Bosnian War, two million people were displaced from their original residences because of ethnic cleansing—a calculated effort to remove certain ethnic groups from territories claimed by other groups through violence. The Dayton Peace Agreement guaranteed property restitution. The agreement was designed to undo ethnic cleansing and encourage people to return to their original communities. However, that did not happen. When their homes were returned, Bosnian owners frequently sold them and went to live elsewhere, among their co-ethnics, rather than return to ethnically mixed communities.[25] It is not unreasonable that people may want to sell property that is important to them, particularly after a war that has shifted their life plans and changed the social equilibrium in communities. It is also quite probable that some people wanted to return to their homes but felt unwelcome in their communities, so they sold their homes and lived elsewhere. Toal and Dahlman note that the return of refugees and displaced people in Bosnia sometimes sparked riots and violence.[26] Returns in Kosovo are similar as returning Serbs are not always welcome and sometimes experience vandalism and violence in their home communities.[27] On describing a visit to her previous home in Kosovo, one Serb woman highlighted the damage done to her relationship with her Albanian neighbors by the violence that occurred. "People pretended not to know us. They were afraid because of themselves, because of what they had done."[28]

In Bosnia, there was a decision made to forgo compensation—monetary payment for the loss of a house or business—and only return property. While the lack of resources for compensation was an issue, the choice to return actual property that was lost resulted from the overarching goal of recreating a Bosnia where people lived in mixed communities, as they did before the war.

> A general fear that a choice between compensation and return of property would undermine the fundamental goal of the Dayton Peace Agreement, namely undo the ethnic cleansing and recreate a multi-ethnic society, resulted in opposition to support the fund.

In addition, critics argued that a compensation plan would reward those groups who obstructed the return process.[29]

Giving people their houses back did not achieve the restoration of the multiethnic communities of Serbs, Croats, and Bosnians that existed before the war. The decision to restore property rather than provide compensation elevated a return to the status quo before the war over the interests of displaced people. Scholars caution against this approach, which seeks to replicate the very social situation that gave rise to the conflict.[30] Normative theorists also raise concerns about rights to reclaim immovable property after displacement or political upheaval because of the ways in which war changes both life plans and resource claims across an entire society.[31]

We can categorize property restitution after conflict into three general categories: the restitution of specific property, compensation with equivalent property, and monetary compensation. Bosnia is a case of the restitution of the specific property lost. South Africa, Guatemala, and Rwanda all provided comparable land or houses if a specific property could not be restored or had a competing claim.[32] In Iraq the state also provided monetary compensation. This third strategy is less common and worth further discussion.

In Iraq, the government led by Saddam Hussein from 1979 to 2003 forcibly displaced its political opponents, confiscated homes and businesses, and sometimes destroyed whole villages. Targets of these displacements were Kurds, Shia Muslims (particularly during the Iran-Iraq War), Assyrians, or just those who disagreed with the regime. After the overthrow of the government in 2003, occupying forces under the Coalition Provisional Authority feared that there would be a rush to reclaim homes and property that had been stripped by the state.[33] Since these homes and land were occupied by others, the potential for property disputes was high and addressing competing claims was imperative to securing peace. The Iraqi Property Claims Commission, established in 2004, resolved property claims resulting from waves of forced displacements from 1968 to 2003. Though Coalition Forces initiated the process, it became completely Iraqi and transformed in 2006 into the Commission for the Resolution of Real Property Disputes. This program gave people the option of having their property restored to them or receiving compensation. Compensation claims were initially funded by the United States, and later by the Iraqi government.

One of the most significant hurdles to monetary compensation is identifying a source of funding. The Iraqi case was unusual in that there was substantial investment in monetary compensation. Not all governments are willing to compensate for wrongs committed by a previous regime, and indeed there is an argument that in the Iraqi case property losses were privileged over other losses suffered in the conflict and other social priorities. During the years preceding the war in Kosovo, the government fired Albanians from their government jobs because of their ethnicity. When they lost their jobs, Albanians also lost their rights to socially owned government apartments. Those apartments were then given to Serbs. After the war, an Albanian government displaced Serbs from the apartments. In a subsequent mass claims process, led by the Kosovo Property Agency (KPA), a resolution was proposed that ethnic Albanians should get the apartments (or compensation if the property was destroyed) and ethnic Serbs should receive compensation for their property loss.[34] However, the KPA had no funding to pay anyone compensation. So while a legal decision was made, there was no available money for a remedy until 2017, eighteen years after the war, when the government of Kosovo allocated three hundred thousand euros for compensation for these claims. This small amount could do little to provide just compensation to those who lost their property, but as no international funders stepped up, the claims became moot.

International policy guidance identifies monetary compensation for lost property as a right but provides no source of funding or assumes it will come from the existing political regime. Time impacts fairness in compensation and how property claims should be weighed in terms of opportunity costs. Some political theorists have argued that restitution claims for property losses should be limited and symbolic the further in the past they occur.[35] Others flag competing beneficiaries and claims on resources in postwar societies where basic needs such as food and education may be unmet.[36] An additional problem with the right to compensation is how it applies to people who have untitled property claims such as in customary land tenure systems. I discuss this problem in more detail later in this chapter.

The Right to Have Property Returned versus the Right to Return

Buried within the principle of restitution is the implicit right to return to place of origin. The 1948 UDHR guaranteed people the right to leave their country of origin and the right to return to it in Article 13. The right to return has been controversial for two reasons. First, states involved in forced displacement and ethnic cleansing do not want people to return.

The most well-known example are Palestinians who have claimed the right to return and are blocked by the Israeli state. More recently Rohingyas, native to Myanmar, were rendered legally stateless then forcibly displaced by actions of the Myanmar government and armed forces.[37] They are not welcome back. Second, there has been no further development of the right to return outside of the UDHR. Nevertheless, we have in international public policy a right to property restitution that is on its way to becoming customary international law. How are we to understand this? The right of return has been legally developed as the right of the return of property with the unspecified implication that people will return as well. Scholars point out that international law has been construed as the right to return to one's former home.[38] Yet the lack of explicit detail tying property return to the restoration of citizenship rights leaves a gap that states, like Israel and Myanmar, have exploited for their political interests.[39] In other post-conflict states there is a similar reluctance to restore property to minority populations and thereby encourage their repatriation; again the Western Balkans provide an example.

Sarajevo Process

The disintegration of Yugoslavia, beginning in 1991, sparked wars throughout that decade in Slovenia, Croatia, Serbia, Bosnia, and Kosovo and displaced people across the Western Balkans. While the last war ended in 1999, many displaced people in the region remained in temporary housing without durable solutions years afterward. After the Croatian war, the Croatian government adopted legislation to prevent the return of non-Croat minorities and restricted property restitution to citizens of Croatian ethnicity.[40] While not as obvious in other countries, the law is indicative of broadly held sentiments. At a regional ministerial conference in 2005, Croatia, Bosnia and Herzegovina, and Serbia and Montenegro agreed to facilitate the return of displaced people. The 2005 meeting began what was dubbed the "Sarajevo Process" a program of cooperation and funding for durable solutions, with states agreeing to the voluntary repatriation of those who wanted to return and the provision of local integration solutions for those that wanted to stay. But an auspicious start and EU funding did not lead to immediate solutions. It was 2013—eight years after the first agreement—before voluntary repatriations began. States lacked enthusiasm for the return of minority communities. For example, in addition to the law noted above, the Croatian government made the return of Croatian Serbs, resident in Serbia after the war, difficult by blocking compensation for their lost apartments in socially owned buildings.[41] It took eight years and pressure from the EU for states to be able to negotiate in good faith and work together on program coordination.

While the Sarajevo Process was effective in the troublesome area of minority repatriation, the Dayton Peace Agreement illustrates the challenge of incentivizing postconflict minority return to places of origin. Even though Bosnia was a "successful" project of property restitution, communities did not return to their ethnic composition prior to the war. Toal and Dahlman refer to the effort by the international community to recreate the status quo ante in Bosnia as "an ambitious, unnecessary, and expensive project of social engineering";[42] it was also a failure.

A century after the Greco-Turkish War there has been a sea change in the rights of those impacted by conflict. International public policy gives people the right to reclaim property and the implicit right to return to their homes. Yet both normative theory and revealed preferences of displaced people should lead us to interrogate when and how the return of specific property in postconflict settings is desirable. It took a very long time for property to be fully restored to people after wars in the Western Balkans, and even that restoration of property did not recreate ethnically integrated prewar communities.

Property Restitution in Customary Tenure Systems

Property restitution in the Western Balkan states was complex, but there were existing property records and documentation of transactions. Property records were held by local municipalities across Yugoslavia since the 1931 transition from the Ottoman land registration system. Where records are absent, stolen, or tampered with, there are more significant challenges. During the Kosovo war, the property registers were taken to Serbia by departing Serb officials, creating a host of postwar property claims and restitution issues.[43] Kosovo was compelled to reconstruct a cadaster based on what records it did have. Only in 2016 did Kosovo and Serbia begin the process of sharing property records to facilitate a functioning land market in Kosovo. In rural customary tenure systems, such as those in northern Uganda or Afghanistan, there is no property register, as claims to land are informal and frequently undocumented, determined by traditional leaders who know families and communities.[44] This can be an advantage, as a lack of documentation after a conflict will not impede resource access. But customary tenure systems have other challenges. In the following section, I examine population return after conflict in customary systems and the definition of legitimate land claims under customary law. Emphasizing customary tenure systems is important because it determines land and housing access in rural areas of many countries where there is currently violent conflict: Central African Republic, Democratic Republic of the Congo, Myanmar, Nigeria, and Syria.

In the best-regulated land systems, resolving property issues after conflict is challenging. The destruction of property, illegal occupation, theft of records, and other issues are the detritus of the conflict. Land disputes surge where property rights are insecure, or when documentation is inconsistent or inaccessible. Customary land tenure systems rarely have titled land and frequently no written record of ownership. As illustrated in Chapter 4, this has been the source of significant conflict when return home becomes possible. Yet the lack of documentation can make customary land tenure systems favorable for returnees. There are no legal hurdles to reclaiming land; it is not necessary to have proof of previous occupation such as a deed, tax records, or a title. In Liberia after the war, communities granted use rights to returnees from other parts of the country and even to people who were refugees from other countries. In a 2013 visit to Tienni, Grand Cape Mount County, in Liberia, I spoke with a group of Sierra Leonean refugees now living in Liberia.[45] They are ethnically Mende and fled into Liberia in 1992 when the Sierra Leonean civil war became too dangerous. They found refuge across the border among a Mende community in Liberia. The Liberians gave them land to farm and to live on. After the war, the Liberian Refugee Repatriation and Resettlement Commission applied for a certificate of customary ownership on behalf of the refugees and worked to convert that to full legal title. Refugees did not receive title to their own land individually, but they owned their own houses and there were intermarriages and friendly relationships between the refugees and the local community. While not every postconflict customary setting is so flexible, it is hard to imagine such a thing happening in a situation with formalized land rights.

Authority Structures

Traditional leaders manage customary tenure systems. Where traditional leaders are efficient and accountable, customary tenure systems work well, but violent conflict can result in leadership changes at all levels of governance.[46] In most customary systems it is the local-level leadership that is most important for resource access. Shifts in leadership during and after conflict create difficulty for returnees. Leaders can die, leave the community, or lose legitimacy because they are on the wrong side.[47] Traditional leaders can use the ambiguity that exists in postconflict rural settings for their own gain. They can sell land that they might not have full authority to control and otherwise use their "office" to engage in rent-seeking behavior. There are some cases where the actions of postconflict "traditional" leaders have been so egregious that people create competing institutions to circumvent them. For example, in Liberia, several communities established locally elected land committees with structures parallel to the traditional authorities to constrain the ability of the new leaders to sell land and forest rights to commercial enterprises.[48] People who have no real claims to traditional leadership can set themselves up as leaders if they happen to be the "winners" in the conflict. In postwar Côte d'Ivoire, young men who had been soldiers returned to some communities and established their own "traditional leaders," refusing to recognize the people who had previously been in these positions.[49] Under the customary system prior to the war, youth would have had no voice in community leadership.

Some scholars note that opaque customary tenure rules in postconflict settings can protect land rights from a predatory government.[50] They argue that community land allocation mechanisms may have an undesirable intricacy when viewed by outsiders, but that complexity serves a purpose in enabling local enforcement mechanisms without relying on the state. This is vital where the state may be unpredictable or simply unable to enforce property rights even if it wanted to do so. Given the prevalence of land grabs in sub-Saharan Africa, this additional guarantee is salient only to the extent that the government recognizes those customary tenure rules.[51]

Timing and Nature of Return in Liberia

When and how people return to their communities of origin varies across contexts. The return experience in Liberia highlights the benefits and challenges of customary tenure systems in accommodating returnees after lengthy displacements. In northern Uganda (Chapter 4), after peace was established, most of those internally displaced people returning home did so over a relatively short period of time (three to four years), although they did not necessarily rebuild their houses where they were previously located.[52] Liberian return migration was different, with people returning to their communities of origin sporadically over many years, often with long sojourns in intermediate locations.

In Liberia, violent conflict began in 1989 in a struggle for power to replace Samuel Doe. This first civil war ended in 1996 with the election of Charles Taylor as president. Most people displaced after the first civil war went back to their homes in rural areas. But this was not the end to the violence. Conflict resumed in 1999 and the second civil war ended in 2003. Returns began shortly thereafter and continued sporadically for some time. During the two civil wars, approximately 80% of the population was displaced, both internally and internationally.[53] There was no tracking of individual returns within Liberia once people repatriated, but multiple informed reports suggest a particular stepwise or punctuated manner of return to rural areas in which people moved first to Monrovia, then to larger cities and towns in their home counties as services were reestablished, then to their previous residences.[54] At each step in this punctuated process, some people decided to stay where they were. This created a shift in the population distribution in Liberia before and after the conflict. While it is difficult to get accurate statistics for specific areas of the countryside, some facts we do know. In 1974 the population of Liberia was estimated by the government to be 1,503,368, with 14% (204,210) living in Monrovia. In 1984, the government estimated a population of 2,101,628. The 2008 census puts the population of the country at 3,476,608, with about 30% (1,021,762) in Monrovia.[55] The great increase in Monrovia's population relative to Liberia as a whole, in both absolute and percentage terms, between 1974 and 2008 strongly suggests that a disproportionate number of returnees came to Monrovia after being displaced.[56] However, the experience of Monrovia was not the same as in the rest of the country. Some rural counties of Liberia saw a relative *depopulation* and a decrease in the percentage of the county population resident in urban areas, while others saw an increase of their urban populations.[57]

These results suggest that people were not returning to their places of origin when they repatriated. Reports from interviews further illustrate that even those who did return to their home communities did so in steps with intermediate stays in other communities. For example, in Nimba County both Mandingo and Lome people lived intermixed in a town bordering Guinea. During the war, this area saw a lot of fighting, and civilians fled the violence. When refugees from the conflict first began to return, they lived in a resettlement town a few kilometers from their place of origin. As they became financially secure and local services were reestablished, they moved again—this time back to their original homes.[58] It all took time as people developed confidence that they could recreate their lives in their communities of origin.

A second example comes from a focus group interview with farmers

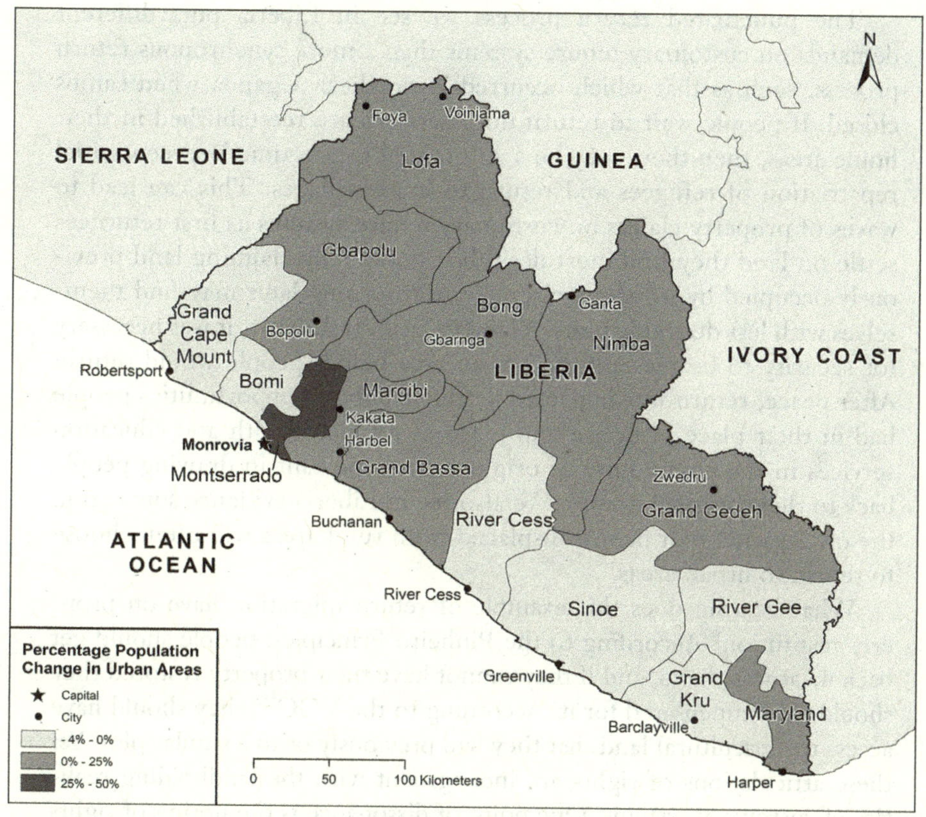

Figure 8. Liberian Urban Population Change, 1974–2008

from Lofa County who were cultivating land just outside Monrovia.[59] All focus group members voiced a strong attachment to Lofa County and an intent eventually to return. At the same time, they wanted to remain in Monrovia for the immediate future. This group of farmers made a point of going to Lofa County to vote in the local elections. While they expected eventually to return to Lofa, many of them had children in school in Monrovia, and the local Bassa community had given them land to farm while they remained near Monrovia.[60] As long as their children were in school in Monrovia, there was little incentive for them to return to Lofa County. Yet another man I interviewed in Monrovia said that he could not go back to his county and village of origin for security reasons. The young men he grew up with "became my enemies and destroyed my house." He did not want to return to his home, so when he returned to the country after the war, he stayed in Monrovia.[61]

The punctuated return process we see in Liberia puts different demands on customary tenure systems than a more synchronous return process, such as that which occurred in northern Uganda when camps closed. If people wait to return until services are reestablished in their home areas, then there may be a substantial gap in time between initial repatriation of refugees and return to home villages. This can lead to waves of property claims on customary tenure systems as first returnees settle on land they find most desirable, potentially claiming land previously occupied by someone else. Those returning later may find themselves with less desirable plots of land to farm. In Liberia, it was necessary for security to be reestablished in an area before people would return. After peace, return was impacted by the livelihood opportunities people had in their place of origin and place of refuge. Health and education services in the community of origin were important in drawing people back to their original homes. We also see in Liberia evidence supporting the observation that people displaced from rural areas will often choose to return to urban areas.

What bearing does this example of return migration have on property restitution? According to the Pinheiro Principles, people should get back what was theirs, and if they cannot have their property restored they should be compensated for it. According to the VGGT, they should have access to agricultural land that they had previously or to a similar plot. Yet these articulations of rights are incongruent with the landholding realities of customary systems. One point of dissonance is the noting of rights to specific and discrete property, rather than a general right to resources. Second, these articulations of rights imply that a person need not be present to have a rightful claim to restitution or the compensation for loss of resources. Compensation as a possible resolution to property claims in postconflict situations might work well in contexts like Iraq, where there are property registers, but it is difficult to imagine an effective system of compensation claims in customary property systems. Compensation works best in contexts with formalized landholding—documentation, land valuation, and cadastral registries—that permit identification of individuals and valuing of property.

In customary tenure systems land rights accrue and diminish over time due to habitation, use, and family circumstances. Therefore, presence and timing are important. Displaced people need to first return home and then make a property claim; in many places this need not be the specific property that they previously possessed.[62] If people choose not to return to their community after conflict, no restitution for loss of property is available.

Physical presence is necessary to make a claim on the resources of the group. It is not possible, for example, to claim customary land in northern Uganda or Liberia without returning there, or to hold that land against other claims to it without the presence of family.[63]

These characteristics of customary tenure complicate the idea of restitution of the exact property lost. Restitution of similar property or monetary compensation also is incongruous with customary rights. In customary tenure systems resource claims are contingent on group membership. For example, in northern Uganda, because I am Acholi from a particular clan, I have the right to land in a specific area. Clan leaders state that if they give a person customary land and that person sells it, they will never give the person land again, precluding the latter's ability to farm and live in the traditional clan area.[64] Presumably, compensation requires a similar relinquishing of claims to the group's resources. While compensation severs the locational tie to the clan area, it is unclear what impact it has in the long term on group membership. There has traditionally been a strong link between land and identity. In rural communities "access to rural land is often a symbol as well as a consequence of membership in a descent group or rural polity, maintaining such access serves to validate membership in the group, as well as vice versa."[65] Further research is needed to determine the identity impact of severing ties to the resource-based community.

International law and policy measures are replete with generalizable rights that accrue to individuals. While there is much to recommend this universal approach, the generalizability of international law can be at odds with customary systems, which are malleable, particularistic, contingent, and communitarian. International legal standards place obligations on state actors, while customary land issues are negotiated within specific localities and communities—often in contexts where state involvement is absent or undesirable. UN organizations and aid agencies are attentive to international law and standards regarding property restitution. These organizations will seek policy outcomes that are unlikely to be achieved in many customary tenure areas.[66] Moreover, property restitution may undermine the customary tenure system if, as in northern Uganda, youth and others who have no wish to return to subsistence agriculture sell the land they reclaim and thereby move it out of the customary system and into the formal market.[67] Investment in job-training programs or the provision of agricultural tools, livestock, or small business startup loans might be more helpful ways of assisting those displaced from customary tenure systems without threatening their community membership or undermining the tenure system.[68]

Conclusion

This chapter began with an epigraph noting that it takes fourteen years for economies to recover from civil war—an unsurprising statistic given the variability of population return and slowness of property restitution. Property restitution has been recognized as a human right in the UDHR, in the Pinheiro Principles (2005), and the VGGT (2012). These guidelines create a norm of property restitution and sharply contrast with the property takings and victor's justice observable prior to World War II. Property losses from war and ethnic cleansing in a conflict are no longer without remedy.

A functioning economy requires people and property; without houses, people have nowhere to return; without farms, they have nowhere to grow food; without factories and shops, they have nowhere to conduct business. The restitution of property in the Western Balkans is among the most successful cases we have of postconflict property restitution. Yet the Sarajevo Process was agreed upon more than ten years after the end of the conflict, and the effective implementation of policies came around the twenty-year mark. This is a substantial time lag given the importance of housing to repatriation or return and property restitution to economic development. There are empirical lessons to be learned from these cases. First, property restitution after conflict is possible. Second, it does not recreate communities as they were. Rather, property restitution empowers people to self-finance the transition to a community where they want to live. The experiences of the Western Balkans suggest a more appropriate end game for property restitution. Success should not be understood as restoring communities to their preconflict state. Success is facilitating individual and family choices in finding workable durable solutions.

Large-scale land claims processes, such as those in Kosovo, Bosnia, South Africa, and Iraq, are increasingly part of the postconflict landscape. These processes consider classes of claims with relaxed standards of evidence to allow for the challenges of a postconflict environment in which documents may be missing or incomplete. Yet they function slowly, and often suffer from a lack of funding. Establishment of an international fund to provide compensation for property claims after conflict would be a helpful step in enabling a focus on the preferences of displaced people in creating durable solutions for themselves. While compensation is not appropriate in every setting, in most it allows people who have been displaced by conflict to make decisions regarding where they would like to settle. Absent an international fund, focusing on issues of land and property claims within peace agreements and seeking ad hoc arrangements for funding them are options that achieve the same goal.

There is no single best solution to property restitution because there is no single property system and no unique experience of conflict. In Cyprus, where both Greek and Turkish Cypriots suffered property losses in intercommunal conflicts between 1963 and 1974, the two communities' different preferences about how to address the property issue impedes conflict resolution. Greek Cypriot IDPs favor a return of all properties, while Turkish Cypriots IDPs prefer an exchange of houses and land or monetary compensation.[69] It is simplistic to assume that people will want to return to localities in which they have been victims of violence; there is a parallel simplicity in assuming that years and sometimes decades of displacement will not change livelihood choices. People who are displaced for a few years might be eager to return to rural livelihoods, particularly if they have valuable agricultural resources such as orchards, vineyards, coffee plants, or other high-value crops. Those who have been displaced for decades may wish to take whatever compensation they can get and use it to rebuild their life elsewhere. Postconflict property restitution should enable choice for displaced people, neither compelling, nor precluding their return to former homes or livelihoods.

SIX

Global Governance and the International Migration Regime

At the time of this writing in early 2022, millions of Ukrainians are refugees in Europe and millions more are internally displaced. In Afghanistan, Myanmar, Syria, Ethiopia, and South Sudan recent or renewed conflicts created large numbers of refugees and IDPs. These are the countries with the highest numbers of conflict-displaced people. Forced migration is one of the most pressing international political issues of this century. Though Ukrainian refugees are currently being welcomed in countries across Europe, it is currently unclear how long the doors of Europe will remain open and what will happen to the Ukrainian refugees should they be unable to return home quickly. There are few places for people to legally go once they leave the country where they have citizenship. Forced migration demands both scholarly investigation and attention to international policies.

This book differs from other approaches that consider return migration from the perspective of human rights, ethics, or state interests. The contributions here add to the growing body of literature examining individual and household choices after conflict-induced displacement. We live in a world in which state sovereignty limits the impact of international agreements and nationalism is resurgent. States do not want open door policies for refugees or other migrants, and state sovereignty precludes a migration regime based exclusively on humanitarian principles. What benefit is there in looking at individual preferences regarding return migration when displaced people do not make the rules? First, we gain an understanding of what factors impact their motivation to go home and can observe how preferences change over time and as displacement impacts subsequent generations. Political changes at home may make return less desirable and children raised in places of refuge do not have the same attachment to "home" or the same preferences as their parents. Second, we gain insight into the kinds of policy changes that might best facilitate return home or another durable solution.

Restoring postconflict communities to economic vibrancy entails the return of both people and property. The preceding chapters have identified ways in which the international migration regime is misaligned with the preferences, needs, and choices of the displaced. Figure 1 in Chapter 1 illustrates that in a refugee regime designed to facilitate repatriation, few people go back to their communities and countries of origins. Does it matter that these policies do not align with the preferences and choices of people after conflicts? The incongruity of policies and preferences impacts three main areas: decision-making, funding, and programming. A family anticipating a quick return home has a different calculus regarding decisions pertaining to jobs, education, housing, and other life choices than a family that realizes that an immediate or even intermediate return home is unlikely. Policies and programs that year on year communicate to people that they will go home are ineffective if the opportunity to return does not materialize. This misalignment is most visible in those cases when return home is only possible so far into the future that it becomes a decision both for those who were displaced and for their adult children, raised in places of refuge.

Expectations matter in another way. Many refugees in the Global South hope for resettlement in northern countries. They want a future somewhere with freedom from violence and secure livelihoods. But opportunities for resettlement are extremely limited, and that is unlikely to change. People anticipating resettlement in a third country may not make the best choices for their households. We saw an example of this in Chapter 5 with Liberian refugees who lingered in camps long after the end of the civil war due to their hope for resettlement.

If the goal of international organizations is to return displaced people to their countries and homes of origin, then resources should be channeled into incentives and programs that prioritize return. Currently, most of the funding goes to resettlement—the durable solution for the fewest people.[1] Below are some ideas gathered from both literature and practice on policies that encourage other durable solutions.

Place of Origin

Critical to incentivizing return is providing services and programs in the places of origin. Investments in medical services, schools, and economic development make them more attractive places for returnees. Two decades ago, James Hathaway argued that "we need . . . to offset the costs to the communities that will receive refugees back, particularly at the local level, and to provide positive incentives to promote the meaningful reintegration of returning refugees in the communities they left behind."[2] The UNHCR increasingly focuses funding on projects and services that benefit everyone in the place of origin both to encourage repatriation and so that the community sees a benefit to welcoming returnees.

Displacements since the 1990s show the importance of asset restitution in facilitating durable solutions, but perhaps not in the ways previously thought. Returning property taken, abandoned, or damaged in a conflict does not restore communities in the full sense of that word. It is important to restitute property losses, but this can be done with greater attention to the preferences of the original owners. More flexible property restitution policies enable returnees to choose where they would like to live, and it may not be the area they left. In areas with formalized property records and cadastral systems, compensation for lost property or the restitution of the actual lost or damaged home, land, or business provides both choice and autonomy to households trying to determine their best paths for the future. Chapter 5 identified how this has worked in Iraq, and how in other places, such as Bosnia, compensation was specifically rejected because of the desire of external actors to return the country to its previously mixed ethnic communities. The intent of the Bosnian property restitution policy was to eliminate any gains made from efforts to ethnically cleanse an area. But many Bosnians did not want to go back to their communities of origin, and this policy created difficulty for those most affected by ethnic cleansing.

Property restitution is vital to the reconstruction of communities after conflict. Addressing housing, land, and property issues early in a peace process is desirable, but restoring property necessitates land administration systems and adjudicatory structures which may be contested or nonexistent. Absent or deficient land administration mechanisms create an environment for illegal land acquisition during and after a conflict and can exacerbate underlying tensions. Special protections are needed for vulnerable households and populations that may have difficulty making land claims. In communities with customary land tenure, attention also needs to be given to land access for women whose experience of conflict might preclude them from resource claims.

There is no "one size fits all" model for addressing issues of land access and property restitution—not all property systems are alike. In customary land tenure systems, which exist across much of sub-Saharan Africa, Central Asia, and other areas where we have seen mass displacements, the promise of compensation for lost resources or even return to a specific home and farm can be unrealistic. In customary systems, postconflict property restitution that simply gives people back what was lost may force people into a particular livelihood (farming). Yet, alternatives such as compensation in customary tenure systems is complicated by a lack of records and overlapping rights. To maximize choice, it is helpful to think more broadly about what sorts of compensation for customary land might be appropriate. Restitution solutions should focus on responses that allow people to pursue new livelihoods, such as job training in high-demand fields and small-business opportunities. Studies of refugee preferences suggest their desire for training in construction, electrical, and plumbing trades, enabling displaced people to assist with rebuilding their communities.[3]

The Importance of the Local

These strategies to encourage return migration are costly. Finding or developing the necessary knowledge for effective return or restitution programs takes time and local expertise. It also requires significant financial investments in areas devastated by war and depopulated by displacement. Return migration is a local political challenge as well as being a national concern. While national political structures designed to give minority populations voice within democratic systems are important, people need security at the local level, in their neighborhoods and communities. The cases from the Western Balkans are instructive. In both Bosnia and Kosovo, conflicts were ethnic in nature, and people returned to communities where they felt safe. In both cases, living among co-ethnics for personal security appeared to be at least as important as property restitution and more important than political structures providing representation to minority communities.

Places of Refuge

The most natural action when people are fleeing violence is for them to go to the closest place of safety. Few people leave their homes and choose a place of refuge thousands of miles away in a country where they do not speak the language. However, insufficient resources for refugee camps, lack of food rations, and limited education for children in places of refuge incentivize people to move again to a place where they can thrive. The surge of Syrian refugees into Europe in 2015 was caused, in part, by the removal of assistance in their first places of refuge. Underfunding of the World Food Program led to a drastic cut in rations for Syrian refugees in Lebanon, Jordan, and Turkey.[4] In Lebanon, food vouchers were reduced to US$13.50 per person per month, half of their previous amount. In Jordan more than 230,000 Syrian refugees living outside of camps lost their food aid entirely.[5] Families were forced to make impossible decisions to survive: taking children out of school; skipping meals; going into debt; or fleeing to Europe. Many chose dangerous travel and an uncertain future rather than remain and starve. On foot and by boat they flooded into Europe via Greece, Italy, and the Balkans countries.[6] More robust funding for places of refuge is necessary. While food aid is a bare minimum, host communities also benefit from funding for roads, schools, and medical facilities that they can also use. Where it is politically possible, these investments could be tied to host country policies that allow displaced people to find their own solutions such as the freedom to work and/or temporary or permanent legal residency.

Policies that encourage people to remain in their place of first refuge can prevent dangerous journeys to the Global North.[7] There are other reasons why proximity to the place of origin is preferable, the most important is that it facilitates rapid return. People who are close to their homes can monitor local security and the condition of homes and other capital resources. Similarity of language, business connections, and ethnic ties in proximate places of refuge mean that people are more autonomous and able to engage in economic activities even while in exile.[8] Host countries often fear that refugees will be a drain on their economic resources, take jobs from locals, and create security problems, but this need not be the case. Refugees who are engaged in the economy, rather than simply receiving assistance in a camp, can provide labor, start businesses, and contribute to development and growth.[9]

Refugee Compacts

Local integration of refugees involves awarding people the right to live in their country of refuge on a long-term basis with the legal right to work, educate their children, and otherwise participate in the economy. While local integration can take a variety of forms, its strongest manifestation is naturalization—the awarding of full citizenship rights to refugees. Naturalization is politically challenging. In some countries such as Jordan, a country of 7.5 million people with 655,000 registered refugees, the number of refugees as a percentage of the population is so high as to make naturalization politically untenable and basic service provision expensive. Elsewhere the prospect of naturalization is contentious because the people who are refugees are viewed as a security threat (Somalis in Kenya). Innovation in local integration efforts is evident in refugee compacts. Compact agreements are country-specific interventions designed to provide durable solutions for refugees. They bring governments, humanitarian organizations, and the private sector together to create opportunities that both help refugees and benefit host communities. The 2016 EU-Jordan Compact targeted the living conditions of Syrian refugees by providing access to employment and education for children while benefiting the economy, security, and stability of Jordan. Compact financing came from the EU, World Bank, and other private regional banks. Jordan agreed to issue thirty-nine thousand work permits and in return received trade incentives from the EU.[10] This innovative economic model benefits the host community and was intended to promote the autonomy of refugees, though there have been concerns raised in its implementation.[11]

Building on the compact model, the UNHCR led the development of the 2018 Global Compact on Refugees to address the rising numbers of refugees and their needs for durable solutions. The compact reiterates the goal of voluntary repatriation in conditions of safety and dignity, and notes, "The need to foster a positive atmosphere for resettlement, and to enhance capacity for doing so, as well as to expand its base, cannot be overstated."[12] It is difficult to imagine states agreeing to additional resettlement opportunities, and the Compact is not legally binding. These compacts improve on past policies by advocating for support of host countries and the economic autonomy of forcibly displaced people.[13] As a result of the conversations around the 2018 Global Compact on Refugees, the UN has begun to talk about options beyond the three durable solutions. Language regarding "complementary pathways" for admission to third countries as distinct from the three durable solutions is now part of the international humanitarian lexicon. These pathways are options such as educational programs or targeted labor schemes, which do not involve the intervention of humanitarian organizations.[14] The movement toward refugee compacts is part of a wider effort on the part of the United Nations and other humanitarian organizations to improve responses to a surge in forced migration.[15] When these solutions align with the interests of states, they add to the narrow set of options for the displaced. Refugee compacts are innovative, but countries do not always fulfill their obligations under these compacts, and there is little to compel them to do so.

Changes in International Law

One significant change in recent migration patterns is the growing number of children migrating alone, a development unanticipated at the time of the writing of the Refugee Convention. Unaccompanied children face physical harm, lack of education, absence of guardianship, and challenging legal hurdles to attain recognition as refugees. Minimal protections, such as legal representation, are frequently absent, even in developed countries like the United States, leaving minors to navigate complex legal situations on their own. Better protection for children is necessary and should be scaled depending on their age. At a minimum, children seeking refuge should receive legal representation and care appropriate to their age. Yet there is no international law requiring legal representation and no obligation to treat minors differently than adults under the Refugee Convention. This protection gap could be addressed in multiple ways. Individual states could develop specific procedures targeted at protecting minors migrating independently. Some do this now, but other states choose not to, often with a deleterious impact on the children involved. Another option would be an international agreement on the treatment of child migrants to allow their prima facia recognition as refugees under the 1951 Convention. Even if this recognition was conditional or limited, it would be an improvement on the current absence of law. In 2017 the European Commission outlined a set of objectives related to dealing the problem of child migrants and specifically addressing the protection gaps that exist. Their goals were, inter alia, to provide guardianship, address physical and mental health needs, trace families, and provide education with an emphasis on the best interests of the child. This is a good first step, but it only addresses EU countries and the needs have no geographic boundaries. Other countries should adopt similar measures and provide legal assistance and guardianship arrangements.

Data Problems and Data Solutions

Beyond the policy changes proposed above, the international migration regime could be improved by better data. Data availability will not open the doors for resettlement to new countries, but it can improve existing policy interventions and increase the likelihood of property restitution or compensation. Little data is available on local integration. Without this information it is impossible to know how many people need services or to evaluate the effectiveness of policies and programs. Smartphones are now pervasive in refugee camps as well as centers of urban displacement, creating new ways of tracking people, assessing their needs, and tracing family members. Data that was difficult to get in the past, is now far more accessible.

New technologies also allow the recording of property documents of displaced families such as deeds, wills, and tax records. This data can be collected from refugees and the displaced as a part of the intake processes of aid organizations and stored in a form that can travel with people as they move through their displacement. A portable portfolio of documentation can prevent asset loss. Digital portfolios of oral testimony, cell phone photos, satellite images, and documentation of the activities of the conflict collected in the media and by the government can create an "alternative" cadaster and facilitate claims to property at some point in the future. This evidence can enable mass claims for restitution after the conflict ends and document family assets for future generations.[16] Early identification of land and property losses of refugees and displaced people can facilitate later restitution of housing, land, and property rights.[17] Displaced people move frequently in search of refuge and can often reside in multiple locations prior to returning home or settling in a place of refuge.[18] At each step in their displacement they can lose evidence of assets. Distributed ledger or blockchain technology is a secure, online data system that permanently stores information across a network of computers and is particularly useful in any sort of record-keeping that involves the need for privacy and protection of data integrity.[19] Blockchain technology has already been used in land registries in Honduras, the Republic of Georgia, and, most recently, Sweden and could be adapted for use in storing vital personal and property records for displaced people.

A Growing Research Agenda

While these suggestions for policy changes are modest in their scope, the data and research needs on return migration and property restitution are considerable. Below, I identify outstanding research areas where there is either insufficient knowledge or where findings from a very limited pool of cases need additional substantiation. This section begins with two observations about the state of current research. First, most academic research has been conducted on cases with relatively small numbers of displaced people. If one considers the scope of cases in Table 2 of Chapter 3, and those discussed throughout this book, the academic literature is biased toward cases such as Bosnia, Kosovo, and Cyprus or displaced people who live in camps. Many of the highly studied cases are frozen conflicts in democratic and/or middle-income states; the generalizability of their findings to nondemocratic or lower-income states is unclear. It is more difficult to study other large, displaced populations from conflicts in Afghanistan, Central African Republic, and Yemen. Syria is the one exception, as it has been highly studied and had large numbers of displaced people.[20] We need more research in challenging settings with large numbers of displaced people and more theorizing about institutional innovations in nondemocratic settings.

The second observation elevates a criticism first made by Oliver Bakewell.[21] Social scientists studying refugees and displaced people have been too tied to the legal and humanitarian categories created by states and international organizations, so much so that it impedes other insights and observations of conflict-related displacement. To choose a different frame of reference is to risk being accused of not supporting human rights or the broader humanitarian endeavor. Thankfully, this is beginning to change, and additional social science research on displacement and return migration outside the humanitarian framework will broaden our knowledge and contribute constructively to humanitarian responses.

What are necessary areas of further research? One pertains to the preferences of displaced people. Do refugees and internally displaced people have similar preferences for return home? Or does the experience of crossing a border and gaining refugee status change people's goals and decisions? Because these two groups of people exist in radically different legal categories, their preferences are rarely compared. Yet the circumstances of their displacement and the desire for safety are similar. Investigation of this issue and the variables of time and opportunity would add a great deal to our understanding of preferences after forced displacement.

Another area of necessary research is the preference for return as it relates to the ethnic composition of the home community. The Kosovo research in Chapter 3 and recent studies of the preferences of Syrians and Greek Cypriots suggest that the ethnic composition of the local community after a conflict (co-ethnics, original neighbors) is more important in the decision to return than the experience of trauma during the conflict.[22] Research from Lebanon suggests that both the presence of co-ethnics and trauma are important.[23] More study on the ethnic composition of the home community and how that relates to trauma and local/national political protections in preferences for return would be welcome.

My hope is that careful readers of this book will never think about forced displacement again without considering its impact across multiple generations. While there has been notable policy work on educational opportunities for displaced children, there are larger understudied questions surrounding their livelihood choices, asset losses, citizenship, identity, and return preferences. Children may be minors when forcibly displaced, but they grow up and become adults in places of refuge, developing different identities and livelihood preferences than their parents. Children can lose family assets that would facilitate durable solutions elsewhere or, in customary tenure systems, face constrained livelihood choices. Since customary land tenure is prevalent throughout sub-Saharan Africa and Central Asia, this is a relevant and much-overlooked issue in previous studies of postconflict property restitution. Further research is needed on the identity implications of adult children who sell customary land or sever their ties to the resource-based community.

There is a related empirical question not addressed here. Does it matter from the perspective of economic development and growth whether the property taken or abandoned in war is returned to its original owners? We know generally that well-defined property rights are fundamental for economic growth,[24] and restoring property is important after a conflict, but does it matter if the property is restored to the original owners prior to the conflict? Could recognizing the property rights of secondary occupants achieve the same economic impact/growth? A somewhat related theoretical question is when, if ever, do claims of general social justice take precedence over individual compensation?

Conclusion

Forced migration is one of the most visible and persistent humanitarian problems of our time. The numbers of displaced people are rising, and the international system for addressing their needs is showing its age. Rising nativism across the Global North limits opportunities for both refuge and resettlement, pitting state interests against those of individuals seeking protection. The time that people spend displaced from their homes without a durable solution is rising, while new political and environmental crises drive further displacement. Yet we now know more about the preferences of displaced people and have technologies that enable better communication, assessment, and protection. The refugee crisis of the past decade is propelling policy innovation and highlights research opportunities that would enable better humanitarian responses.

In the introduction I noted that the goals of this book are modest. This reflects a certain pragmatism; a recognition that states are unwilling to adopt large changes to the existing international migration regime. Yet pragmatism is not pessimism. Small changes can make a difference, wars do end, and people show a remarkable resiliency in rebuilding communities after conflict. The policy innovations evident in the refugee compacts, regional agreements on IDPs, and even the VGGT make a difference at the margins and potentially large differences in the lived experience of displaced people.

More than a decade after peace came to northern Uganda, the region is booming. People have returned, many of the family land conflicts which characterized the early postconflict years have been resolved, the cities are thriving, and the countryside is producing food for the population. The area is not the same as it was before the conflict. Many former residents displaced by the conflict live elsewhere in Uganda or overseas. More young adults choose to pursue business over agriculture than in previous generations. The city of Gulu, for years isolated by the war, is now home to a regional university and vibrant economy. Northern Uganda is nearing the fourteen-year mark, at which point we could expect its level of economic development to equal what it was prior to the conflict. The goal of improving policies around return migration and property restitution should not be recreating communities as they existed prior to conflict but shortening the timeline of recovery by expanding the choices of individuals searching for durable solutions.

Appendix

List of Interviews

As noted in the preface, if there were circumstances that suggested there might be any threat of harm to the interview subject, the interviews are completely anonymized or listed with just an indicator of their role. When there was no obvious threat of harm, I gave interview subjects a choice as to whether they wanted me to cite them directly or to keep their names confidential. I conducted all human subjects research with the approval of the university Institutional Review Board.

Kosovo

1. Albina Baledimaj Basha, Prishtinë/Priština, November 7, 2012.
2. John Chesnut, Country Representative, Pristina High School, Prishtinë/Priština, November 8, 2012.
3. Julie Kolgjini, Professor of English, American University of Kosovo, Prishtinë/Priština, November 9, 2012.
4. William Donovan, Resident Adviser, Housing Finance, US Treasury, Office of Technical Assistance, Prishtinë/Priština, November 12, 2012.
5. Arben Limani, Privatization Department, Prishtinë/Priština, November 12, 2012.
6. Nita Luci, Professor of Anthropology, American University of Kosovo and University of Pristina, Prishtinë/Priština, November 12, 2012.

7. Education official, Gjilan/Gnjilane, November 13, 2012.
8. Katherine Nobbs and Silke Nebenfuhr, OSCE, Prishtinë/Priština, November 14, 2012.
9. Michelle A. Pinkowski, Construction Reform Expert, USAID Business Enabling Environment Program in Kosovo, Prishtinë/Priština, November 17, 2012.
10. Beate Dastel, UNICEF, Prishtinë/Priština, November 19, 2012.
11. Kristen Stec, Danish Refugee Council, Prishtinë/Priština, November 20, 2012.
12. Blerim Agani, National Property Officer, Human Rights and Communities Department, OSCE, Prishtinë/Priština, November 20, 2012.
13. Grese Caka, Democracy and Governance Specialist, USAID, Prishtinë/Priština, November 23, 2012.
14. Jorge Baca, Chief of Mission and Agron Ajazi, Programme Manager EU Return and Reintegration in Kosovo, International Organization for Migration, Prishtinë/Priština, November 23, 2012.
15. Arben Citaku, General Secretary, Ministry of Environment and Spatial Planning, Prishtinë/Priština, November 26, 2012.
16. Terry Slywka, Chief of Party, USAID Business Enabling Environment Program in Kosovo, Prishtinë/Priština, December 4, 2012.
17. Agathe More, PhD student, University of Edinburgh, Prishtinë/Priština, December 4, 2012.
18. Andrea J. Tomaszewicz, Senior Economic Adviser, US Embassy, Board Member, Kosovo Property Agency, Prishtinë/Priština, December 6, 2012.
19. Mimoza Jupa, Political/Human Rights Adviser, US Embassy, Prishtinë/Priština, December 6, 2012.
20. Murat Meta, Chief Executive Officer, Kosovo Cadastral Agency, Prishtinë/Priština, December 6, 2012.
21. Darden Makolli, NORMA, Prishtinë/Priština, December 8, 2012.
22. Arben Hoti, County Representative, Water for Life, Prishtinë/Priština, December 10, 2012.
23. Linn Slattengren, Attorney, Interlex Associates, former member of the Special Chamber of the Supreme Court, Prishtinë/Priština, December 10, 2012.

24. Jan-Peter Olters, Country Manager, World Bank, Prishtinë/ Priština, December 11, 2012.
25. Zenun Zeqa, Deputy Mayor, Klinë/Klina, December 20, 2012.
26. Milorad Sarkovic, Municipal Officer for Communities and Return, Klinë/Klina, December 20, 2012.
27. Remzije Maloku, Municipal Officer for Gender Issues, Klinë/ Klina, December 20, 2012.
28. Declan O'Mahoney, Property Coordinator, EULEX, Prishtinë/Priština, December 21, 2012.
29. Violeta Rexha, EULEX Gender Officer, Prishtinë/Priština, December 21, 2012.
30. Besim Tafa, Senior Legal Adviser Human Rights, EULEX, Prishtinë/Priština, December 21, 2012.
31. Louis Sell, former US Ambassador, Prishtinë/Priština, January 16, 2013.
32. Agim Alim, Mayor, Ferizaj/Uroševac, January 17, 2013.
33. Qazime Vata, Director of Urbanism, Ferizaj/Uroševac, January 17, 2013.
34. Ajet Muslina and Fadil Ibishi, Municipal Cadaster Office, Ferizaj/Uroševac, January 17, 2013.
35. Mustafe Grainca, Director of Economy, Finance and Budget, Ferizaj/Uroševac, January 17, 2013.
36. Vjolla Krasniqi, Municipal Gender Officer, Ferizaj/Uroševac, January 17, 2013.
37. Xhevdine Dervishe-Rexhepie, Municipal Officer for Communities and Returns, Ferizaj/Uroševac, January 17, 2013.
38. Hazer Tara, Deputy Mayor, Rahovec/Orahovac, February 5, 2013.
39. Kaplan Goshi, Municipal Cadaster Officer, Rahovec/Orahovac, February 5, 2013.
40. Fatmir Iska, Director of the Cadaster, Rahovec/Orahovac, February 5, 2013.
41. Slavisa Kolaseimac, Municipal Officer for Communities and Returns, Rahovec/Orahovac, February 5, 2013.
42. Habibe Haxhimustfa, Municipal Coordinator for Human Rights, Rahovec/Orahovac, February 5, 2013.
43 Lee Norgaard, Mercy Corps, Prishtinë/Priština, February 7, 2013.
44. Alexander Borg Olivier, former UNMIK Senior Legal Adviser, Prishtinë/Priština, February 13, 2013.

45. Djordje Djordjevic, Municipal Cadaster Office, Gracanicë/ Gračanica, February 14, 2013.
46. Nebojsa Peric, Adviser to the Mayor, Gracanicë/Gračanica, February 14, 2013.
47. Gordana Djone, Director of NGO, Laplje Selo, Gracanicë/ Gračanica, Municipality, February 22, 2013.
48. Avni Vula, lawyer, Gracanicë/Gračanica, February 22, 2013.

Liberia

49. Gregory Kitt and Alexandra Hartman, Norwegian Refugee Council, Monrovia, October 1, 2012.
50. Jonathan Greenham, DAI, Chief of Party, Food and Enterprise Development, Monrovia, October 2, 2012.
51. John Saah Nyumah, lawyer and former Deputy Director of the Liberian Refugee Repatriation and Resettlement Commission, Monrovia, October 3, 2012.
52. Alfred Brownell and Francis Collee, Office of Green Advocates, Monrovia, October 3, 2012.
53. Isaac Boe Doe, Monrovia, October 4, 2012.
54. Focus Group Paynesville, Paynesville Women's Initiative, October 4, 2012.
55. James Nyenkan, Managing Partner, PCG Liberia, Monrovia, October 5, 2012.
56. Jim and Lyn Gray, Monrovia, October 5, 2012.
57. Mark Marquardt, Chief of Party, Land Policy Institutional Support Project, Liberia Land Commission, Tetra Tech ARD, Monrovia, October 6, 2012.
58. Adarkwah Antwi, Land Tenure Expert, Land Conflict Resolution Expert, Liberia Land Commission and Tetra Tech ARD, Monrovia, October 7, 2012.
59. Focus Group Montserrado, Gbalian Women's Initiative, October 8, 2012.
60. Jimmy T. Toe and Kojo Ross, Liberia Refugee Repatriation and Resettlement Commission, Monrovia October 9, 2012.
61. Matthew Siakor Jr., Center for Research and Development Initiative, Monrovia, October 9, 2012.

Serbia

62. Member of OSCE Mission to Serbia, Belgrade, May 19, 2016.
63. Marina Cremonese, Danish Refugee Council, Representative for Serbia/Montenegro, Belgrade, May 26, 2016.
64. Miloslava Smiljanic, Danish Refugee Council, Protection/Monitoring Coordinator, Belgrade, May 26, 2016.
65. Ivana Milanovic-Dukic, Danish Refugee Council, Program Manager, Belgrade, May 26, 2016.
66. Massimo Moratti, Danish Refugee Council, Protection Manager, Belgrade, May 26, 2016.
67. UNHCR Representative, Belgrade, May 16, 2016.
68. Dejan Milisavljević, Adviser, Department for Reception, Accommodation and Returnees upon Readmission, Commissariat for Refugees and Migration of the Republic of Serbia, Belgrade, May 26, 2016.
69. Interview with displaced Serbian family, Belgrade, October 3, 2016.
70. Interview with displaced Serbian family, Belgrade, October 3, 2016.
71. Interview with displaced Serbian family, Belgrade, October 3, 2016.
72. Interview with displaced Serbian man, Belgrade, October 3, 2016.
73. Interview with displaced Serbian man, Belgrade, October 7, 2016.
74. Interview with displaced Serbian family, Belgrade, October 7, 2016.
75. Interview with displaced Serbian woman, Belgrade, October 7, 2016.
76. Big Swamp, Roma Focus Group, Novi Sad, October 11, 2016.
77. Grmech, Roma Focus Group, Belgrade, October 11, 2016.
78. Antenna, Roma Focus Group, Belgrade, October 11, 2016.
79. Interview with displaced Serbian woman, Belgrade, October 13, 2016.
80. Interview with displaced Serbian man, Belgrade, October 13, 2016.
81. Interview with displaced Serbian family, Belgrade, October 13, 2016.

Uganda

82. Rita Laker-Ojok, Tetra Tech, Kampala, May 19, 2015.
83. Mary Baganizi, Programme Officer, Trocaire, Kampala, May 20, 2015.
84. Sabiti Omara, Advocate, Head of Land Rights Information Center, Amuru, Uganda Land Alliance, Gulu, May 25, 2015.
85. Representative of the Acholi Religious Leaders Peace Initiative, Gulu, May 25, 2015.
86. Senior Administrative Officer for Amuru, Gulu, May 25, 2015.
87. Susan Mildred Aber, Senior Land Management Officer, Amuru District Local Government, Gulu, May 26, 2015.
88. Julian Hopwood, local land consultant and PhD student, Gulu, May 26, 2015.
89. Ezangu Bosco, Program Manager, Gulu Women's Economic Development and Globalization, May 27, 2015.
90. Patrick Ong'ara, Sub-county Chief, and Zakeo Lubeja, Parish Chief, May 27, 2015.
91. Amos Canwat, former District Land Committee Chairman for Gulu, May 27, 2015.
92. Focus group of elders from Zoro Parish, representing fifty-seven clans, Gulu, May 27, 2015.
93. Simon Ogenrwot, Legal Officer, Center for Repatriation and Rehabilitation, Gulu, May 28, 2015.
94. Stephen Langole, PhD student, Gulu University, Institute for Peace and Strategic Studies, May 28, 2015.
95. Rabbin Drabe, UNICEF, Gulu, May 28, 2015.
96. Ambrose Olaa, Minister of Finance Planning and Economic Development, Acting Prime Minister, Cultural Institutions, with Rev. Willy Olango, Minister, Gulu, May 29, 2015.
97. Fr. Joe Okumu, Gulu, May 29, 2015.
98. Teresa Eilu, Programme Director, Law and Equality Movement Uganda, Kampala, June 1, 2015.
99. David Zac Nirengiye, Kampala, June 1, 2015.

Other

100. Mamadou Dian Balde, Division of Internal Protection, UNHCR, Geneva, Switzerland, March 10, 2011.

101. Barbara McCallin, via Skype, February 11, 2011.
102. Marzia Montemurro, Internal Displacement Monitoring Centre, Geneva, Switzerland, March 10, 2011.
103. Elizabeth Ferris, Brookings Institution, Project on Internal Displacement, December 15, 2011.
104. Peter Van der Auweraert, Head, Land, Property and Reparations Division, International Organization on Migration, via Skype, March 4, 2011.
105. Erica Harper, International Development Law Organization, Geneva, Switzerland, March 8, 2011.
106. Senior Research Officer, UNHCR, Geneva, Switzerland, March 8, 2011.

Glossary

Asylum. Permission given to a noncitizen to stay in a country because of a
threat of persecution.

Asylum seeker. A person applying for refugee status in a country other
than the person's own. The burden of proof is on individuals to substantiate that they have a "well-founded fear of persecution." Not all
asylum seekers are eventually recognized as refugees.

Compensation. Money awarded as restitution for loss of property.

Customary international law. A general practice, rather than a principle
stemming from a treaty or legal agreement. It is a fundamental component of international humanitarian law, and many of the "laws of
war," such as the importance of distinguishing between civilians and
soldiers in combat, are based in customary international law.

Customary land. Untitled land often undocumented, controlled and allocated by an ethnic group according to customary law.

Customary law. A body of social rules, usually unwritten, governing
personal status, access to community resources, and local organization. Prevalent across Central Asia, Oceania, and sub-Saharan Africa
in addition to other areas.

Durable solutions. Resolution of refugee situations. There are three
recognized by the UN and humanitarian organizations as solutions
to forced displacement: voluntary repatriation to country of origin,
integration into place of refuge, or resettlement in a third country.

Ethnic cleansing. Violence against a particular population intended to
remove them from specific geographic area.

Forced migration. People moving involuntarily due to violence, natural disasters, climate change, famine, and development projects.

Internally displaced person (IDP). Someone forced to flee from home who has not crossed an international border.

International migration regime. The collection of international laws, norms, and policies regarding migration.

Local integration. A durable solution in which refugees permanently remain in the country where they have sought refuge. This includes long-term permission to remain, but rarely naturalization. Distinct from resettlement, this is usually in a country nearest to the country of habitual residence.

Minorities Treaties. Treaties made after World War I designed to grant citizenship rights and protection to religious and ethnic minority groups within new states formed in the wake of the dissolving Austro-Hungarian and Ottoman Empires in exchange for the international recognition of those states. They were largely ineffective.

Naturalization. The granting of citizenship to someone from a different country of origin.

Non-refoulement. The principle that refugees should not be returned to a dangerous place where they have a risk of harm. First recognized in the Convention Relating to the International Status of Refugees of 1933.

Prima facie refugees. Group determination of refugee status by a state or the UNHCR based on "objective criteria related to the circumstances of their country of origin." This is typically awarded to people fleeing an active conflict because of the presumption that they meet the criteria. Proof of persecution is not the responsibility of the individual, and this status does not require the same degree of scrutiny in terms of an asylum claim unless evidence to the contrary is presented. It may be temporary in nature, can be revoked, and often comes with restrictions that those seeking asylum do not face.

Refugee. In common usage this is someone who has crossed an international boundary fleeing a threat. Legally, "a person who, owing to a well-founded fear of persecution for reasons of race, religion, nationality, membership of a particular social group or political opinion, is outside the country of his nationality and is unable or, owing to such fear, is unwilling to avail himself of the protection of that country; or who, not having a nationality and being outside the country of his former habitual residence as a result of such events, is unable or, owing to such fear, is unwilling to return to it."[1]

Repatriation. Return to country of origin/nationality, though not necessarily to home community within that country.

Resettlement. Transfer of refugees from the country in which they have sought protection to another state that has agreed to admit them—as refugees—with permanent residence status.[2]

Return migration. Movement of people back to their place of habitual residence.

Statelessness. The condition of not being considered as a national by any state.[3]

VGGT. Voluntary Guidelines on the Responsible Governance of Tenure of Land, Fisheries and Forests in the Context of National Food Security (VGGT) resulting in 2012 from a consultative process led by the UN Committee on World Food Security.

Voluntary repatriation. The safe, dignified, and chosen return of refugees to their country of origin.

Notes

Chapter 1

1. UNHCR, "Figures at a Glance," 2021, https://www.unhcr.org/en-us/figures-at-a-glance.html

2. Milana is a pseudonym. Interview 1013161, October 13, 2016.

3. Roque Planas, "How El Salvador Became the World's Most Violent Peacetime Country," *Huffington Post*, March 4, 2016.

4. Xavier Devictor and Quy-Toan Do, "How Many Years Have Refugees Been in Exile," World Bank Policy Research Working Paper (Washington, DC: World Bank, 2016), 2.

5. James C. Hathaway, "The Meaning of Repatriation," *International Journal of Refugee Law* 9, no. 4 (1997).

6. Margaret E. Peters, *Trading Barriers: Immigration and the Remaking of Globalization* (Princeton, NJ: Princeton University Press, 2017).

7. Ana M. Ibáñez and Andrés Moya, "Who Stays and Who Leaves during Mass Atrocities?," in *Economic Aspects of Genocide, Other Mass Atrocities, and Their Prevention*, ed. Charles H. Anderton and Jurgen Bauer (New York: Oxford University Press, 2016); Michael A. Clemens, "Violence, Development, and Migration Waves: Evidence from Central American Child Migrant Apprehensions," Working Paper 459 (Washington, DC: Center for Global Development, 2017); Will H. Moore and Stephen M. Shellman, "Whither Will They Go? A Global Study of Refugees' Destinations, 1965–1995," *International Studies Quarterly* 51, no. 4 (2007); Will H. Moore and Stephen M. Shellman, "Fear of Persecution: Forced Migration, 1952–1995," *Journal of Conflict Resolution* 48, no. 5 (2004); Christian A. Davenport, Will H. Moore, and Steven C. Poe, "Sometimes You Just Have to Leave: Domestic Threats and Forced Migration, 1964–1989," *International Interactions* 29, no. 1 (2003).

8. Prakash Adhikari, "Conflict-Induced Displacement: Understanding the Causes of Flight," *American Journal of Political Science* 57, no. 1 (2013).

129

"

9. UNHCR, "UNHCR Warns 2020 Risks Lowest Resettlement Levels in Recent History," news release, November 19, 2020, https://www.unhcr.org/en-us/news/press/2020/11/5fb4e6f24/unhcr-warns-2020-risks-lowest-resettlement-levels-recent-history.html

10. The UNHCR counts those people who come to them for services or register as refugees.

11. Forced Displacement and Development Study Group, "Refugee Compacts: Addressing the Crisis of Protracted Displacement" (Washington, DC: Center for Global Development and International Rescue Committee, 2017).

12. It is a tragedy worthy of note that people who fled one war were caught up in another conflict in their place of refuge. UNHCR, "Assessment on Returns to Iraq amongst the Iraqi Refugee Population in Syria" (Syria: UNHCR Syria, Public Information Unit, 2008), 3.

13. Azose and Raftery argue that "when aggregated across the globe, we find that a majority of international migration consists of emigration from the place of birth, but return migration is also substantial, making up 26–31% of movements in each time period." Jonathan J. Azose and Adrian E. Raftery, "Estimation of Emigration, Return Migration, and Transit Migration between All Pairs of Countries," *Proceedings of the National Academy of Sciences of the United States of America* 116, no. 1 (2019), 118. While "aggregation across the globe" is not very helpful for specific conflict settings, it does suggest that there might be more return migration than is currently counted.

14. Sometimes reported in refugee statistics are Palestinians who became refugees in 1948, before the 1951 Refugee Convention came into effect. The UNHCR is careful to note in its documents and data exactly whom it is counting.

15. The difference between return and repatriation is discussed further in chapter 2.

16. World Bank, "Forcibly Displaced: Toward a Development Approach Supporting Refugees, the Internally Displaced, and Their Hosts" (Washington, DC: World Bank, 2016).

17. Amy Weiss-Meyer, "Apps for Refugees: How Technology Helps in a Humanitarian Crisis," *The Atlantic*, May 2017.

18. Niels Harild, Asger Christensen, and Roger Zetter, "Sustainable Refugee Return: Triggers, Constraints, and Lessons on Addressing the Development Challenges of Forced Displacement," Global Program on Forced Displacement Issue Note (Washington, DC: World Bank, 2015), 44.

19. Stathis N. Kalyvas, *The Logic of Violence in Civil War* (New York: Cambridge University Press, 2006), inter alia.

20. World Bank, *World Development Report 2011* (World Bank, 2011), https://doi.org/10.1596/978-0-8213-8439-8

21. Samir Elhawary, "Security for Whom? Stabilisation and Civilian Protection in Colombia," *Disasters* 34 (2010).

22. Samir Elhawary and Sara Pantuliano, "Land Issues in Post-conflict Return and Recovery," in *Land and Post-conflict Peacebuilding*, ed. Jon D. Unruh and Rhodri C. Williams (London: Earthscan, 2013).

23. Deborah Isser and Peter Van der Auweraert, *Land, Property, and the Challenge of Return for Iraq's Displaced* (Washington, DC: US Institute of Peace, 2009);

Anneke Smit, *The Property Rights of Refugees and Internally Displaced Persons* (New York: Routledge, 2012); Anneke Smit, "Housing and Property Restitution and IDP Return in Kosovo," *International Migration* 44, no. 3 (2006); Gerard Toal and Carl T. Dahlman, *Bosnia Remade: Ethnic Cleansing and Its Reversal* (New York: Oxford University Press, 2011).

24. Alexander Betts and Paul Collier, *Refuge: Transforming a Broken Refugee System* (New York: Allen Lane, 2017).

25. The suggestion of compensation as a possible resolution to property claims in postconflict situations might work well in contexts like Iraq, where there are property registers, but it is difficult to imagine an effective system of compensation claims in customary property systems, such as Liberia and Uganda, which lacked the trappings of formalized landholding—documentation, land valuation, and cadastral registries that permit identification of individuals who might receive compensation.

26. Eric Posner, *The Twilight of Human Rights Law* (New York: Oxford University Press, 2014).

27. Kathryn Sikkink, *Evidence for Hope: Making Human Rights Work in the 21st Century* (Princeton, NJ: Princeton University Press, 2017).

Chapter 2

1. Devictor and Do, "How Many Years?"

2. Named after those rendered minorities in new states after the dissolution of the Austro-Hungarian or Ottoman Empires. Carole Fink, "The League of Nations and the Minorities Question," *World Affairs* 157, no. 4 (1995), 198.

3. Article 1(2) of the 1920 Treaty between the Principal Allied and Associated Powers and Greece.

4. There remains a group of twenty-five countries in which the citizenship of a child is determined by the citizenship of the father alone.

5. Keith Lowe, *Savage Continent: Europe in the Aftermath of World War II* (New York: St. Martin's Press, 2012), 27.

6. Gilbert Jaeger, "On the History of International Protection of Refugees," *International Review of the Red Cross* 83 (2001).

7. Gil Loescher, "The International Refugee Regime: Stretched to the Limit?," *Journal of International Affairs* 47, no. 2 (1994), 357.

8. Article I (A)(2).

9. Vanessa Holtzer, "The 1951 Refugee Convention and the Protection of People Fleeing Armed Conflict and Other Situations of Violence," Legal Protection Policy Research Series (Geneva: UNHCR, 2012), 11.

10. Holtzer, "1951 Refugee Convention," 10.

11. "Seven of the 17 countries—Argentina, Bolivia, Chile, El Salvador, Guatemala, Mexico and Nicaragua—have directly imported the definition contained in the Cartagena Declaration into their national regimes, with six other countries using slightly different wording. Only three countries, Costa Rica, Panama, and Venezuela, have not incorporated the regional refugee definition into their national regime in any way." Michael Reed-Hurtado, "The Cartagena Declaration on Refugees and the Protection of People Fleeing Armed Conflict and Other Situations of Violence in Latin America," Legal and Protection Policy Research Series (Geneva: Division of International Protection, 2013), 16.

12. Customary international law is a general practice, rather than a principle stemming from a treaty or legal agreement. It is a fundamental component of international humanitarian law, and many of the "laws of war," such as the importance of distinguishing between civilians and soldiers in combat, are based in customary international law.

13. I&N Dec. 316 (A.G.2018), Interim Decision #3929.

14. Hathaway, "The Meaning of Repatriation," 555.

15. European Commission, "New Pact on Migration and Asylum" (Brussels: European Union, 2020).

16. "Five Years after Arrival, Germany's Refugees Are Integrating," *The Economist*, August 25, 2020.

17. Deutsche Welle, "Ukraine: EU agrees protection plan for refugees" https://www.dw.com/en/ukraine-eu-agrees-protection-plan-for-refugees/a-60997378

18. Heather Faulkner, interview, October 26, 2016.

19. Martin Gottwald, "Back to the Future: The Concept of 'Comprehensive Solutions,'" *Refugee Survey Quarterly* 31, no. 3 (2012).

20. Catherine-Lune Grayson, "Durable Solutions: Perspectives of Somali Refugees Living in Kenyan and Ethiopian Camps and Selected Communities of Return" (Danish Refugee Council: Nairobi, Kenya, 2013).

21. UNHCR, "Global Trends: Forced Displacement in 2020," https://www.unhcr.org/flagship-reports/globaltrends/

22. Katy Long, "State, Nation, Citizen: Rethinking Repatriation" (University of Oxford: Refugee Studies Centre, 2008), 4.

23. UNHCR, "Voluntary Repatriation," http://www.unhcr.org/en-us/voluntary-repatriation-49c3646cfe.html

24. Katy Long, "Back to Where You Once Belonged: A Historical Review of UNHCR Policy and Practice on Refugee Repatriation" (Geneva: Policy Development and Evaluation Service, 2013), 8.

25. B. S. Chimni, "From Resettlement to Involuntary Repatriation: Towards a Critical History of Durable Solutions to Refugee Problems," *Refugee Survey Quarterly* 23, no. 3 (2004).

26. UNHCR, *The State of the World's Refugees: A Humanitarian Agenda* (New York: Oxford University Press, 1997), 147.

27. Daniel P. Sullivan, "Shared Obstacles to Return: Rohingya and South Sudanese," *Forced Migration Review*, no. 62 (2019); Jeff Crisp, "Repatriation Principles under Pressure," *Forced Migration Review*, no. 62 (2019).

28. Mollie Gerver addresses the ethics of return, voluntary and coerced, to countries that may still be risky or lacking in basic services. Mollie Gerver, *The Ethics and Practice of Refugee Repatriation* (Edinburgh: Edinburgh University Press, 2018).

29. Obi Anyadike, "The Grinch's Not-So-Festive Guide to Food Ration Cuts," news release, December 17, 2016, http://www.irinnews.org/news/2016/12/27/grinch%E2%80%99s-not-so-festive-guide-food-ration-cuts?utm_source=IRIN+-+the+inside+story+on+emergencies&utm_campaign=58100fe216-RSS_EMAIL_CAMPAIGN_ENGLISH_AFRICA&utm_medium=email&utm_term=0_d842d98289-58100fe216-29273553

30. Controversially, the Rwandan government ended this problem by attacking

the refugee camps. See Gerard Prunier, *Africa's World War: Congo, the Rwandan Genocide and the Making of a Continental Catastrophe* (New York: Oxford University Press, 2011); Fiona Terry, *Condemned to Repeat? The Paradox of Humanitarian Action* (Ithaca, NY: Cornell University Press, 2002).

31. Simon Allison, "World's Largest Refugee Camp Scapegoated in Wake of Garissa Attack," *The Guardian*, 14 April 2015.

32. Norwegian Refugee Council, "Dadaab's Broken Promise: A Call to Reinstate Voluntary, Safe and Dignified Returns for the Dadaab Refugee Community" (Oslo: Norwegian Refugee Council, 2016).

32. Betts and Collier, *Refuge*, 55.

34. Gottwald, "Back to the Future."

35. Nicholas Van Hear, Oliver Bakewell, and Katy Long, "Push-Pull Plus: Reconsidering the Drivers of Migration," *Journal of Ethnic & Migration Studies* 44, no. 6 (2018).

36. UNHCR, "Resettlement."

37. Lewis Turner, "Who Will Resettle Single Syrian Men?," *Forced Migration Review*, no. 54 (2017).

38. In the revised executive order, Iraq was dropped from the list.

39. Department of Homeland Security, "Protecting the Nation from Foreign Terrorist Entry to the United States," Fact Sheet (Washington DC: US Government Printing Office, 2017).

40. Hathaway, "The Meaning of Repatriation," 551.

41. Substantial progress has been made in encouraging and enabling states to protect the interests of IDPs by the Brookings-Bern Project in Internal Displacement, a public-private partnership, and by the Internal Displacement and Monitoring Center, which provides data and analysis about internally displaced people. While both organizations receive some funding from the UN, they are not UN agencies, which illustrates the difference between refugees and IDPs.

42. Kosovo formally declared independence in 2008, but it did so unilaterally, without the recognition of Serbia. It has since struggled to obtain international recognition and does not currently hold a seat in the UN General Assembly.

43. Iain King and Whit Mason, *Peace at Any Price: How the World Failed Kosovo* (Ithaca, NY: Cornell University Press, 2006).

44. Interview 107162, October 7, 2016.

45. Sandra F. Joireman and Laura S. Meitzner Yoder, "A Long Time Gone: Postconflict Rural Property Restitution under Customary Law," *Development and Change* 47, no. 3 (2016). The Ugandan government also gave people the opportunity to stay around the camps and locally integrate there, though few chose this option.

46. Sebastián Albuja and Marcela Ceballos, "Urban Displacement and Migration in Colombia," *Forced Migration Review*, no. 34 (2010).

47. Ana María Ibáñez and Andrés Moya, "Vulnerability of Victims of Civil Conflicts: Empirical Evidence for the Displaced Population in Colombia," *World Development* 38, no. 4 (2010).

48. This is an area where statistics to back up my argument would be very helpful, but they do not exist across countries and contexts.

49. Megan Bradley, "Durable Solutions and the Right of Return for IDPs: Evolving Interpretations," *International Journal of Refugee Law* 30, no. 2 (2018).

50. Barbara E. Harrell-Bond, "Repatriation: Under What Conditions Is It the Most Desirable Solution for Refugees? An Agenda for Research," *African Studies Review* 32, no. 1 (1989), 44.

51. Médecins Sans Frontières, "Dadaab to Somalia: Pushed Back into Peril" (Geneva: Médecins Sans Frontières, 2016).

52. Amnesty International, "Nowhere Else to Go: Forced Returns of Somali Refugees from Dadaab Refugee Camp, Kenya" (London: Amnesty International, 2016).

53. Melissa Fleming and Dana Hughes, "In Kenya, UNHCR Chief Assured Refugee Return Will Not Contravene International Obligations" (Geneva: UNHCR, 2016).

54. Jacob Poushter, "European Opinions of the Refugee Crisis in 5 Charts" (Washington, DC: Pew Research Center, 2016).

55. Emily Tamkin, "Once Again, Slovakia Makes Life Harder for Muslims," December *Foreign Policy* (2016).

56. European Union, "Operational Implementation of the EU-Turkey Statement," https://ec.europa.eu/home-affairs/sites/homeaffairs/files/what-we-do/policies/european-agenda-migration/press-material/docs/state_of_play_-_eu-turkey_en.pdf

57. Executive Order Protecting the Nation from Foreign Terrorist Entry into the United States, March 6, 2017.

58. Mujib Mashal and Zahra Naderjan, "A Third of Afghans Will Need Aid This Year, U.N. Says," *New York Times*, January 21, 2017.

59. Human Rights Watch, "Pakistan Coercion, UN Complicity: The Mass Forced Return of Afghan Refugees" (New York: Human Rights Watch, 2017).

60. Ruchi Kumar, "Forced Repatriation to Afghanistan: 'We Didn't Think It Would Happen to Us,'" *The Guardian*, March 9, 2017.

61. Kumar, "Forced Repatriation to Afghanistan."

62. Chimni, "Resettlement to Involuntary Repatriation," 73.

63. Megan Bradley, *Refugee Repatriation: Justice, Responsibility and Redress* (Cambridge: Cambridge University Press, 2013), 7–8.

64. Naohiko Omata, "The Complexity of Refugees' Return Decision-Making in a Protracted Exile: Beyond the Home-Coming Model and Durable Solutions," *Journal of Ethnic and Migration Studies* 39, no. 8 (2013).

Chapter 3

1. UNHCR, *Global Trends: Forces Displacement in 2020* (Geneva: UNHCR, 2021), 3.

2. UNHCR, "Figures at a Glance," 2021.

3. Harrell-Bond, "Repatriation"; Khalid Koser and Richard Black, "The End of the Refugee Cycle?," in *The End of the Refugee Cycle? Refugee Repatriation and Reconstruction*, ed. Richard Black and Khalid Koser (New York: Berghahn Books, 1999).

4. Laura Hammond, "Examining the Discourse of Repatriation: Towards a More Proactive Theory of Return Migration," n *The End of the Refugee Cycle? Refugee Repatriation and Reconstruction*, ed. Richard Black and Khalid Koser (New York: Berghahn Books, 1999), 233.

5. Oliver Bakewell, "Research beyond the Categories: The Importance of Policy Irrelevant Research into Forced Migration," *Journal of Refugee Studies* 21, no. 4 (2008).

6. "A Nation of Victims," *The Economist*, October 31, 2015.

7. Elizabeth Ferris, Erin Mooney, and Chareen Star, *From Responsibility to Response: Assessing National Approaches to Internal Displacement* (Washington, DC: Brookings Institution, 2011), 139.

8. Sandra F. Joireman, "Ethnic Violence, Local Security and Return Migration: Enclave Communities in Kosovo," *International Migration* 55, no. 5 (2017); Toal and Dahlman, *Bosnia Remade*.

9. Klaus Deininger, Ana M. Ibáñez, and Pablo Querubin, "Towards Sustainable Return Policies for the Displaced Population: Why Are Some Displaced Households More Willing to Return Than Others," HiCN Working Papers 07, Households in Conflict Network (Sussex, UK: University of Sussex, 2004); Joireman and Meitzner Yoder, "A Long Time Gone."

10. David Turton, "The Meaning of Place in a World of Movement: Lessons from Long-Term Field Research in Southern Ethiopia," *Journal of Refugee Studies* 18, no. 3 (2005), 277.

11. Van Hear, Bakewell, and Long, "Push-Pull Plus."

12. Deininger, Ibáñez, and Querubin, "Towards Sustainable Return Policies"; Kara Ross Camarena and Nils Hagerdal, "When Do Displaced Persons Return? Postwar Migration among Christians in Mount Lebanon," *American Journal of Political Science* 64, no. 2 (2020); Katy Long, "Home Alone? A Review of the Relationship between Repatriation, Mobility and Durable Solutions for Refugees," Policy Development and Evaluation Service (Geneva: UNHCR, 2010); Deniz Sert, "Property Rights in Return and Resettlement of Internally Displaced Persons (IDPs): A Quantitative and Comparative Case Study" (PhD dissertation, City University of New York, 2008).

13. Howard Adelman and Ezekial Barkan, *No Return, No Refuge: Rites and Rights in Minority Repatriation* (New York: Columbia University Press, 2011); Toal and Dahlman, *Bosnia Remade*.

14. Statistics on length of displacement come from the UNHCR and are reported differently based on who is counted. An excellent analysis of the length of displacement is in Devictor and Do, who show how the numbers change over time and based on who is included. Devictor and Do, "How Many Years?"

15. Liz Alden Wily, "Tackling Land Tenure in the Emergency to Development Transition in Post-conflict States: From Restitution to Reform," in *Uncharted Territory*, ed. Sara Pantuliano (Bourton on Dunsmore, UK: Practical Action Publishing, 2009), 34.

16. Oliver Bakewell, "'Keeping Them in Their Place': The Ambivalent Relationship between Development and Migration in Africa," *Third World Quarterly* 29, no. 7 (2008); Turton, "The Meaning of Place"; Laura Hammond, "Tigrayan Returnees' Notions of Home: Five Variations on a Theme," in *Homecomings: Unsettling Paths of Return*, ed. Fran Markowitz and Anders H. Stefansson (New York: Lexington Books, 2004); Liisa Malkki, "National Geographic: The Rooting of Peoples and the Territorialization of National Identity among Scholars and Refugees," *Cultural Anthropology* 7, no. 1 (1992).

17. María Alejandra Arias, Ana María Ibáñez, and Pablo Querubin, "The Desire to Return during Civil War: Evidence for Internally Displaced Populations in Colombia," *Peace Economics, Peace Science and Public Policy* 20, no. 1 (2014); Ratnin Dewaraja and Noriyuki Kawamura, "Trauma Intensity and Posttraumatic Stress: Implications of the Tsunami Experience in Sri Lanka for the Management of Future Disasters," *International Congress Series* 1287 (2006).

18. Grayson, "Durable Solutions," 39.

19. Deininger, Ibáñez, and Querubin, "Towards Sustainable Return Policies"; Ibáñez and Moya, "Who Stays?"

20. Turton, "The Meaning of Place."

21. Interview 1013163, with family, October 13, 2016.

22. Interview 107162, October 7, 2016.

23. Faten Ghosn et al., "The Journey Home: Violence, Anchoring, and Refugee Decisions to Return," *American Political Science Review* 115, no. 3 (2021); Joireman, "Ethnic Violence, Local Security."

24. James Jeffrey, "Europe Pays Out to Keep a Lid on Ethiopia Migration" (Geneva: IRIN, 2016).

25. World Bank data.

26. Roger Zetter and Héloïse Ruaudel, "Refugees' Right to Work and Access to Labour Markets: Constraints, Challenges and Ways Forward," *Forced Migration Review* no. 58 (June 2018).

27. Heng Zhu et al., "Economic Impact of Refugee Settlements in Uganda" (Rome: World Food Program, 2016).

28. Claire MacPherson and Olivier Sterck, "Empowering Refugees through Cash and Agriculture: A Regression Discontinuity Design," *Journal of Development Economics* 149 (2021); J. Edward Taylor et al., "Economic Impact of Refugees," *Proceedings of the National Academy of Sciences* 113, no. 27 (2016).

29. Diana Furchtgott-Roth, "Does Immigration Increase Economic Growth?" Economic Policies for the 21st Century (New York: Manhattan Institute, 2014).

30. Hein De Haas, "Turning the Tide? Why Development Will Not Stop Migration," *Development & Change* 38, no. 5 (2007); Hein De Haas, "The Myth of Invasion: The Inconvenient Realities of African Migration to Europe," *Third World Quarterly* 29, no. 7 (2008); Jonas Gamso and Farhod Yuldashev, "Targeted Foreign Aid and International Migration: Is Development-Promotion an Effective Immigration Policy?," *International Studies Quarterly* 62, no. 4 (2018).

31. Harild, Christensen, and Zetter, "Sustainable Refugee Return"; Arias, Ibáñez, and Querubin, "Desire to Return."

32. Gottwald, "Back to the Future"; Nicholas Van Hear, Rebecca Brubaker, and Thais Bessa, "Managing Mobility for Human Development: The Growing Salience of Mixed Migration," Human Development Reports (Geneva: United Nations Development Program, 2009).

33. Camarena and Hagerdal, "When Do Displaced Persons Return?"; World Bank, "Forcibly Displaced."

34. Londa Schiebinger, "Gendered Innovations: Harnessing the Creative Power of Sex and Gender Analysis to Discover New Ideas and Develop New Technologies," *Triple Helix* 1, no. 1 (2014).

35. Arias, Ibáñez, and Querubin, "Desire to Return."

36. Peggy Levitt, "'You Know, Abraham Was Really the First Immigrant': Religion and Transnational Migration," *International Migration Review* 37, no. 3 (2003). There are some places of refuge where social networks are extremely limited because children cannot go to school and there are no opportunities for work outside of camps.

37. Monica Boyd, "Family and Personal Networks in International Migration: Recent Developments and New Agendas," *International Migration Review* 23 (1989), 642.

38. Patricia Weiss Fagan, "Uprooted and Unrestored: A Comparative Review of Durable Solutions for People Displaced by Conflict in Colombia and Liberia" (Geneva: Policy Development and Evaluation Service, 2011); Gottwald, "Back to the Future"; Omata, "Complexity of Refugees' Return."

39. Z. O. E. Robertson, Raelene Wilding, and Sandra Gifford, "Mediating the Family Imaginary: Young People Negotiating Absence in Transnational Refugee Families," *Global Networks* 16, no. 2 (2016).

40. Smit, *Property Rights of Refugees*; Toal and Dahlman, *Bosnia Remade*.

41. "Dayton Peace Agreement" (1995).

42. Toal and Dahlman, *Bosnia Remade*.

43. Camarena and Hagerdal, "When Do Displaced Persons Return?"

44. Adelman and Barkan, *No Return, No Refuge*, 20.

45. Anders H. Stefansson, "Homecomings to the Future: From Diasporic Mythographies to Social Projects of Return," in *Homecomings: Unsettling Paths of Return*, ed. Fran Markowitz and Anders H. Stefansson (New York: Lexington Books, 2004), 57.

46. Hammond, "Examining the Discourse"; Richard Black, "Conceptions of 'Home' and the Political Geography of Refugee Repatriation: Between Assumption and Contested Reality in Bosnia-Herzegovina," *Applied Geography* 22, no. 2 (2002); Daniel Warner, "Voluntary Repatriation and the Meaning of Return to Home: A Critique of Liberal Mathematics," *Journal of Refugee Studies* 7, nos. 2–3 (1994); Hammond, "Tigrayan Returnees' Notions"; Koser and Black, "End of Refugee Cycle"; Stefansson, "Homecomings to the Future"; Anders H. Stefansson, "Homes in the Making: Property Restitution, Refugee Return, and Senses of Belonging in a Post-war Bosnian Town," *International Migration* 44, no. 3 (2006).

47. Office for the Coordination of Humanitarian Affairs, "Liberia 2007: Common Humanitarian Action Plan" (Geneva: United Nations, 2007).

48. UNHCR, "Implementation of the Comprehensive Strategy for the Liberian Refugee Situation, Including UNHCR'S Recommendations on the Applicability of the 'Ceased Circumstances' Cessation Clauses" (Geneva: UNHCR, 2012), 2.

49. John Sah Nyumah, interview, October 3, 2012.

50. Abeeku Essuman-Johnson, "When Refugees Don't Go Home: The Situation of Liberian Refugees in Ghana," *Journal of Immigrant & Refugee Studies* 9, no. 2 (2011): 119.

51. Naohiko Omata, "Forgotten People: Former Liberian Refugees in Ghana," *Forced Migration Review*, no. 52 (2016).

52. Fagan, "Uprooted and Unrestored"; Zurab Elzarov, "Emerging Options for Durable Solutions in Darfur," *Forced Migration Review*, no. 62 (2019).

53. Maria Eastmond and Joakim Öjendal, "Revisiting a 'Repatriation Success': The Case of Cambodia," in *The End of the Refugee Cycle? Refugee Repatriation and Reconstruction*, ed. Richard Black and Khalid Koser (New York: Berghahn Books, 1999), 44.

54. UNHCR, "Cambodian Refugee Camps in Thailand Now Empty" (Geneva: UNHCR, 1999).

55. This case study was originally published in a different form in Joireman, "Ethnic Violence, Local Security."

56. Kosovo Agency of Statistics, *Statistical Yearbook of the Republic of Kosovo* (Pristina: Kosovo Agency of Statistics, 2020).

57. Besnik Pula, "The Emergence of the Kosovo 'Parallel State,' 1988–1992," *Nationalities Papers* 32, no. 4 (2004).

58. David L. Phillips, *Liberating Kosovo: Coercive Diplomacy and U.S. Intervention* (Cambridge, MA: Belfer Center Studies in International Security and MIT Press, 2012), 81.

59. Phillips, *Liberating Kosovo*, 106.

60. US Department of State, "Erasing History: Ethnic Cleansing in Kosovo" (Washington, DC: US Department of State, 1999).

61. Adelman and Barkan, *No Return, No Refuge*.

62. King and Mason, *Peace at Any Price*, 50.

63. Adelman and Barkan, *No Return, No Refuge*; Elton Skendaj, *Creating Kosovo: International Oversight and the Making of Ethical Institutions* (Washington, DC: Woodrow Wilson Center Press, 2014).

64. OSCE Mission in Kosovo, "An Assessment of the Voluntary Returns Process in Kosovo" (Pristina, Kosovo: Organization for Security and Cooperation, 2014).

65. Tatjana Perič and Martin Demirovski, "Unwanted: The Exodus of Kosovo Roma (1998—2000)," *Cambridge Review of International Affairs* 13, no. 2 (2000).

66. Nando Sigona, "Between Competing Imaginaries of Statehood: Roma, Ashkali and Egyptian (RAE) Leadership in Newly Independent Kosovo," *Journal of Ethnic and Migration Studies* 38, no. 8 (2012).

67. Richard Allen, "Support for IDPs in Serbia: Consolidated Report and Programme Strategy" (Belgrade: UNHCR, 2016), 109.

68. King and Mason, *Peace at Any Price*, 155.

69. Dejan Milisavljević, interview, May 26, 2016.

70. There are four mechanisms in each municipality that are designed to protect the interests of minority populations in the municipality: the Communities Committee; the Municipal Office for Communities and Returns; the Deputy Chairperson of the Municipal Assembly for Communities; and the Deputy Mayor for Communities.

71. OSCE Mission in Kosovo, "Assessment of Voluntary Returns," 22.

72. International Labor Organization data.

73. Kosovo Agency of Statistics, *Statistical Yearbook*.

74. Emmanuela C. del Re, "When Our Men Arrive: UNMIK's Post-conflict Administration of Kosovo," in *International Intervention in the Balkans since 1995*, ed. Peter Siani-Davies (New York: Routledge, 2003).

75. Although all recent ACLED data is from Africa, the first version of the data set included data from the Balkans.

76. Kristine Eck, "In Data We Trust? A Comparison of UCDP GED and ACLED Conflict Events Datasets," *Cooperation and Conflict* 47, no. 1 (2012).

77. This data set is based on the Soviet Atlas Narodov Mira (ARM) ethnic data. Cederman et al., "Representing Ethnic Groups in Space: A New Dataset," *Journal of Peace Research* 47, no. 4 (2010), discuss the methods used in the development of the georeferenced data set. In the GREG data set the two main ethnic groups in Kosovo are Serbs and Albanians, with two small enclave communities of Croats near Pristina and Kacanik. There are occasional problems with identification in the data set, as Slavic Muslims in Dragas are included in the Serbian data even though they would not identify as Serbs.

78. Data problems are challenging in Kosovo, as is typical in postconflict settings where data is scarce or politicized. Having worked on return migration in other settings such as Uganda and Liberia, I found data to be comparatively abundant, albeit inconsistent, in Kosovo largely because of international interest in tracking returns. That said, I follow a multimethod technique using statistical analysis, mapping, and interviews to develop a comprehensive picture of the situation.

79. While this double notation of names in Albanian and Serbian is awkward, it is widely used and respectful of the two national languages in Kosovo and the Serbian minority.

80. John O'Loughlin and Frank D. W. Witmer, "The Localized Geographies of Violence in the North Caucasus of Russia, 1999–2007," *Annals of the Association of American Geographers* 101, no. 1 (2011), 184.

81. This is further complicated by the fact that five municipalities were created relatively recently in an attempt to give better minority representation and follow through on the Ahtisaari plan: Mamuşa/Mamushë/Mamuša, created in 2005; Gračanica/Graçanicë, Hani I Elezit / Djenerel Jankovic, Junik, and Partesh/Partes all created in 2010. Using georeferenced data on violent incidents with the current municipality boundaries allows us to ascertain the impact of violent incidents by location.

82. There is no available data on returns or population for the four northern Serb municipalities.

83. OSCE Mission in Kosovo, "Assessment of Voluntary Returns in Kosovo" (Pristina, Kosovo: OSCE, 2019), 24.

84. Interview 103162, October 3, 2016; Interview 103163, October 3, 2016.

85. Interview 103163, October 3, 2016.

86. Interview 107161, October 7, 2016.

87. Jose M. Garzon et al., "Kosovo Conflict Assessment: Breaking Down Invisible Walls" (Pristina, Kosovo: USAID, 2012).

88. Slavisa Kolaseimac, interview, February 5, 2013.

89. Ghosn et al., "The Journey Home."

90. Charis Psaltis et al., "Transitional Justice and Acceptance of Cohabitation in Cyprus," *Ethnic & Racial Studies* 42, no. 11 (2019).

91. Some put the number as high as two hundred thousand, but all numbers are

estimates. Wanda Troszczynska-van Genderen, "Rights Displaced: Forced Returns of Roma, Ashkali and Egyptians from Western Europe to Kosovo" (New York: Human Rights Watch, 2010).

92. Sigona, "Between Competing Imaginaries," 1218.

93. Progress, "Improving the Tools for the Social Inclusion and Non-discrimination of Roma in the EU" (Luxembourg: European Commission Directorate-General for Employment, Social Affairs and Equal Opportunities, 2010).

94. Field notes, October 2017.

95. Sigona, "Between Competing Imaginaries," 1219.

96. Troszczynska-van Genderen, "Rights Displaced."

97. Field notes, October 11, 2017.

98. Field notes, October 11, 2017.

99. Slobodan Cvejić, "Assessment of the Needs of Internally Displaced Roma in Serbia" (Belgrade: UNHCR 2015), 4.

100. Troszczynska-van Genderen, "Rights Displaced."

101. Verena Knaus, "No Place to Call Home—Repatriation from Germany to Kosovo as Seen and Experienced by Roma, Ashkali and Egyptian Children" (Pristina, Kosovo: UNICEF, 2011), 8.

102. Knaus, "No Place to Call Home," 23.

103. Allen, "Support for IDPs in Serbia," 109.

Chapter 4

1. UNHCR, *Global Trends: Forced Displacement in 2019*, 4.

2. Rachel Pannett, "Ukrainian boy, 11, traveled hundreds of miles alone to Slovakia, with only a passport and a plastic bag," The Washington Post, March 8, 2022.

3. Inter-agency Working Group on Unaccompanied and Separated Children, *Inter-Agency Guiding Principles on Unaccompanied and Separated Children*, ed. ICRC Central Tracing Agency and Protection Division (Geneva: International Committee of the Red Cross, 2004), 13.

4. Gabriel Bol Deng, "The Narrow Escape: The Facts of My Life," *Voices* 32, nos. 3–4 (2006), 20.

5. Deng, "The Narrow Escape."

6. Everett M. Ressler, Neil Boothby, and Daniel J. Steinbock, *Unaccompanied Children: Care and Protection in Wars, Natural Disasters and Refugee Movements* (New York: Oxford University Press, 1988), 119.

7. Adam Nossiter, "'I Am Alone': Migrant Children in Calais 'Jungle' Face an Uncertain Fate," *New York Times*, October 21, 2016.

8. Lara Marlowe, "Calais's Migrant Children Suffer as Europe Procrastinates," *Irish Times*, March 12, 2016.

9. Marlowe, "Calais's Migrant Children."

10. As a Syrian minor in 2016 Yousef would have been recognized as a prima facie refugee. In other words, the assumption would be that he was a legitimate refugee; he would not have to prove that he was persecuted. Prima facie status holds for designated groups, unless evidence to the contrary is presented. UNHCR, "Protection of Refugees in Mass Influx Situations: Overall Protection Framework,"

Background Paper Prepared for the Global Consultation on International Protection (Geneva: United Nations, 2001).

11. Children's ability to comprehend complex situations changes with age. There is a significant difference in the ability of a ten-year-old to understand the full context of their situation compared to a fifteen-year-old. Older children can make decisions, exert their will, and act independently—what social scientists refer to as agency. Most child migrants are in their older teens.

12. Ressler, Boothby, and Steinbock, *Unaccompanied Children*, 255.

13. Jacqueline Bhabha, *Child Migration and Human Rights in a Global Age* (Princeton, NJ: Princeton University Press, 2014), 205.

14. Mirian Jordan and Ron Nixon, "Trump Administration Threatens Jail and Separating Children from Parents for Those Who Illegally Cross Southwest Border," *New York Times*, May 7, 2018, https://www.nytimes.com/2018/05/07/us/politics/homeland-security-prosecute-undocumented-immigrants.html

15. Inter-agency Working Group on Unaccompanied and Separated Children, "Inter-Agency Guiding Principles on Unaccompanied and Separated Children," 16.

16. Nick Cumming-Bruce, "Taking Migrant Children from Parents Is Illegal, U.N. Tells U.S.," *New York Times*, June 5, 2018.

17. UNHCR, "UNHCR Guidelines on Determining the Best Interests of the Child" (Geneva: UNHCR, 2008); "Field Handbook for the Implementation of UNHCR Bid Guidelines" (Geneva: UNHCR, 2011).

18. The idea of individually determined refugee status was part of the 1951 Convention, but circumstances forced the broadening of the status to include prima facie refugees as the Refugee Convention was put into practice. Large-scale movements of people due to war or natural disasters rendered individual assessments in all cases untenable. States and the UNHCR began to make group determinations of refugee status that are referred to as prima facie—meaning based on first impression. This shifts the burden of proof away from the individual and does not require the same degree of scrutiny in terms of the asylum claim.

19. Bhabha, *Child Migration*.

20. Sandra F. Joireman, "Future Rights for Future Citizens: Children's Property Rights in Fragile Environments," *Oxford Development Studies* 46, no. 4 (2018).

21. Julia Vorhölter, *Youth at the Crossroads: Discourses on Socio-cultural Change in Post-war Northern Uganda* (Göttingen, the Netherlands: Göttingen University Press, 2014), 155.

22. Sandra F. Joireman, "Intergenerational Land Conflict in Northern Uganda: Children, Customary Law and Return Migration," *Africa* 88, no. 1 (2018).

23. UNHCR, "UNHCR Reports Crisis in Refugee Education" (Geneva: UNHCR, 2016).

24. Preethi Nallu, "Syrian Refugee Children Appeal for Education" (Geneva: News Deeply, 2016).

25. Miriam George, Wendy Kliewer, and Sebastan Irudaya Rajan, "'Rather Than Talking in Tamil, They Should Be Talking to Tamils': Sri Lankan Tamil Refugee Readiness for Repatriation," *Refugee Survey Quarterly* 34, no. 2 (2015).

26. Amaya Valcárcel Silvela, "Sri Lankan Tamil Refugees in India: Return or Integration?," *Forced Migration Review*, no. 62 (2019), 13.

27. Interview 107162.

28. Hammond, "Tigrayan Returnees' Notions," 48.

29. Malkki, "National Geographic"; Stefansson, "Homes in the Making"; Turton, "The Meaning of Place."

30. Johnathan Bascom, "Reconstituting Households and Reconstructing Home Areas: The Case of Returning Eritreans," in *In Search of Cool Ground: War, Flight and Homecoming in Northeast Africa*, ed. Tim Allen (Trenton, NJ: Africa World Press, 1996); Julius Holt, "Looking beyond the Towns: Facts & Conjectures about Rural Returnees in the Ogaden & 'Somaliland'"; Bascom, "Reconstituting Households"; Gearoid Ó Tuathail, "Localizing Geopolitics: Disaggregating Violence and Return in Conflict Regions," *Political Geography* 29, no. 5 (2010).

31. Fagan, "Uprooted and Unrestored," 8.

32. Edith Honan, "U.N. Expands Refugee Camp in Kenya as South Sudan Conflict Rages," Reuters, June 20, 2015.

33. Joireman, "Future Rights."

34. Marion A. Kaplan, *Between Dignity and Despair: Jewish Life in Nazi Germany* (New York: Oxford University Press, 1998).

35. Joireman, "Future Rights."

36. Phuong Pham, Patrick Vinck, Marieke Wierda, Eric Stover, and Adrian di Giovanni, *Forgotten Voices: A Population-Based Survey of Attitudes about Peace and Justice in Northern Uganda* (New York: International Center for Transitional Justice and the Human Rights Center, University of California, Berkeley, 2005). The statistic of 1.8 million displaced people encompassed only those officially counted in the IDP camps, not those who moved to cities for security.

37. "A Catastrophe Ignored," *The Economist*, July 22, 2004, 46; Bayard Roberts, Kaducu Felix Ocaka, John Browne, Thomas Oyok, and Egbert Sondorp, "Factors Associated with Post-traumatic Stress Disorder and Depression amongst Internally Displaced Persons in Northern Uganda," *BMC Psychiatry* 8 (2008).

38. Chris Dolan, *Social Torture: The Case of Northern Uganda, 1986–2006* (New York: Berghahn Books, 2009); Vorhölter, *Youth at the Crossroads*; Justine Nannyonjo, "Conflicts, Poverty and Human Development in Northern Uganda," WIDER Working Paper (New York: United Nations World Institute for Development Economics Research, 2005).

39. This section of the chapter is based on Joireman, "Intergenerational Land Conflict."

40. Francis M. Deng, "Customary Law in the Cross Fire of Sudan's War of Identities," in *Customary Justice and the Rule of Law in War-Torn Societies*, ed. Deborah Isser (Washington, DC: United States Institute of Peace, 2011); Manfred O. Hinz, *Customary Law Ascertained: The Customary Law of the Owambo, Kavango and Caprivi Communities of Namibia*, vol. 1 (Windhoek: Namibia Scientific Society in association with the Human Rights and Documentation Centre, 2010); Gordon R. Woodman, "A Survey of Customary Laws in Africa in Search of Lessons for the Future," in *The Future of African Customary Law*, ed. Jeanmarie Fenrich, Paolo Galizzi, and Tracy E. Higgins (New York: Cambridge University Press, 2011).

41. Sandra F. Joireman, "Rebuilding Communities after Violent Conflict: Informal Justice Systems and Resource Access," *Online Symposium*, November 2014,

http://harvardhrj.com/2014/11/rebuilding-communities-after-violent-conflict-informal-justice-systems-and-resource-access/

42. Susan Mildred Aber, interview, May 26, 2015; Patrick Ong'ara and Zakeo Lubeja, interview, May 27, 2015.

43. "Uganda: Escalating Land Disputes in the North" (Geneva: IRIN 2011); Levis Onegi, "Post-conflict Land Insecurity Threatens Re-displacement in Northern Uganda," *Forced Migration Review*, no. 41 (December 2012). There is evidence to suggest that not everyone returned to the original location of their homes and land. Sandra F. Joireman, Adam Sawyer, and Juliana Wilhoit, "A Different Way Home: Resettlement Patterns in Northern Uganda," *Political Geography* 31, no. 4 (2012). Interview evidence suggests that some people were aware that their land claims were not justified by previous occupation.

44. Ronald R. Atkinson, "Afterword: A Perspective on the Last Thirty Years," in *The Roots of Ethnicity: Origins of the Acholi of Uganda before 1800* (Kampala: Fountain Publishers, 2010), 333.

45. IRIN, "Uganda."

46. NGO official, interview, May 25, 2015.

47. Ong'ara and Lubeja, interview.

48. LC V official, interview, May 25, 2015; NGO official, interview; Simon Ogenrwot, interview, May 28, 2015; Sabiti Omara, interview, May 25, 2015.

49. Koro Elders Focus Group, interview, May 27, 2015. The Koro Elders Focus group was a group of two women and four men representing the heads of fifty-seven clans. In Acholi they are called the Rwodi Kweri (plural, chiefs of the hoe) and are engaged in resolving conflicts regarding land issues and customary law. This focus group meeting occurred in Acholi with Mirriam Lakote translating. Many of the problems around land issues that occurred with return migration would engage the Rwot Kweri (chief) as a first step.

50. Sandra F. Joireman, "The Mystery of Capital Formation in Sub-Saharan Africa: Women, Property Rights and Customary Law," *World Development* 36, no. 7 (2008).

51. Amos Canwat, interview, May 27, 2015; Koro Elders Focus Group, interview; NGO official, interview; Ogenrwot, interview; Omara, interview.

52. Lindsay McClain Opiyo, "Alone Like a Tree: Reintegration Challenges Facing Children Born of War and Their Mothers in Northern Uganda," JRP Situational Brief (Gulu, Uganda: Justice and Reconciliation Project, 2015), 3.

53. Koro Elders Focus Group, interview; NGO official, interview.

54. Opiyo, "Alone Like a Tree: Reintegration Challenges Facing Children Born of War and Their Mothers in Northern Uganda," 6.

55. Julian Hopwood, interview, May 26, 2015.

56. Ogenrwot, interview.

57. Susan Reynolds Whyte et al., "Remaining Internally Displaced: Missing Links to Security in Northern Uganda," *Journal of Refugee Studies* 26, no 2 (2012), 295.

58. Omara, interview.

59. Koro Elders Focus Group, interview.

60. Ogenrwot, interview.

Chapter 5

1. Anke Hoeffler, Syeda Shahbano Ijaz, and Sarah von Billerbeck, "Post Conflict Recovery and Peace Building," World Development Report Background Papers (Washington, DC: World Bank, 2011), 4.

2. Interview 103162, October 3, 2016.

3. The section of this chapter on return migration to Liberia was originally published in a slightly different form in Joireman and Meitzner Yoder, "A Long Time Gone."

4. See the note on methods at the beginning of Chapter 3 for a deeper description of the Liberia research.

5. Joanna Berendt, "In Poland, 'a Narrow Window to Do Justice' for Those Robbed by Nazis," *New York Times*, June 12, 2018.

6. Lydia Tomkiw, "Holocaust Survivor Stories in 2015: In Poland, the Fight to Get Their Property Back," *International Business Times*, November 14, 2015. World War II compensation claims are a minority of property restitution claims in Poland, most of which are from the Communist era.

7. BBC News, "Polish Law on Property Stolen by Nazis Angers Israel," August 16, 2021, https://www.bbc.com/news/world-europe-58218750

8. Gerver, *Ethics and Practice*; Tyler Cowen, "How Far Back Should We Go? Why Restitution Should Be Small," in *Retribution and Reparation in the Transition to Democracy*, ed. Jon Elster (New York: Cambridge University Press, 2006); Pablo Kalmanovitz, "Corrective Justice versus Social Justice in the Aftermath of War," in *Distributive Justice in Transitions*, ed. Morten Bergsmo et al. (Oslo: Torkel Opsahl Academic EPublisher, 2010); Anna Stilz, "Nations, States, and Territory," *Ethics* 121, no. 3 (2011); Jeremy Waldron, "Superseding Historic Injustice," *Ethics* 103, no. 1 (1992).

9. Norwegian Refugee Council et al., "Dangerous Ground: Syria's Refugees Face an Uncertain Future" (Oslo: Norwegian Refugee Council, 2018), 15.

10. Emily Stubblefield and Sandra F. Joireman, "Law, Violence, and Property Expropriation in Syria: Impediments to Restitution and Return," *Land* 8, no. 11 (2019).

11. Adesoji Adelaja and Justin George, "Terrorism and Land Use in Agriculture: The Case of Boko Haram in Nigeria," *Land Use Policy* 88 (2019).

12. Jutta Bakonyi, Peter Chonka, and Kirsti Stuvøy, "War and City-Making in Somalia: Property, Power and Disposable Lives," *Political Geography* 73 (2019).

13. Margaret Jane Radin, "Property and Personhood," *Stanford Law Review* 34 (1982).

14. John Steinbeck, *The Grapes of Wrath* (New York: Penguin Group, 1939), 37.

15. Bernadette Atuahene, *We Want What's Ours: Learning from South Africa's Land Restitution Program* (Oxford: Oxford University Press, 2014).

16. Bradley, *Refugee Repatriation*.

17. Hannah Arendt, *The Origins of Totalitarianism* (New York: Schocken Books, 2004), 370.

18. Lausanne Peace Treaty VI, Convention Concerning the Exchange of Greek and Turkish Populations Signed at Lausanne, January 30, 1923, Article I.

19. Bruce Clark, *Twice a Stranger: The Mass Expulsions That Forged Modern Greece and Turkey* (Cambridge, MA: Harvard University Press, 2006), 191.

20. Nansen has a saint-like reputation and led an incredible and very public life as an Arctic explorer and then as a champion for refugees and displaced people. This was not his finest moment.

21. Catherine Lu, *Justice and Reconciliation in World Politics* (Cambridge: Cambridge University Press, 2017), 230.

22. Megan J. Ballard, "Post Conflict Property Restitution: Flawed Legal and Theoretical Foundations," *Berkeley Journal of International Law* 28 (2010).

23. Voluntary Guidelines on the Responsible Governance of Tenure of Land, Fisheries and Forests in the Context of National Food Security, Article 14.2.

24. Harild, Christensen, and Zetter, "Sustainable Refugee Return."

25. Toal and Dahlman, *Bosnia Remade*.

26. Toal and Dahlman, *Bosnia Remade*, 170.

27. OSCE Mission in Kosovo, "Assessment of Voluntary Returns in Kosovo."

28. Interview 107163, October 7, 2016.

29. International Organization for Migration, *Property Restitution and Compensation: Practices and Experiences of Claims Programmes*, online ed. (Geneva: International Organization for Migration, 2008), 16.

30. Kalmanovitz, "Corrective Justice."

31. Gerver, *Ethics and Practice*; Michael Heller and Christopher Serkin, "Revaluing Restitution: From the Talmud to Postsocialism," *Michigan Law Review* 97, no. 6 (1999); Kalmanovitz, "Corrective Justice"; Anna Stilz, "Occupancy Rights and the Wrong of Removal," *Philosophy & Public Affairs* 41, no. 4 (2013).

32. Paulo Sérgio de M. S. Pinheiro, "Housing and Property Restitution in the Context of the Return of Refugees and Internally Displaced Persons," in *Sub-Commission on the Promotion and Protection of Human Rights*, ed. Commission on Human Rights (New York: Economic and Social Council 2003); Cherryl Walker, *Landmarked: Land Claims and Land Restitution in South Africa* (Athens: Ohio University Press, 2008).

33. Peter Van der Auweraert, "Property Restitution in Iraq" (Washington, DC: US Department of State, 2007).

34. Ministry of Justice, "Kosovo National Strategy on Property Rights" (Pristina: Republic of Kosovo, 2016), 33.

35. Waldron, "Superseding Historic Injustice"; Cowen, "How Far Back?"

36. Kalmanovitz, "Corrective Justice"; Lu, *Justice and Reconciliation*.

37. Shehmin Awan, "The Statelessness Problem of the Rohingya Muslims Notes," *Washington University Global Studies Law Review* 19, no. 1 (2020).

38. Ballard, "Post Conflict Property Restitution: Flawed Legal and Theoretical Foundations"; Agnes Hurwitz, "Beyond Restitution: Housing, Land, Property and the Rule of Law," in *Civil War and the Rule of Law*, ed. Agnes Hurwitz and Reyko Huang (Boulder: Lynne Rienner, 2008).

39. The expulsion of the Arab population from Israel also occurred before all these rights became international policy. Under international law Israel is also obligated to pay compensation to Palestinians who lost their land due to construction related to a security fence. Legal Consequences of the Construction of a Wall in the Occupied Palestinian Territory, Advisory Opinion, 2004 I.C.J. 131, at 152 (July 9).

40. Pinheiro, "Housing and Property Restitution," 6.

41. Olga Mitrović, "Resolving a Protracted Refugee Situation through a Regional Process," *Forced Migration Review* 50 (September 2015).

42. Toal and Dahlman, *Bosnia Remade*, 302.

43. There are competing narratives as to why the property registers were taken back to Serbia. One is that the Serb officials were fulfilling their duty as civil servants to protect the property records in a time of war. The alternative is that the property records were taken to undermine the property system of the nascent state.

44. Uganda is now moving toward a more formalized system for both customary and freehold tenure.

45. See Chapter 4 for a discussion of methods in the Liberia research.

46. Pauline Peters warns of an excessively positive interpretation of the flexibility of customary tenure systems as this very feature lends those systems to manipulation. Pauline E. Peters, "Challenges in Land Tenure and Land Reform in Africa: Anthropological Contributions," *World Development* 37, no. 8 (2009).

47. Harry G. West and Scott Kloeck-Jenson, "Betwixt and Between: 'Traditional Authority' and Democratic Decentralization in Post-war Mozambique," *African Affairs* 98, no. 393 (1999).

48. Alfred Brownell, interview, October 3, 2012.

49. Barbara McCallin, "Restitution and Legal Pluralism in Contexts of Displacement," in *Case Studies on Transitional Justice and Displacement* (Washington, DC: International Center for Transitional Justice, 2012); Montemurro, interview.

50. Daniel Fitzpatrick, Andrew McWilliam, and Susana Barnes, *Property and Social Resilience in Times of Conflict: Land, Custom and Law in East Timor* (Burlington, VT: Ashgate, 2012).

51. Liz Alden Wily and Jeffrey Hatcher, "Rights to Resources in Crisis: Reviewing the Fate of Customary Tenure in Africa" (Washington, DC: Rights and Resources Initiative, 2012); Pauline E. Peters, "Conflicts over Land and Threats to Customary Tenure in Africa," *African Affairs* 112, no. 449 (2013).

52. Joireman, Sawyer, and Wilhoit, "A Different Way Home: Resettlement Patterns in Northern Uganda."

53. Office for the Coordination of Humanitarian Affairs, "Liberia 2007."

54. Adarkwah Antwi, interview, October 7, 2012; Mamadou Dian Balde, interview, March 11, 2011; Mark A. Butman, "Urbanization vs. Rural Return in Post-conflict Liberia" (MA thesis, George Washington University, 2009); Nyumah, interview.

55. Liberia Institute of Statistics and Geo-Information Services, "2008 Population and Housing Census: Final Results" (Monrovia: Liberia Institute of Statistics and Geo-Information Services, 2009).

56. See also the case study of Liberia in Harild, Christensen, and Zetter, "Sustainable Refugee Return."

57. Percentage change was calculated using the 1974 urban population vs. the 2008 urban populations in the major cities of each county. While inexact, this method illustrates the dissimilarity of urbanization and return across the counties.

58. Antwi, interview.

59. This group consisted of three women and one man all of whom were from Lofa County before the war and had been given land to farm outside of Monrovia.

60. Montserrado Focus Group, Montserrado County, Liberia, 2012. There

are alternative narratives from the period immediately following the conflict. Jon Unruh has noted that in some areas of Liberia, earlier on in the resettlement process, access to rural land was a problem Jon D. Unruh, "Land Rights in Postwar Liberia: The Volatile Part of the Peace Process," *Land Use Policy* 26, no. 2 (2009).

61. Paynesville Focus Group, October 4, 2012. This was a group of eight women and one man all displaced by the war and living in the Paynesville area of Monrovia.

62. Joireman, Sawyer, and Wilhoit, "A Different Way Home."

63. Joireman and Meitzner Yoder, "A Long Time Gone"; Koro Elders Focus Group, interview.

64. Koro Elders Focus Group, interview.

65. Sara S. Berry, "The Food Crisis and Agrarian Change in Africa: A Review Essay," *African Studies Review* 27, no. 2 (1984): 91.

66. See Bakewell for a discussion of the ways in which categories and criteria around refugees can render invisible those who do not fit neatly into them. Bakewell, "Research Beyond the Categories."

67. Koro Elders Focus Group, interview.

68. Patricia Weiss Fagan, "Refugees and IDPS after Conflict: Why They Do Not Go Home," Special Report (Washington DC: United States Institute of Peace, 2011).

69. Deniz Senol Sert, "Cyprus: Peace, Return and Property," *Journal of Refugee Studies* 23, no. 2 (2010).

Chapter 6

1. Betts and Collier, *Refuge.*

2. Hathaway, "The Meaning of Repatriation," 556.

3. Catherine Huser et al., "South Sudanese Returns: Perceptions and Responses," *Forced Migration Review*, no. 62 (2019).

4. World Food Programme, "WFP Forced to Make Deeper Cuts in Food Assistance for Syrian Refugees Due to Lack of Funding," news release, July 1, 2015, https://www.wfp.org/news/news-release/wfp-forced-make-deeper-cuts-food-assistance-syrian-refugees-due-lack-funding

5. Steven Erlanger and Kimiko De Freytas-Tamura, "UN Funding Shortfalls and Cuts in Refugee Aid Fuel Exodus to Europe," *New York Times*, September 19, 2015.

6. The travel necessary to get to Europe in this situation, as in other cases of irregular immigration, was extremely dangerous. Orla Guerin, "Aid Cuts Driving Jordan's Syrian Refugees to Risk All," September 11 BBC News, 2015; Reece Jones, *Violent Borders: Refugees and the Right to Move* (New York: Verso, 2016). Manny Fernandez, "A Path to America, Marked by More and More Bodies," *New York Times*, May 4, 2017.

7. In the wake of the 2015 migration crisis, the European Union acted to keep people from entering its territory. The EU pact with Turkey, discussed in Chapter 2, returns any refugees showing up in Italy and Greece back to Turkey. In exchange the EU committed to provide more resettlement opportunities, financial support for Turkey, and visa liberalization for Turkish citizens. A similar agreement provided EU funding to Niger to keep people in the country and meet their needs

there. This agreement protects those displaced by violence—in this case as a result of Boko Haram activities in both Nigeria and Niger—from undertaking perilous journeys to Europe. It also benefits the political needs of northern states that do not want to take in large numbers of refugees or have economic migrants pouring across their borders.

8. Betts and Collier, *Refuge*.

9. Heng Zhu et al., "Economic Impact."

10. European Commission, "EU-Jordan Partnership: The Compact" (Brussels: Commission of the European Union, 2017); "Donors Pledge around $40-Billion Aid to Syrian Refugees' Hosts,"April 10 *Jordan Times*, 2017.

11. Katharina Lenner and Lewis Turner, "Learning from the Jordan Compact," *Forced Migration Review*, no. 57 (2018); Jennifer Gordon, "The International Governance of Refugee Work: Reflections on the Jordan Compact," *Global Public Policy and Governance* (2021), https://doi.org/10.1007/s43508-021-00019-6

12. UNHCR, "The Global Compact on Refugees" (Geneva: UNHCR, 2018), 17–18.

13. The Global Compact has also been criticized for "externalizing" borders and undermining the global responsibility for asylum. Penelope Mathew, "Killing Asylum Softly or Leaving No One Behind? The New York Declaration and Global Compacts in a Divided World," *Globalizations* (2021), https://tandfonline.com/doi/full/10.1080/14747731.2021.1974207

14. UNHCR, "Complementary Pathways for Admission to Third Countries," https://www.unhcr.org/en-us/complementary-pathways.html, accessed February 17, 2022.

15. Jeff Crisp has argued that the scale and speed of the Syrian refugee crisis has done more to change humanitarian policy responses than the Global Compact. Jeff Crisp, "The Syrian Emergency: A Catalyst for Change in the International Refugee Regime," *Journal of Refugee Studies* 34, no. 2 (2021).

16. Jon D. Unruh, "Assembling Evidence for a Land and Property Restitution Database during the Syrian Civil War," presented to World Bank Land and Poverty Conference, Washington, DC, 2016; Jacomijn J. van Haersolte-van Hof, "Innovations to Speed Mass Claims: New Standards of Proof," in *Redressing Injustices through Mass Claims*, ed. International Bureau of the Permanent Court of Arbitration (New York: Oxford University Press, 2006); Joireman, "Future Rights."

17. Jon D. Unruh, "Evidencing the Restitution Landscape: Pre-emptive and Advance Techniques for War-Torn Land and Property Rights Reacquisition," *Land Use Policy* 38 (2014); Scott Leckie and Chris Huggins, *Conflict and Housing, Land, and Property Rights: A Handbook on Issues, Frameworks, and Solutions* (New York: Cambridge University Press, 2011).

18. Joireman and Meitzner Yoder, "A Long Time Gone."

19. David Shrier, Weige Wu, and Alex Pentland, "Blockchain & Infrastructure (Identity, Data Security)," *MIT Connection Science*, Part 3 of 4, May 2016.

20. This is likely due to the relative accessibility of refugee populations in Germany, Turkey, and Jordan, or this may be yet another area where Syria is a game-changer, as Crisp argues. Crisp, "The Syrian Emergency: A Catalyst for Change in the International Refugee Regime."

21. Bakewell, "Research beyond the Categories."

22. Ghosn et al., "The Journey Home"; Psaltis et al., "Transitional Justice."

23. Camarena and Hagerdal, "When Do Displaced Persons Return?"

24. Terry L. Anderson and Laura E. Huggins, *Property Rights: A Practical Guide to Freedom and Prosperity* (Stanford, CA: Hoover Institution Press, 2003); Christopher Clague et al., "Contract-Intensive Money: Contract Enforcement, Property Rights, and Economic Performance," *Journal of Economic Growth* 4 (June 1999); Erica Field, "Property Rights and Investment in Urban Slums," *Journal of the European Economic Association* 2–3 (2005).

Glossary

1. 1951 Refugee Convention.

2. UNHCR, *UNHCR Resettlement Handbook* (Geneva: UN Refuge Agency, 2011), 3.

3. 1954 United Nations Convention relating to the Status of Stateless Persons.

Bibliography

Adelaja, Adesoji, and Justin George. "Terrorism and Land Use in Agriculture: The Case of Boko Haram in Nigeria." *Land Use Policy* 88 (2019), 104116.

Adelman, Howard, and Ezekial Barkan. *No Return, No Refuge: Rites and Rights in Minority Repatriation.* New York: Columbia University Press, 2011.

Adhikari, Prakash. "Conflict-Induced Displacement, Understanding the Causes of Flight." *American Journal of Political Science* 57, no. 1 (2013), 82–89.

Albuja, Sebastián, and Marcela Ceballos. "Urban Displacement and Migration in Colombia." *Forced Migration Review*, no. 34 (2010), 10.

Allen, Richard. "Support for IDPs in Serbia: Consolidated Report and Programme Strategy." Belgrade, Serbia, 2016.

Amnesty International. "Nowhere Else to Go: Forced Returns of Somali Refugees from Dadaab Refugee Camp, Kenya." London: Amnesty International, 2016.

Anderson, Terry L., and Laura E. Huggins. *Property Rights: A Practical Guide to Freedom and Prosperity.* Stanford, CA: Hoover Institution Press, 2003.

Anyadike, Obi. "The Grinch's Not-So-Festive Guide to Food Ration Cuts." News release, December 17, 2016. http://www.irinnews.org/news/2016/12/27/grin ch%E2%80%99s-not-so-festive-guide-food-ration-cuts?utm_source=IRIN+ -+the+inside+story+on+emergencies&utm_campaign=58100fe216-RSS_EMA IL_CAMPAIGN_ENGLISH_AFRICA&utm_medium=email&utm_term=0 _d842d98289-58100fe216-29273553

Arendt, Hannah. *The Origins of Totalitarianism.* New York: Schocken Books, 2004. 1948.

Arias, María Alejandra, Ana María Ibáñez, and Pablo Querubin. "The Desire to Return during Civil War: Evidence for Internally Displaced Populations in Colombia." *Peace Economics, Peace Science and Public Policy* 20, no. 1 (2014), 209–33.

Asiimwe, Agnes. "Why Idi Amin Expelled the Asians." *New African*, no. 521 (2012), 32–35.

Atuahene, Bernadette. *We Want What's Ours: Learning from South Africa's Land Restitution Program*. Oxford: Oxford University Press, 2014.

Awan, Shehmin. "The Statelessness Problem of the Rohingya Muslims Notes." *Washington University Global Studies Law Review* 19, no. 1 (2020), 85–112.

Azose, Jonathan J., and Adrian E. Raftery. "Estimation of Emigration, Return Migration, and Transit Migration between All Pairs of Countries." *Proceedings of the National Academy of Sciences of the United States of America* 116, no. 1 (2019), 116–22.

Bakewell, Oliver. "'Keeping Them in Their Place': The Ambivalent Relationship between Development and Migration in Africa." *Third World Quarterly* 29, no. 7 (2008), 1341–58.

Bakewell, Oliver. "Research beyond the Categories: The Importance of Policy Irrelevant Research into Forced Migration." *Journal of Refugee Studies* 21, no. 4 (2008), 432–53.

Bakonyi, Jutta, Peter Chonka, and Kirsti Stuvøy. "War and City-Making in Somalia: Property, Power and Disposable Lives." *Political Geography* 73 (2019), 82–91.

Ballard, Megan J. "Post Conflict Property Restitution: Flawed Legal and Theoretical Foundations." *Berkeley Journal of International Law* 28 (2010), 462–96.

Bascom, Johnathan. "Reconstituting Households and Reconstructing Home Areas: The Case of Returning Eritreans." In *In Search of Cool Ground: War, Flight and Homecoming in Northeast Africa*, edited by Tim Allen, 66–79. Trenton, NJ: Africa World Press, 1996.

BBC News. "Polish Law on Property Stolen by Nazis Angers Israel." August 16, 2021, https://www.bbc.com/news/world-europe-58218750

Berendt, Joanna. "In Poland, 'a Narrow Window to Do Justice' for Those Robbed by Nazis." *New York Times*, June 12, 2018.

Berry, Sara S. "The Food Crisis and Agrarian Change in Africa: A Review Essay." *African Studies Review* 27, no. 2 (1984), 59–112.

Betts, Alexander, and Paul Collier. *Refuge: Transforming a Broken Refugee System*. New York: Allen Lane, 2017.

Bhabha, Jacqueline. *Child Migration and Human Rights in a Global Age*. Princeton, NJ: Princeton University Press, 2014.

Black, Richard. "Conceptions of 'Home' and the Political Geography of Refugee Repatriation: Between Assumption and Contested Reality in Bosnia-Herzegovina." *Applied Geography* 22, no. 2 (2002), 123.

Boyd, Monica. "Family and Personal Networks in International Migration: Recent Developments and New Agendas." *International Migration Review* 23, no. 3 (1989), 638–70.

Bradley, Megan. "Durable Solutions and the Right of Return for IDPS: Evolving Interpretations." *International Journal of Refugee Law* 30, no. 2 (2018), 218–42.

Bradley, Megan. *Refugee Repatriation: Justice, Responsibility and Redress*. Cambridge: Cambridge University Press, 2013.

Brownell, Alfred. Interview. Monrovia, Liberia, 2012.

Butman, Mark A. "Urbanization vs. Rural Return in Post-conflict Liberia." MA these, George Washington University, 2009.

Camarena, Kara Ross, and Nils Hagerdal. "When Do Displaced Persons Return? Postwar Migration among Christians in Mount Lebanon." *American Journal of Political Science* 64, no. 2 (2020), 223–39.

Cederman, Lars-Erik, Jan Ketil Rød, and Nils B. Weidmann. "Representing Ethnic Groups in Space: A New Dataset." *Journal of Peace Research* 47, no. 4 (2010), 491–99.

Chimni, B. S. "From Resettlement to Involuntary Repatriation: Towards a Critical History of Durable Solutions to Refugee Problems." *Refugee Survey Quarterly* 23, no. 3 (2004), 55–73.

Clague, Christopher, Philip Keefer, Stephen Knack, and Mancur Olson. "Contract-Intensive Money: Contract Enforcement, Property Rights, and Economic Performance." *Journal of Economic Growth* 4 (June 1999), 185–211.

Clark, Bruce. *Twice a Stranger: The Mass Expulsions That Forged Modern Greece and Turkey*. Cambridge, MA: Harvard University Press, 2006.

Clemens, Michael A. "Violence, Development, and Migration Waves: Evidence from Central American Child Migrant Apprehensions." Washington, DC: Center for Global Development Working Paper 459, 2017.

Cohen, Roberta. "The Guiding Principles on Internal Displacement: An Innovation in International Standard Setting." *Global Governance* 10, no. 4 (2004), 459–80.

Cowen, Tyler. "How Far Back Should We Go? Why Restitution Should Be Small." In *Retribution and Reparation in the Transition to Democracy*, edited by Jon Elster, 17–32. New York: Cambridge University Press, 2006.

Crisp, Jeff. "Repatriation Principles under Pressure." *Forced Migration Review*, no. 62 (2019), 19–23.

Crisp, Jeff. "The Syrian Emergency: A Catalyst for Change in the International Refugee Regime." *Journal of Refugee Studies* 34, no. 2 (2021), 1441–53.

Cumming-Bruce, Nick. "Taking Migrant Children from Parents Is Illegal, U.N. Tells U.S." *New York Times*, June 5, 2018.

Cvejić, Slobodan. "Assessment of the Needs of Internally Displaced Roma in Serbia." UNHCR, Belgrade, Serbia, 2015.

Davenport, Christian A., Will H. Moore, and Steven C. Poe. "Sometimes You Just Have to Leave: Domestic Threats and Forced Migration, 1964–1989." *International Interactions* 29, no. 1 (2003), 27–55.

de Haas, Hein. "The Myth of Invasion: The Inconvenient Realities of African Migration to Europe." *Third World Quarterly* 29, no. 7 (2008), 1305–22.

de Haas, Hein. "Turning the Tide? Why Development Will Not Stop Migration." *Development & Change* 38, no. 5 (2007), 819–41.

Deininger, Klaus, Ana M. Ibanez, and Pablo Querubin. "Towards Sustainable Return Policies for the Displaced Population: Why Are Some Displaced

Households More Willing to Return Than Others?" HiCN Working Papers 07, Households in Conflict Network. Sussex, UK: University of Sussex, 2004.

del Re, Emmanuela C. "When Our Men Arrive: UNMIK's Post-Conflict Administration of Kosovo." 5 In *International Intervention in the Balkans since 1995*, edited by Peter Siani-Davies, 88–104. New York: Routledge, 2003.

Deng, Gabriel Bol. "The Narrow Escape: The Facts of My Life." *Voices* 32, nos. 3–4 (2006), 20–24.

Department of Homeland Security. "Protecting the Nation from Foreign Terrorist Entry to the United States." Washington, DC: US Government Printing Office, 2017.

Deutsche Welle, "Ukraine: EU agrees protection plan for refugees" https://www.dw.com/en/ukraine-eu-agrees-protection-plan-for-refugees/a-60997378

Devictor, Xavier, and Quy-Toan Do. "How Many Years Have Refugees Been in Exile?" World Bank Policy Research Working Paper. Washington, DC: World Bank, 2016.

Dewaraja, Ratnin, and Noriyuki Kawamura. "Trauma Intensity and Posttraumatic Stress: Implications of the Tsunami Experience in Sri Lanka for the Management of Future Disasters." *International Congress Series* 1287 (2006), 69–73.

Dolan, Chris. *Social Torture: The Case of Northern Uganda, 1986–2006*. New York: Berghahn Books, 2009.

"Donors Pledge around $40-Billion Aid to Syrian Refugees' Hosts." *Jordan Times*, April 10, 2017.

Eastmond, Maria, and Joakim Öjendal. "Revisiting a 'Repatriation Success': The Case of Cambodia." In *The End of the Refugee Cycle? Refugee Repatriation and Reconstruction*, edited by Richard Black and Khalid Koser, 38–55. New York: Berghahn Books, 1999.

Eck, Kristine. "In Data We Trust? A Comparison of UCDP, GED and ACLED Conflict Events Datasets." *Cooperation and Conflict* 47, no. 1 (March 2012), 124–41.

Elhawary, Samir. "Security for Whom? Stabilisation and Civilian Protection in Colombia." *Disasters* 34 (2010), S388–S405.

Elhawary, Samir, and Sara Pantuliano. "Land Issues in Post-conflict Return and Recovery." *In Land and Post-Conflict Peacebuilding*, edited by Jon D. Unruh and Rhodri C. Williams. London: Earthscan, 2013, 115–20.

Elzarov, Zurab. "Emerging Options for Durable Solutions in Darfur." *Forced Migration Review*, no. 62 (2019), 55–57.

Erlanger, Steven, and Kimiko De Freytas-Tamura. "U.N. Funding Shortfalls and Cuts in Refugee Aid Fuel Exodus to Europe." *New York Times*, September 19, 2015.

Essuman-Johnson, Abeeku. "When Refugees Don't Go Home: The Situation of Liberian Refugees in Ghana." *Journal of Immigrant & Refugee Studies* 9, no. 2 (2011), 105–26.

European Commission. "EU-Jordan Partnership: The Compact." Brussels: Commission of the European Union, 2017.

European Commission. "New Pact on Migration and Asylum." Brussels: European Union, 2020.

European Union. "Operational Implementation of the EU-Turkey Statement." European Union. https://ec.europa.eu/home-affairs/sites/homeaffairs/files/what-we-do/policies/european-agenda-migration/press-material/docs/state_of_play_-_eu-turkey_en.pdf

Executive Order Protecting the Nation from Foreign Terrorist Entry into the United States. March 6, 2017.

Fagan, Patricia Weiss. "Refugees and IDPs after Conflict: Why They Do Not Go Home.'" Special Report. Washington, DC: United States Institute of Peace, 2011.

Fagan, Patricia Weiss. "Uprooted and Unrestored: A Comparative Review of Durable Solutions for People Displaced by Conflict in Colombia and Liberia." Geneva: Policy Development and Evaluation Service, 2011.

Fakhoury, Tamirace, and Derya Ozkul. "Syrian Refugees' Return from Lebanon." *Forced Migration Review*, no. 62 (2019), 26–28.

Fernandez, Manny. "A Path to America, Marked by More and More Bodies." *New York Times*, May 4, 2017.

Ferris, Elizabeth, Erin Mooney, and Chareen Star. *From Responsibility to Response: Assessing National Approaches to Internal Displacement*. Washington, DC: Brookings Institution, 2011.

Field, Erica. "Property Rights and Investment in Urban Slums." *Journal of the European Economic Association* 2–3 (2005), 279–90.

Fink, Carole. "The League of Nations and the Minorities Question." *World Affairs* 157, no. 4 (1995), 197–205.

Fitzpatrick, Daniel, Andrew McWilliam, and Susana Barnes. *Property and Social Resilience in Times of Conflict: Land, Custom and Law in East Timor*. Burlington, VT: Ashgate, 2012.

"Five Years after Arrival, Germany's Refugees Are Integrating." *The Economist*, August 25, 2020.

Fleming, Melissa, and Dana Hughes. "In Kenya, UNHCR Chief Assured Refugee Return Will Not Contravene International Obligations." Geneva: UNHCR, 2016.

Forced Displacement and Development Study Group. "Refugee Compacts: Addressing the Crisis of Protracted Displacement." Washington, DC: Center for Global Development and International Rescue Committee, 2017.

Furchtgott-Roth, Diana. "Does Immigration Increase Economic Growth?" Economic Policies for the 21st Century. New York: Manhattan Institute, 2014.

Gamso, Jonas, and Farhod Yuldashev. "Targeted Foreign Aid and International Migration: Is Development-Promotion an Effective Immigration Policy?" *International Studies Quarterly* 62, no. 4 (2018), 809–20.

Garzon, Jose M., Urim Ahmeti, Lulijete Gjonbala, and Lejla Kolenovic. "Kosovo Conflict Assessment: Breaking Down Invisible Walls." Pristina, Kosovo: USAID, 2012.

George, Miriam, Wendy Kliewer, and Sebastan Irudaya Rajan. "Rather Than Talking in Tamil, They Should Be Talking to Tamils": Sri Lankan Tamil Refugee Readiness for Repatriation." *Refugee Survey Quarterly* 34, no. 2 (2015), 1–22.

Gerver, Mollie. *The Ethics and Practice of Refugee Repatriation*. Edinburgh: Edinburgh University Press, 2018.

Ghosn, Faten, Tiffany S. Chu, Miranda Simon, Alex Braithwaite, Michael Frith, and Joanna Jandali. "The Journey Home: Violence, Anchoring, and Refugee Decisions to Return." *American Political Science Review* 115, no. 3 (2021), 982–98.

Gordon, Jennifer. "The International Governance of Refugee Work: Reflections on the Jordan Compact." *Global Public Policy and Governance* (2021). https://doi.org/10.1007/s43508-021-00019-6

Gottwald, Martin. "Back to the Future: The Concept of 'Comprehensive Solutions.'" *Refugee Survey Quarterly* 31, no. 3 (2012), 101–36.

Grayson, Catherine-Lune. "Durable Solutions: Perspectives of Somali Refugees Living in Kenyan and Ethiopian Camps and Selected Communities of Return." Nairobi, Kenya: Danish Refugee Council, 2013.

Guerin, Orla. "Aid Cuts Driving Jordan's Syrian Refugees to Risk All." BBC News, September 11, 2015.

Hammond, Laura. "Examining the Discourse of Repatriation: Towards a More Proactive Theory of Return Migration." In *The End of the Refugee Cycle? Refugee Repatriation and Reconstruction*, edited by Richard Black and Khalid Koser, 227–44. New York: Berghahn Books, 1999.

Hammond, Laura. "Tigrayan Returnees' Notions of Home: Five Variations on a Theme." In *Homecomings: Unsettling Paths of Return*, edited by Fran Markowitz and Anders H. Stefansson, 36–53. New York: Lexington Books, 2004.

Harild, Niels, Asger Christensen, and Roger Zetter. "Sustainable Refugee Return: Triggers, Constraints, and Lessons on Addressing the Development Challenges of Forced Displacement." Global Program on Forced Displacement Issue Note. Washington, DC: World Bank, 2015.

Harrell-Bond, Barbara E. "Repatriation: Under What Conditions Is It the Most Desirable Solution for Refugees? An Agenda for Research." *African Studies Review* 32, no. 1 (1989), 41–69.

Hathaway, James C. "The Meaning of Repatriation." *International Journal of Refugee Law* 9, no. 4 (1997), 551–58.

Heller, Michael, and Christopher Serkin. "Revaluing Restitution: From the Talmud to Postsocialism." *Michigan Law Review* 97, no. 6 (1999), 1385–412.

Heng Zhu, Mateusz Filipski, Jaakko Valli, Ernesto Gonzalez, Anubhab Gupta, and J. Edward Taylor. "Economic Impact of Refugee Settlements in Uganda." Rome: World Food Program, 2016.

Hoeffler, Anke, Syeda Shahbano Ijaz, and Sarah von Billerbeck. "Post Conflict Recovery and Peace Building." World Development Report Background Papers. Washington, DC: World Bank, 2011.

Holt, Julius. "Looking beyond the Towns: Facts and Conjectures about Rural Returnees in the Ogaden and 'Somaliland." In *In Search of Cool Ground: War, Flight and Homecoming in Northeast Africa, edited by* Tim Allen, 143–52. Trenton, NJ: Africa World Press, 1996.

Holtzer, Vanessa. "The 1951 Refugee Convention and the Protection of People Fleeing Armed Conflict and Other Situations of Violence." Legal Protection Policy Research Series. Geneva: UNHCR, 2012.

Honan, Edith. "U.N. Expands Refugee Camp in Kenya as South Sudan Conflict Rages." Reuters, June 20, 2015.

Human Rights Watch. "Pakistan Coercion, UN Complicity: The Mass Forced Return of Afghan Refugees." New York: Human Rights Watch, 2017.

Hurwitz, Agnes. "Beyond Restitution: Housing, Land, Property and the Rule of Law." In *Civil War and the Rule of Law*, edited by Agnes Hurwitz and Reyko Huang, 193–224. Boulder: Lynne Rienner Publishers, 2008.

Huser, Catherine, Andrew Cunningham, Christine Kamau, and Mary Obara. "South Sudanese Returns: Perceptions and Responses." *Forced Migration Review*, no. 62 (2019), 7–10.

Ibáñez, Ana María, and Andrés Moya. "Who Stays and Who Leaves during Mass Atrocities?" In *Economic Aspects of Genocide, Other Mass Atrocities, and Their Prevention*, edited by Charles H. Anderton and Jurgen Bauer. New York: Oxford University Press, 2016, 251–73.

Ibáñez, Ana María, and Andrés Moya. "Vulnerability of Victims of Civil Conflicts: Empirical Evidence for the Displaced Population in Colombia." *World Development* 38, no. 4 (2010), 647–63.

Inter-Agency Working Group on Unaccompanied and Separated Children. *Inter-Agency Guiding Principles on Unaccompanied and Separated Children.* Edited by ICRC Central Tracing Agency and Protection Division. Geneva: International Committee of the Red Cross, 2004.

International Organization for Migration. *Property Restitution and Compensation: Practices and Experiences of Claims Programmes.* Online ed. Geneva: International Organization for Migration, 2008.

"Uganda: Escalating Land Disputes in the North." Geneva: IRIN, 2011.

Isser, Deborah, and Peter Van der Auweraert. *Land, Property, and the Challenge of Return for Iraq's Displaced.* Washington, DC: US Institute of Peace, 2009.

Jaeger, Gilbert. "On the History of International Protection of Refugees." *International Review of the Red Cross* 83 (2001), 727–37.

Jeffrey, James. "Europe Pays Out to Keep a Lid on Ethiopia Migration." Geneva: IRIN, 2016.

Joireman, Sandra F. "Ethnic Violence, Local Security and Return Migration: Enclave Communities in Kosovo." *International Migration* 55, no. 5 (2017), 122–35.

Joireman, Sandra F. "Future Rights for Future Citizens: Children's Property Rights in Fragile Environments." *Oxford Development Studies* 46, no. 4 (2018), 470–82.

Joireman, Sandra F. "Intergenerational Land Conflict in Northern Uganda: Children, Customary Law and Return Migration." *Africa* 88, no. 1 (2018), 81–98.

Joireman, Sandra F. "The Mystery of Capital Formation in Sub-Saharan Africa: Women, Property Rights and Customary Law." *World Development* 36, no. 7 (2008), 1233–46.

Joireman, Sandra F. "Rebuilding Communities after Violent Conflict: Informal Justice Systems and Resource Access." *Online Symposium*, November 2014. http://harvardhrj.com/2014/11/rebuilding-communities-after-violent-conflict-informal-justice-systems-and-resource-access/

Joireman, Sandra F., Adam Sawyer, and Juliana Wilhoit. "A Different Way Home: Resettlement Patterns in Northern Uganda." *Political Geography* 31, no. 4 (2012), 197–204.

Joireman, Sandra F., and Laura S. Meitzner Yoder. "A Long Time Gone: Postconflict Rural Property Restitution under Customary Law." *Development and Change* 47, no. 3 (2016), 563–85.

Jones, Reece. *Violent Borders: Refugees and the Right to Move.* New York: Verso, 2016.

Jordan, Mirian, and Ron Nixon. "Trump Administration Threatens Jail and Separating Children from Parents for Those Who Illegally Cross Southwest Border." *New York Times*, May 7, 2018. https://www.nytimes.com/2018/05/07/us/politics/homeland-security-prosecute-undocumented-immigrants.html

Kalmanovitz, Pablo. "Corrective Justice versus Social Justice in the Aftermath of War." In *Distributive Justice in Transitions*, edited by Morten Bergsmo, César Rodríguez-Garavito, Pablo Kalmanovitz, and Maria Paula Saffon. Oslo: Torkel Opsahl Academic EPublisher, 2010.

Kalyvas, Stathis N. *The Logic of Violence in Civil War.* New York: Cambridge University Press, 2006.

Kaplan, Marion A. *Between Dignity and Despair: Jewish Life in Nazi Germany.* New York: Oxford University Press, 1998.

Kaya, Serdar, and Phil Orchard. "Prospects of Return: The Case of Syrian Refugees in Germany." *Journal of Immigrant & Refugee Studies* 18, no. 1 (2020), 95–112.

King, Iain, and Whit Mason. *Peace at Any Price: How the World Failed Kosovo.* Ithaca, NY: Cornell University Press, 2006.

Knaus, Verena. "No Place to Call Home—Repatriation from Germany to Kosovo as Seen and Experienced by Roma, Ashkali and Egyptian Children." Pristina, Kosovo, UNICEF, 2011.

Koser, Khalid, and Richard Black. "*The End of the Refugee Cycle?*" 1 In *The End of the Refugee Cycle? Refugee Repatriation and Reconstruction*, edited by Richard Black and Khalid Koser, 2–17. New York: Berghahn Books, 1999.

Kosovo Agency of Statistics. *Statistical Yearbook of the Republic of Kosovo.* Pristina: Kosovo Agency of Statistics, 2020.

Kumar, Ruchi. "Forced Repatriation to Afghanistan: 'We Didn't Think It Would Happen to Us.'" *The Guardian*, March 9, 2017.

Leckie, Scott, and Chris Huggins. *Conflict and Housing, Land, and Property Rights: A*

Handbook on Issues, Frameworks, and Solutions. New York: Cambridge University Press, 2011.

Lenner, Katharina, and Lewis Turner. "Learning from the Jordan Compact." *Forced Migration Review*, no. 57 (2018), 48–51.

Levitt, Peggy. "'You Know, Abraham Was Really the First Immigrant': Religion and Transnational Migration." *International Migration Review* 37, no. 3 (2003), 847–73.

Liberia Institute of Statistics and Geo-Information Services. "2008 Population and Housing Census: Final Results." Monrovia: Liberia Institute of Statistics and Geo-Information Services, 2009.

Loescher, Gil. "The International Refugee Regime: Stretched to the Limit?" *Journal of International Affairs* 47, no. 2 (1994), 351–77.

Long, Katy. "Back to Where You Once Belonged: A Historical Review of UNHCR Policy and Practice on Refugee Repatriation." Geneva: Policy Development and Evaluation Service, 2013.

Long, Katy. "Home Alone? A Review of the Relationship between Repatriation, Mobility and Durable Solutions for Refugees." Geneva: Policy Development and Evaluation Service, UNHCR, 2010.

Long, Katy. "State, Nation, Citizen: Rethinking Repatriation." Oxford: Refugee Studies Centre, University of Oxford, 2008.

Lowe, Keith. *Savage Continent: Europe in the Aftermath of World War II*. New York: St. Martin's Press, 2012.

Lu, Catherine. *Justice and Reconciliation in World Politics*. Cambridge: Cambridge University Press, 2017.

MacPherson, Claire, and Olivier Sterck. "Empowering Refugees through Cash and Agriculture: A Regression Discontinuity Design." *Journal of Development Economics* 149 (2021), 102614.

Malkki, Liisa. "National Geographic: The Rooting of Peoples and the Territorialization of National Identity among Scholars and Refugees." *Cultural Anthropology* 7, no. 1 (1992), 24–44.

Maniraguha, Jean Pierre. "Challenges of Reintegrating Returning Refugees: A Case Study of Returnee Access to Land and to Basic Services in Burundi." Master's thesis, University of Tromsø, 2011.

Marlowe, Lara. "Calais's Migrant Children Suffer as Europe Procrastinates." *Irish Times*, March 12, 2016.

Mashal, Mujib, and Zahra Naderjan. "A Third of Afghans Will Need Aid This Year, U.N. Says." *New York Times*, January 21, 2017.

Mathew, Penelope. "Killing Asylum Softly or Leaving No One Behind? The New York Declaration and Global Compacts in a Divided World." *Globalizations* (2021), 1–15.

McCallin, Barbara. "Restitution and Legal Pluralism in Contexts of Displacement." Case Studies on Transitional Justice and Displacement. Washington, DC: International Center for Transitional Justice, 2012.

Médecins Sans Frontières. "Dadaab to Somalia: Pushed Back into Peril." Geneva: Médecins Sans Frontières, 2016.

Metivier, Sean, Djordje Stefanovic, and Neophytos Loizides. "Struggling for and within the Community: What Leads Bosnian Forced Migrants to Desire Community Return?" *Ethnopolitics* 17, no. 2 (2018), 147–64.

Ministry of Justice. "Kosovo National Strategy on Property Rights." Pristina: Republic of Kosovo, 2016.

Mitrović, Olga. "Resolving a Protracted Refugee Situation through a Regional Process." *Forced Migration Review* 50 (September 2015), 12–15.

Moore, Will H., and Stephen M. Shellman. "Fear of Persecution: Forced Migration, 1952–1995." *Journal of Conflict Resolution* 48, no. 5 (2004), 723–45.

Moore, Will H., and Stephen M. Shellman. "Whither Will They Go? A Global Study of Refugees' Destinations, 1965–1995." *International Studies Quarterly* 51, no. 4 (2007), 811–34.

Nallu, Preethi. "Syrian Refugee Children Appeal for Education." News Deeply, September 21, 2016.

Nannyonjo, Justine. "Conflicts, Poverty and Human Development in Northern Uganda." WIDER Working Paper. New York: United Nations World Institute for Development Economics Research, 2005.

"A Nation of Victims." *The Economist*, October 31, 2015.

Norwegian Refugee Council. "Dadaab's Broken Promise: A Call to Reinstate Voluntary, Safe and Dignified Returns for the Dadaab Refugee Community." Oslo: Norwegian Refugee Council, 2016.

Norwegian Refugee Council, Save the Children, Action Against Hunger, CARE International, International Rescue Committee, and Danish Refugee Council. "Dangerous Ground: Syria's Refugees Face an Uncertain Future." Oslo: Norwegian Refugee Council, 2018.

Nossiter, Adam. "'I Am Alone': Migrant Children in Calais 'Jungle' Face an Uncertain Fate." *New York Times*, October 21, 2016.

Ó Tuathail, Gearoid. "Localizing Geopolitics: Disaggregating Violence and Return in Conflict Regions." *Political Geography* 29, no. 5 (2010), 256–65.

O'Loughlin, John, and Frank D. W. Witmer. "The Localized Geographies of Violence in the North Caucasus of Russia, 1999–2007." *Annals of the Association of American Geographers* 101, no. 1 (2011), 178–201.

Office for the Coordination of Humanitarian Affairs. "Liberia 2007: Common Humanitarian Action Plan." Geneva: United Nations, 2007.

Omata, Naohiko. "The Complexity of Refugees' Return Decision-Making in a Protracted Exile: Beyond the Home-Coming Model and Durable Solutions." *Journal of Ethnic and Migration Studies* 39, no. 8 (2013), 1281–97.

Omata, Naohiko. "Forgotten People: Former Liberian Refugees in Ghana." *Forced Migration Review* 1, no. 52 (2016), 10–12.

Onegi, Levis. "Post-conflict Land Insecurity Threatens Re-displacement in Northern Uganda." *Forced Migration Review*, no. 41 (December 2012), 31–32.

Opiyo, Lindsay McClain. "Alone Like a Tree: Reintegration Challenges Facing Children Born of War and Their Mothers in Northern Uganda." JRP Situational Brief. Gulu, Uganda: Justice and Reconciliation Project, 2015.

OSCE Mission in Kosovo. "An Assessment of the Voluntary Returns Process in Kosovo." Pristina, Kosovo: Organization for Security and Cooperation, 2014.

OSCE Mission in Kosovo. "Assessment of Voluntary Returns in Kosovo." Pristina, Kosovo: Organization for Security and Cooperation, 2019.

Özkan, Zafer, Naif Ergün, and Hüseyin Çakal. "Positive versus Negative Contact and Refugees' Intentions to Migrate: The Mediating Role of Perceived Discrimination, Life Satisfaction and Identification with the Host Society among Syrian Refugees in Turkey." *Journal of Community & Applied Social Psychology* 31, no. 4 (2021), 438–51.

Pannett, Rachel "Ukrainian boy, 11, traveled hundreds of miles alone to Slovakia, with only a passport and a plastic bag," *The Washington Post*, March 8, 2022

Paynesville Focus Group. Interview October 4, 2012.

Perič, Tatjana, and Martin Demirovski. "Unwanted: The Exodus of Kosovo Roma (1998–2000)." *Cambridge Review of International Affairs* 13, no. 2 (2000), 83–96.

Peters, Margaret E. *Trading Barriers: Immigration and the Remaking of Globalization.* Princeton, NJ: Princeton University Press, 2017.

Peters, Pauline E. "Challenges in Land Tenure and Land Reform in Africa: Anthropological Contributions." *World Development* 37, no. 8 (2009), 1317–25.

Peters, Pauline E. "Conflicts over Land and Threats to Customary Tenure in Africa." *African Affairs* 112, no. 449 (2013), 543–62.

Pham, Phuong, Patrick Vinck, Marieke Wierda, Eric Stover, and Adrian di Giovanni. *Forgotten Voices: A Population-Based Survey of Attitudes about Peace and Justice in Northern Uganda.* New York: International Center for Transitional Justice and the Human Rights Center, University of California, Berkeley, 2005.

Phillips, David L. *Liberating Kosovo: Coercive Diplomacy and U.S. Intervention.* Cambridge, MA: Belfer Center Studies in International Security and MIT Press, 2012.

Pinheiro, Paulo Sérgio de M. S. "Housing and Property Restitution in the Context of the Return of Refugees and Internally Displaced Persons." *Sub-Commission on the Promotion and Protection of Human Rights*, Commission on Human Rights. New York: Economic and Social Council, 2003.

Planas, Roque. "How El Salvador Became the World's Most Violent Peacetime Country." *Huffington Post*, March 4, 2016.

Posner, Eric. *The Twilight of Human Rights Law.* New York: Oxford University Press, 2014.

Poushter, Jacob. "European Opinions of the Refugee Crisis in 5 Charts." Washington, DC: Pew Research Center, 2016.

Progress. "Improving the Tools for the Social Inclusion and Non-discrimination of Roma in the EU." Luxembourg: European Commission Directorate-General for Employment, Social Affairs and Equal Opportunities, 2010.

Prunier, Gerard. *Africa's World War: Congo, the Rwandan Genocide and the Making of a Continental Catastrophe*. New York: Oxford University Press, 2011.

Psaltis, Charis, Huseyin Cakal, Neophytos Loizides, and Işık Kuşçu Bonnenfant. "Internally Displaced Persons and the Cyprus Peace Process." *International Political Science Review* 41, no. 1 (2019), 138–54.

Psaltis, Charis, Neophytos Loizides, Alicia LaPierre, and Djordje Stefanovic. "Transitional Justice and Acceptance of Cohabitation in Cyprus." *Ethnic & Racial Studies* 42, no. 11 (2019), 1850–69.

Pula, Besnik. "The Emergence of the Kosovo 'Parallel State,' 1988–1992." *Nationalities Papers* 32, no. 4 (2004), 797–826.

Radin, Margaret Jane. "Property and Personhood." *Stanford Law Review* 34 (1982), 957–1015.

Reed-Hurtado, Michael. "The Cartagena Declaration on Refugees and the Protection of People Fleeing Armed Conflict and Other Situations of Violence in Latin America." Legal and Protection Policy Research Series. Geneva: Division of International Protection, 2013.

Ressler, Everett M., Neil Boothby, and Daniel J. Steinbock. *Unaccompanied Children: Care and Protection in Wars, Natural Disasters and Refugee Movements*. New York: Oxford University Press, 1988.

Rincon, Jairo Munive. "Ex-Combatants, Returnees, Land and Conflict in Liberia." Copenhagen: Danish Institute for International Studies, 2010.

Roberts, Bayard, Kaducu Felix Ocaka, John Browne, Thomas Oyok, and Egbert Sondorp. "Factors Associated with Post-traumatic Stress Disorder and Depression amongst Internally Displaced Persons in Northern Uganda," *BMC Psychiatry* 8 (2008), 1–9.

Robertson, Z. O. E., Raelene Wilding, and Sandra Gifford. "Mediating the Family Imaginary: Young People Negotiating Absence in Transnational Refugee Families." *Global Networks* 16, no. 2 (2016), 219–36.

Schiebinger, Londa. "Gendered Innovations: Harnessing the Creative Power of Sex and Gender Analysis to Discover New Ideas and Develop New Technologies." *Triple Helix* 1, no. 1 (November 7, 2014), 9.

Sert, Deniz. "Cyprus: Peace, Return and Property." *Journal of Refugee Studies* 23, no. 2 (2010), 238–59.

Sert, Deniz. "Property Rights in Return and Resettlement of Internally Displaced Persons (IDPs): A Quantitative and Comparative Case Study." PhD dissertation, City University of New York, 2008.

Shrier, David, Weige Wu, and Alex Pentland. "Blockchain & Infrastructure (Identity, Data Security)." *MIT Connection Science*, Part 3 of 4 (May 2016), 1–18.

Sigona, Nando. "Between Competing Imaginaries of Statehood: Roma, Ashkali and Egyptian (RAE) Leadership in Newly Independent Kosovo." *Journal of Ethnic and Migration Studies* 38, no. 8 (2012), 1213–32.

Sikkink, Kathryn. *Evidence for Hope: Making Human Rights Work in the 21st Century*. Princeton, NJ: Princeton University Press, 2017.

Skendaj, Elton. *Creating Kosovo: International Oversight and the Making of Ethical Institutions.* Washington, DC: Woodrow Wilson Center Press, 2014.

Smit, Anneke. *The Property Rights of Refugees and Internally Displaced Persons.* New York: Routledge, 2012.

Smit, Anneke. "Housing and Property Restitution and IDP Return in Kosovo." *International Migration* 44, no. 3 (2006), 63–88.

Stefanovic, Djordje, and Neophytos Loizides. "Peaceful Returns: Reversing Ethnic Cleansing after the Bosnian War." *International Migration* 55, no. 5 (2017), 217–34.

Stefanovic, Djordje, Neophytos Loizides, and Samantha Parsons. "Home Is Where the Heart Is? Forced Migration and Voluntary Return in Turkey's Kurdish Regions." *Journal of Refugee Studies* 28, no. 2 (2015), 276–96.

Stefansson, Anders H. "Homecomings to the Future: From Diasporic Mythographies to Social Projects of Return." *In Homecomings: Unsettling Paths of Return,* edited by Fran Markowitz and Anders H Stefansson. New York: Lexington Books, 2004, 2–20.

Stefansson, Anders H. "Homes in the Making: Property Restitution, Refugee Return, and Senses of Belonging in a Post-WAR Bosnian Town." *International Migration* 44, no. 3 (2006), 115–39.

Steinbeck, John. *The Grapes of Wrath.* New York: Penguin Group, 1939.

Stilz, Anna. "Nations, States, and Territory." *Ethics* 121, no. 3 (2011), 572–601.

Stilz, Anna. "Occupancy Rights and the Wrong of Removal." *Philosophy & Public Affairs* 41, no. 4 (2013), 324–56.

Stubblefield, Emily, and Sandra F. Joireman. "Law, Violence, and Property Expropriation in Syria: Impediments to Restitution and Return." *Land* 8, no. 11 (2019).

Sullivan, Daniel P. "Shared Obstacles to Return: Rohingya and South Sudanese." *Forced Migration Review,* no. 62 (2019), 4–7.

Sydney, Chloe. "Return Decision Making by Refugees." *Forced Migration Review,* no. 62 (2019), 11–12.

Tamkin, Emily. "Once Again, Slovakia Makes Life Harder for Muslims." *Foreign Policy,* December 2, 2016.

Taylor, J. Edward, Mateusz J. Filipski, Mohamad Alloush, Anubhab Gupta, Ruben Irvin Rojas Valdes, and Ernesto Gonzalez-Estrada. "Economic Impact of Refugees." *Proceedings of the National Academy of Sciences* 113, no. 27 (2016), 7449–53.

Terry, Fiona. *Condemned to Repeat? The Paradox of Humanitarian Action.* Ithaca, NY: Cornell University Press, 2002.

Toal, Gerard, and Carl T. Dahlman. *Bosnia Remade: Ethnic Cleansing and Its Reversal.* New York: Oxford University Press, 2011.

Tomkiw, Lydia. "Holocaust Survivor Stories in 2015: In Poland, the Fight to Get Their Property Back." *International Business Times,* November 14, 2015.

Troszczynska-van Genderen, Wanda. "Rights Displaced: Forced Returns of Roma, Ashkali and Egyptians from Western Europe to Kosovo." New York: Human Rights Watch, 2010.

Turner, Lewis. "Who Will Resettle Single Syrian Men?" *Forced Migration Review*, no. 54 (2017), 29–31.

Turton, David. "The Meaning of Place in a World of Movement: Lessons from Long-Term Field Research in Southern Ethiopia." *Journal of Refugee Studies* 18, no. 3 (2005), 258–80.

UNHCR. "Assessment on Returns to Iraq amongst the Iraqi Refugee Population in Syria." Syria: UNHCR Syria, Public Information Unit, 2008.

UNHCR. "Cambodian Refugee Camps in Thailand Now Empty." Geneva: UNHCR, 1999.

UNHCR. "Complementary Pathways for Admission to Third Countries." https://www.unhcr.org/en-us/complementary-pathways.html

UNHCR. "Field Handbook for the Implementation of UNHCR Bid Guidelines." Geneva: UNHCR, 2011.

UNHCR. "Figures at a Glance." UNHCR. https://www.unhcr.org/en-us/figures-at-a-glance.html

UNHCR. "The Global Compact on Refugees." Geneva: UNHCR, 2018.

UNHCR. "Global Trends: Forced Displacement in 2019." Geneva: UNHCR, 2020.

UNHCR. "Global Trends: Forced Displacement in 2020." UNHCR, https://www.unhcr.org/flagship-reports/globaltrends/

UNHCR. "Implementation of the Comprehensive Strategy for the Liberian Refugee Situation, Including UNHCR'S Recommendations on the Applicability of the 'Ceased Circumstances' Cessation Clauses." Geneva: UNHCR, 2012.

UNHCR. "Protection of Refugees in Mass Influx Situations: Overall Protection Framework." Background Paper prepared for the Global Consultation on International Protection. Geneva: United Nations, 2001.

UNHCR. "Resettlement." https://www.unhcr.org/en-us/resettlement.html

UNHCR. *The State of the World's Refugees: A Humanitarian Agenda*. New York: Oxford University Press, 1997.

UNHCR. "UNHCR Guidelines on Determining the Best Interests of the Child." Geneva: UNHCR, 2008.

UNHCR. "UNHCR Reports Crisis in Refugee Education." Geneva: UNHCR, 2016.

UNHCR. *UNHCR Resettlement Handbook*. Geneva: UNHCR, 2011.

UNHCR. "UNHCR Warns 2020 Risks Lowest Resettlement Levels in Recent History." News release, November 19, 2020. https://www.unhcr.org/en-us/news/press/2020/11/5fb4e6f24/unhcr-warns-2020-risks-lowest-resettlement-levels-recent-history.html

UNHCR. "Voluntary Repatriation." http://www.unhcr.org/en-us/voluntary-repatriation-49c3646cfe.html

Unruh, Jon D. "Assembling Evidence for a Land and Property Restitution Database during the Syrian Civil War." Presented to the World Bank Land and Poverty Conference. Washington, DC, 2016.

Unruh, Jon D. "Evidencing the Restitution Landscape: Pre-emptive and Advance Techniques for War-Torn Land and Property Rights Reacquisition." *Land Use Policy* 38 (2014), 111–22.

Unruh, Jon D. "Land Rights in Postwar Liberia: The Volatile Part of the Peace Process." *Land Use Policy* 26, no. 2 (2009), 425–33.

US Department of State. "Erasing History: Ethnic Cleansing in Kosovo." Washington, DC: US Department of State, 1999.

Valcárcel Silvela, Amaya. "Sri Lankan Tamil Refugees in India: Return or Integration?" *Forced Migration Review*, no. 62 (2019), 13–15.

Van der Auweraert, Peter. "Property Restitution in Iraq." Washington, DC: US Department of State, 2007.

van Haersolte-van Hof, Jacomijn J. "Innovations to Speed Mass Claims: New Standards of Proof." 2 In *Redressing Injustices through Mass Claims*, edited by the International Bureau of the Permanent Court of Arbitration, 13–25. New York: Oxford University Press, 2006.

Van Hear, Nicholas, Oliver Bakewell, and Katy Long. "Push-Pull Plus: Reconsidering the Drivers of Migration." *Journal of Ethnic & Migration Studies* 44, no. 6 (2018), 927–44.

Van Hear, Nicholas, Rebecca Brubaker, and Thais Bessa. "Managing Mobility for Human Development: The Growing Salience of Mixed Migration." Human Development Reports. Geneva: United Nations Development Program, 2009.

Vorhölter, Julia. *Youth at the Crossroads: Discourses on Socio-Cultural Change in Post-War Northern Uganda*. Göttingen, the Netherlands: Göttingen University Press, 2014.

Waldron, Jeremy. "Superseding Historic Injustice." *Ethics* 103, no. 1 (1992), 4.

Walker, Cherryl. *Landmarked: Land Claims and Land Restitution in South Africa*. Athens: Ohio University Press, 2008.

Warner, Daniel. "Voluntary Repatriation and the Meaning of Return to Home: A Critique of Liberal Mathematics." *Journal of Refugee Studies* 7, nos. 2–3 (1994), 160–74.

Weiss-Meyer, Amy. "Apps for Refugees: How Technology Helps in a Humanitarian Crisis." *The Atlantic*, May 2017.

West, Harry G., and Scott Kloeck-Jenson. "Betwixt and Between: 'Traditional Authority' and Democratic Decentralization in Post-war Mozambique." *African Affairs* 98, no. 393 (1999), 455.

Whyte, Susan Reynolds, Sulayman Mpisi Babiiha, Rebecca Mukyala, and Lotte Meinert. "Remaining Internally Displaced: Missing Links to Security in Northern Uganda." *Journal of Refugee Studies*, 26, no 2 (2012), 283–301.

Wily, Liz Alden. "Tackling Land Tenure in the Emergency to Development Transition in Post-conflict States: From Restitution to Reform." In *Uncharted Territory*, edited by Sara Pantuliano, 27–50. Bourton on Dunsmore, UK: Practical Action Publishing, 2009.

Wily, Liz Alden, and Jeffrey Hatcher. "Rights to Resources in Crisis: Reviewing the

Fate of Customary Tenure in Africa." Washington, DC: Rights and Resources Initiative, 2012.

Woodman, Gordon R. "A Survey of Customary Laws in Africa in Search of Lessons for the Future." In *The Future of African Customary Law*, edited by Jeanmarie Fenrich, Paolo Galizzi, and Tracy E. Higgins, 9–30. New York: Cambridge University Press, 2011.

World Bank. "Forcibly Displaced: Toward a Development Approach Supporting Refugees, the Internally Displaced, and Their Hosts." Washington, DC: World Bank, 2016.

World Bank. *World Development Report 2011*. World Bank, 2011. https://doi.org/10.1596/978-0-8213-8439-8

World Food Programme. "WFP Forced to Make Deeper Cuts in Food Assistance for Syrian Refugees Due to Lack of Funding." News release, July 1, 2015. https://www.wfp.org/news/news-release/wfp-forced-make-deeper-cuts-food-assistance-syrian-refugees-due-lack-funding

Zetter, Roger, and Héloïse Ruaudel. "Refugees' Right to Work and Access to Labour Markets: Constraints, Challenges and Ways Forward." *Forced Migration Review* no. 58 (June 2018).

Index